Introduction to the American Legal System

Seventh Edition

Enika H. Schulze
P. Michael Jung, Esq.
Rebecca P. Adams, Esq.

Copyright © 1990, 1992, 1993, 1996, 1998, 2000, and 2002

Pearson Publications Company
Dallas, Texas

Website: Pearsonpub-legal.com

ISBN 0-929563-72-7

This book provides a comprehensive overview of the American legal system for the student, beginning paralegal, or anyone else new to the legal system. The book explains basic legal concepts in a concise, easy-to-grasp way not readily available in current literature. Important concepts are highlighted for ease of comprehension.

This edition includes updates to every chapter, including the important and increasing role of alternative dispute resolution in the American legal system, found at the end of Chapter Three. Discussion of various concepts has been expanded, and new sections have been added to broaden student understanding of the principles underlying our system of justice. More terms have been added to the Glossary, and many existing definitions have been expanded. Finally, the entire book has been carefully edited to render it even more readable than prior editions. This includes the addition of more headings to better identify and subdivide the topics covered by the text.

Introduction to the American Legal System provides a general overview of the structure of the legal system, the criminal justice system, and the federal courts. It includes an extensive glossary as well as specific concepts and examples in the substantive areas of:

- torts
- contracts
- real property
- wills and intestate succession
- legislation.

A chapter on legal research is included to orient the novice on issues of the law, legal material, and techniques of legal research. The United States Constitution—the primary source of U.S. law—can be found in Appendix A.

Introduction to the American Legal System is also a popular study guide for the certificate examinations offered by the National Association of Legal Assistants and the PACE exam offered by the National Federation of Paralegal Associations.

Susan R. Patterson
Editor

ACKNOWLEDGMENTS

The authors wish to express their appreciation to the Honorable Patrick E. Higginbotham, Judge of the United States Court of Appeals for the Fifth Circuit, whose continual insistence upon high standards and quality performance was the impetus for this project.

Appreciation is also extended to Walter E. Steele, Jr., Associate Dean for Clinical Education, Southern Methodist University School of Law, for his guidance in the early stages of this project.

Sincere appreciation for revisions in the recent editions is expressed to Susan R. Patterson, Esq., whose research and attention to detail have added significantly to the quality of this book. Lance Cooper, Esq., provided his editorial skills and scholarship to the current edition.

The Publisher

"The authors have done a superb job of providing a comprehensive and detailed description of the complex American legal system, written in a style that permits even beginning students of the legal system to understand the subject matter thoroughly.

This volume will be a very valuable reference handbook to those whose livelihood is earned in American courts."

George R. Poehner, Former Chairman
Standing Committee on Legal Assistants
State Bar of Texas

"As a straightforward description of the judicial process from beginning to end it is almost ideal for the person who is new to the court system. . . .The book is arranged so that even the complete novice can grasp the basic ideas . . . [The authors] comment on the public's criticism, and then attempt to explain why a particular procedure or law is necessary in order to guarantee citizens their constitutional rights. This frank approach allows readers to look at the material in an intelligent manner, making their own judgments about the law's merits and faults."

Legal Information Alert

TABLE OF CONTENTS

Chapter One

GENERAL INTRODUCTION
TO THE LEGAL SYSTEM

Basic Legal Concepts and Terminology

Sources of American Law

Modern American jurisprudence finds its origins in the small towns and villages of England. There, judges resolved disputes by making decisions that were based on custom, common sense, and fairness. These decisions, although at first not recorded, became part of an ancient tradition known as the **common law** or "the law of the case."

As the common law developed, so did the principles of *stare decisis* (Latin for "to stand by things decided") and **precedent**. When a court made a decision based upon the facts of the case before it, that decision provided guidance for other courts faced with similar sets of facts. Gradually, the courts developed the policy that a decision of a court was binding on that court and on other courts of equal or lower rank when the same or a similar issue arose in the future based on the same or similar facts. The reason for this policy was simple: People functioning in a society needed to know the rules so they could conduct themselves accordingly. They needed to know that a particular decision was the law, would remain the law, and would not be changed the next time a court was faced with the same issue. The principle of *stare decisis* also serves as a check on the power of judges.

In England, although the common law was the primary source of legal rules and principles, statutes began to play an increasingly important role. A **statute** is a law passed by a legislative body; it may be a prohibition, a command, or a declaration. But the meaning of the various statutes was not always clear. And it was not always obvious that a statute applied to a particular set of facts. Thus, courts assumed the responsibility of construing statutes and applying them to various factual situations.

In the United States today, the common law, statutory law, and the principle of *stare decisis* form the backbone of our legal system. The courts of our nation, in resolving disputes or interpreting statutes, are guided by the decisions that other courts have made in the past when faced with the same or similar issues. These decisions are recorded and presented in law books so that lawyers, legal scholars, and judges may refer to them and study them whenever they need guidance.

Substance v. Equity

The rules that are the heart of our system of justice, whether they are legislative enactments or a part of the common law handed down by judges, are rules of **substantive law**. They state the rights and duties of individuals and the circumstances in which a court will grant one person redress against another.[1] Courts are frequently asked to resolve questions of substantive law. In some cases, they may have to determine the meaning of a particular statute. If there is no statute that applies to the facts before it, a court may have to decide what the common law rule should be in that sort of a case; in so doing, the court has made new law. If the rule has already been established by *stare decisis*, courts may have to determine whether the facts of that case fit the rule.

Occasionally, a court may determine that the common law rule, if applied to the facts at hand, would achieve a highly unjust result. In these cases, the court may go around the rule by applying principles of **equity**. In other words, the court will attempt to achieve a fair result when the common law rule is inadequate to achieve justice. Take, for example, the case of an engineer living on the east coast who accepts an oral job offer from a company in Texas. In reliance on the offer, she and her husband quit their jobs, take their children out of school, sell their home and move. After one month on the job, the engineer is fired without good cause. Under the common law she would likely have no remedy, because most states still follow the doctrine of employment-at-will that says an employer, in the absence of a written agreement to the contrary, can fire an employee for a good reason, a bad reason, or no

---

1. R. Field and B. Kaplan, *Materials for a Basic Course in Civil Procedure* 2 (1978).

reason at all. Nevertheless, if she brings suit against the Texas employer, she may be able to win damages based on the equitable doctrine of "detrimental reliance," because she put herself and her family in a vulnerable position in reliance on the job offer. If the court determines that her actions were reasonable, a decision in her favor would most likely stand up on appeal as an equitable remedy for the employer's wrongdoing. Note, however, that equity will generally limit the amount of monetary damages she can obtain and will disallow damages designed to punish the employer. Today, common and statutory law embody principles of equity to a greater extent than in the past. This is the case simply because, over time, legislatures and courts have had to deal with a wider range of circumstances and cases for which they have fashioned remedies that have, in turn, become the rule of law. Nevertheless, courts may still apply principles of equity with confidence, independent of any rule. To the extent that lawmaking cannot keep up with the rate of technological, social and cultural change, courts will continue to be called upon to make equitable decisions in the absence of applicable common law rules and statutes.

Substance v. Procedure

Courts make decisions by studying existing rules of substantive law and by relying on principles of justice and common sense. These rules of substantive law are very different from rules of **procedure**. The rules of procedure establish the step-by-step mechanism that people bringing or defending a lawsuit or criminal prosecution must follow. Each state establishes its own procedure, as do the federal courts. These procedures are the means by which people:

- gain access to the courts
- conduct themselves during preparation for trial
- conduct themselves during the trial itself
- enforce the judgment of a court, once that judgment has been entered.[2]

Rules of procedure are very important. Their goal is to impose order on a dispute so that it will be resolved correctly, fairly, and quickly. They

---

2. *Id* at 3.

provide the method by which each party presents his or her story to the court in the way that is most conducive to a fair decision. Rules of procedure focus the dispute on the relevant issues, thereby saving time and protecting litigants from prejudicial or irrelevant immaterial evidence. They also give to the parties the means of discovering their opponent's position. **Discovery** prevents unfair surprise; it also enables parties to present to the court a more complete story so that the court can better understand the truth. In federal courts, the procedural rules are known as the Federal Rules of Civil Procedure and the Federal Rules of Criminal Procedure.

Civil v. Criminal

There are two basic types of disputes: civil and criminal. In a criminal case, the state or federal government brings an action against an individual to determine if he or she has broken one of its laws and, if so, to punish the person accordingly. In a civil case, on the other hand, a person, called the **plaintiff**, brings a lawsuit seeking some sort of redress for an injury that person claims to have suffered. The person may be an individual, a corporation, or sometimes even the state. The redress, called the **remedy**, that the person seeks is usually in the form of money, called **damages**. The person asks the court to order an opponent, called the **defendant**, to pay monetary compensation for the wrong that the opponent caused. For example, a person who loses an arm in an auto accident cannot ask the court to provide a new arm. A person can, however, ask the court to require the driver who caused the accident to pay monetary compensation for that arm. Of course, the problem with this system is that it is practically impossible to put a dollar value on something as priceless as an arm. How much money is an arm worth? or a person's health? or life? Although we cannot really put a price tag on such things, we can compensate the victim for certain specific losses. Thus, the person who caused the accident can be required to pay to the victim, among other things, whatever the victim's medical bills were or will be in the future, and whatever income the victim has lost or will lose as because of the accident. Of course, not all civil cases are about money. In November of 2000, the two leading presidential candidates, Al Gore and George W. Bush, both filed cases in civil court over the Florida election returns. After more than a month of litigation, the U.S. Supreme Court ruled in favor of Bush.

The Court

A court's primary function is to resolve disputes in an orderly manner. These disputes may be between two private parties, between a private party and the state or federal government, or even between two states. In later chapters we will explore in detail how the courts perform this vital task of resolving disputes. First, however, we will examine several important characteristics of the courts that will give us a perspective on their role in our society.

The Judiciary and the Separation of Powers

In the United States the judicial branch is one of the three branches of government. The other two branches are the executive (the president, or in the various states, the governor) and the legislative. Under the federal as well as the state constitutions, each branch acts as a check on the other two, ensuring that no one branch becomes overly powerful. The legislature, for example, has the power to enact laws. But this power is not absolute: if the president or governor opposes a particular law, he or she may veto it.

Similarly, the courts have the authority to check the power of the other branches. A court may rule that a particular law that the legislature passed and the executive signed is unconstitutional, which voids the law. The party relying on the law will usually appeal the decision to a higher court. If the state's highest court, or the United States Supreme Court, upholds the original decision, the law is permanently nullified.

The Judiciary and Federalism

Just as there are a federal government and fifty different state governments, so there is a system of federal courts and fifty different state courts. The federal Constitution created the federal courts, and the different state constitutions created the state courts. In general, the federal and state courts function independently of each other. Although certain types of cases can be tried in a federal court as well as in a state court, many cases can be tried only in state courts, and many others can be tried only in federal courts.

As a general proposition (although there are exceptions), the federal courts cannot interfere with or contradict the actions of a state court, and vice versa. Thus, if a person does not like a decision received in a federal court, that person cannot go to a state court and try the case a second time in the hopes of obtaining a more favorable ruling.

Courts as Protectors of the Individual and the Oppressed

The courts play the important role of standing between the government and the individual and affording protection to the individual. They make certain that a person accused of a crime is not deprived of rights and receives a fair trial. Courts also ensure that the majority of our citizens does not infringe on the rights of the minority. Legislators who tend to vote the majority views of their constituents may be unresponsive to minority groups who may espouse unpopular causes. The courts must be certain that the majority, acting through the legislatures, does not deprive the minority of the rights to which everyone in this country is entitled. The decisions of the Supreme Court, for example, on abortion, desegregation, and prayer in public schools came about after legislatures failed to resolve these politically volatile issues through legislative action.

In theory, the federal courts are more likely than state courts to make decisions that protect the rights of the individual and of minorities. In recent years, however, state courts have been more responsive than the federal courts to civil rights claims, a reversal of the pattern in the 1960s and 1970s. This new trend may be due to a growing conservatism on the federal bench coupled with increasing public support for minority rights. But bear in mind that in many states state and local judges are elected for a term and then must face reelection, whereas all federal judges are appointed to their posts and serve for life. Thus, the federal judge can make a ruling in favor of unpopular people or causes and not run the risk of losing his or her job in the next election. The elected judge, however, is more prone to being influenced by popular opinion and, as a result, may protect unpopular people or viewpoints less zealously than the appointed judge.

These two methods of selecting judges reflect two sharply differing views about the judiciary. The elected judge is ultimately answerable to the majority, for the judge must ask the majority for reelection. An elected judiciary is based on the theory that even though the majority may sometimes infringe on the rights of the individual or the minority, majority control is nonetheless the best method of governing a nation.

A system in which the executive nominates a judge with the advice and consent of the legislature reflects a different view of judging. The appointed judge who makes an unpopular decision need not fear public outrage, because he or she does not depend on the majority for reelection. An appointed judge is answerable to no one except the judges who sit on a higher court within that judge's judicial line of authority. This approach reflects the view that the majority sometimes does not protect the rights of the minority, that the rights of that minority should be preserved, and that the duty of protecting those rights should be in the hands of persons who do not owe their jobs directly to the voters. Today, more and more jurisdictions are experimenting with hybrid methods of selecting judges that combine appointment with confirmation by the electorate.

Role of the Courts in Making Law

The role of the judicial branch in shaping the laws of the United States is indirect. Its role is confined to:

- reconfirming and strengthening existing law
- widening or narrowing the application of existing law
- overturning existing laws that conflict with laws at a higher level of authority.

While a president, governor, or mayor can propose legislation, and Congress, state legislatures, and city counsels can both propose and enact laws, the courts can do neither. Nor can they institute lawsuits to test the constitutionality of laws. A court may take action only after a party has come to it seeking the resolution of a dispute. Based on our adversarial system of justice, the court listens to the best evidence and arguments that the parties can muster. It then determines what actually happened and decides who should prevail, according to the law that applies. The applicable law may be a statute, common law precedent, or both. Thus, the court's decision reconfirms and strengthens the authority of the law. In situations where the facts of the case are unlike any other case on record, the court's interpretation of the law may widen or narrow its application. In rare instances, a court may overturn the law because it conflicts with higher law, including state or U.S. constitutional principles, which almost guarantees that the case will be appealed to a higher court. Eventually, the case may reach the state's highest court or the United States Supreme Court for a final determination of the law's validity. Whenever a decision to overturn a law is finalized, the legislative group that passed it in the first place has the opportunity to redraft it in a form that will withstand challenge, and their drafting will, of course, be guided by the opinion of the court. Nevertheless, the court itself cannot participate, nor can it propose its own version of the law.

The Judge

The judge, who is the chief officer of a court, presides over the settlement of disputes. In fulfilling this responsibility, the judge must perform three main tasks:

1. Enforce the rules of court procedure to make sure that each side is able to gather and present evidence fairly.

2. Determine the facts (assuming that the parties have not requested a jury). Naturally, in a heated dispute, there will be sharp disagreements as to what actually happened. In a controversy over who is ultimately responsible for damages suffered as a result of a traffic collision, for example, witnesses who were at the scene of the accident may give varying testimony on factual issues such as whether the light was green or red, whether the defendant gave a proper turn signal, or whether the plaintiff was speeding. Additional complications arise when the physical evidence conflicts with the statements made by the witnesses. These are all issues of fact that the judge or jury must resolve.

3. Apply the law to the facts to determine who should prevail. In cases where a jury has been impaneled, the judge will instruct the jury in the law that it must apply in making its decision. In

a simple traffic collision case, if the jury finds that the defendant ran a red light, the judge will instruct the jury whether, under the law, the defendant was obligated to stop at that light. If there is no jury, the judge must apply the law and decide the outcome. When a decision is rendered, whether by the judge or the jury, such findings are reduced to a written order called a **judgment**, which is signed by the judge. This ends the dispute at the trial court, but the judge's order is not irreversible until both parties have exhausted their rights to appeal to a higher court. The judgment has the full power of the government behind it, and the sheriff or marshal will carry it out by force if necessary.

TERMS TO KNOW

common law
stare decisis
precedent
statute
substantive law
equity
procedure
defendant
plaintiff
remedy
damages
judgment

Chapter Two

THE CRIMINAL JUSTICE SYSTEM

Introduction

A **crime** is an action that offends the morality of a society and that a society has determined it will not tolerate. A crime is defined by statute and is composed of elements, each of which must be proven to convict the person accused of the crime. For example, the crime of burglary is usually composed of five elements: (1) the breaking and (2) entering of a (3) dwelling (4) of another (5) with the intent to commit a felony in the structure.

The **criminal justice system** is the system that a society develops to handle those who commit crimes. The term "criminal justice system" applies to the entire process from commission of a crime to punishment. This system necessarily reflects the values of its society, in both the conduct that it punishes and in the way that it treats the accused and the criminal.

Systems that are characterized by strict enforcement of the laws, by a rapid determination of the guilt of the accused, and by harsh punishment are frequently found in nations that grant defendants few rights. When compared to the United States, these nations are more likely to strictly control their citizens and interfere in their private lives.

Since its beginning, the United States has regarded itself as a different sort of society. Many of the people who settled the new nation left their homelands to be free from what they considered to be excessive government intrusion. They recognized the importance of restricting the power of government and protecting the individual citizen from the power of the state. Consequently, the states passed the Bill of Rights, which became the first 10 amendments to the Constitution. Those amendments, which grant the person accused of a crime many vital rights, form the foundation of the nation's criminal justice system.

Our criminal justice system today, however, is the subject of much criticism. Many members of the public believe that they are not safe, that crime is rampant, that the police are not effective in catching the wrongdoer, and that the system—lawyers, judges, and prosecutors—is excessively lenient.

The crime-fearing public that criticizes the courts in this way overlooks a crucial fact: the problems that lie at the root of crime are not lenient judges or clever lawyers, but instead are such things as poverty, poor education, and the breakdown of the family structure. These are conditions that the criminal justice system cannot and should not be expected to correct.

The criminal justice system already has an extraordinarily difficult task. It must strike a delicate balance among the sometimes competing interests in protecting the accused from improper intrusion of the state, vindicating the public morality by punishing the wrongdoer, and enforcing the criminal laws in such a way that society is protected from future crimes. This is indeed a formidable task. To the outsider, the criminal justice system that has evolved to tackle this difficult job may appear to be a confusing maze. There are numerous courts and several sets of criminal laws.

Cases in federal court involve the alleged violation of federal criminal laws and cases in state court involve the alleged violation of state criminal laws.

The vast majority of criminal statutes are state laws. In recent years, however, more and more activity is being criminalized at the federal level, especially drug-related acts and intentional violations of federal regulations dealing with the environment, worker safety, securities, and other commercial activities.

Federal and state laws divide criminal conduct into two categories: **misdemeanors** and **felonies**. Misdemeanors range from traffic violations to such offenses as theft of a small amount of money. A felony is a major crime for which the maximum penalty may be a fine, imprisonment, or both. Felonies include such offenses as homicide, arson, rape, robbery, burglary, and grand larceny.

Federal and most state courts are divided into three levels. At the lowest level is the trial court. In that court, the actual trial is conducted, and the accused is found guilty or not guilty. At the next level are the appeals courts—usually there are several such courts. Finally, each state has a high court, usually called the supreme court. The highest court in the federal system, for example, is the **United States Supreme Court**.

Within the state criminal justice system, there are generally several different types of trial courts. The power of these courts to hear various types of cases depends upon their jurisdiction. **Subject matter jurisdiction** refers to the power or authority of a court to hear and decide a particular kind of case, depending on the topic, the amount of damages claimed, and other factors. **Personal jurisdiction** (also called *"in personam* jurisdiction") gives courts the power over the people involved in a criminal or civil lawsuit based upon where they reside or can be found, or where the allegedly illegal actions of the defendant occurred. In civil cases involving property, personal jurisdiction can also depend upon where the property (personal or real) is located. In order to hear a case, a court must have jurisdiction over (1) the subject matter, and (2) the people or property involved.

The lowest level courts, for example, typically have jurisdiction only over minor crimes such as traffic violations, criminal trespass, and public intoxication. Other courts hear only more serious misdemeanors, such as petit larceny, while the highest level of trial courts hears only felony cases. Some trial courts, especially those in rural counties, hear both civil cases and felony or misdemeanor criminal cases. The civil cases may involve a wide range of topics (e.g., divorce, probate, personal injury, breach of contract) and damages of any amount of money.

Conversely, courts in more heavily populated counties are more likely to hear only civil or only criminal matters. In the case of some civil courts, their jurisdiction is limited by statute to matters involving a certain amount of damages being claimed by the plaintiff, or other criteria. Most appeals courts at the state and federal levels hear both civil and criminal appeals. Likewise, the highest appeals courts in most states hear both types of matters, although in some, such as Texas, there are two "supreme" courts, one for criminal appeals and the other for civil. The United States Supreme Court can consider both types of appeals.

In 1967, the President's Commission on Law Enforcement and Administration of Justice issued a Task Force Report on the Courts.[1] The Commission inquired into the effectiveness and fairness of America's criminal courts and found that the aspects of the criminal court system most in need of reform were the lower criminal courts in urban areas. Because most crimes are committed in the cities, these courts handle the majority of all cases that are tried. Literally millions of persons, called **defendants**, who have been arrested for a crime or have been cited for various misdemeanor violations, appear before these courts, either for trial of misdemeanor or petty offenses or for preliminary proceedings in more serious cases.

Lower level urban courts are less likely to be fair and effective for several reasons:

1. They labor under high work loads, simply because they hear the vast majority of the nation's criminal cases.

2. These courts often operate with meager facilities and with the least trained personnel, as compared with higher courts.

3. Practices by judges, prosecutors, and defense counsel in these courts are often less formal than practices in higher courts and occasionally may violate rules of criminal procedure. Both defense counsels and prosecutors must be vigilant to ensure that lax practices are not detrimental to defendants.

4. Judgeships in such lower courts are often elective offices. Pressures from "friends" and interest groups, and the practice of accepting campaign contributions from lawyers, make impartiality difficult. Studies show that in those cities where judges are appointed and where the salaries are adequate, the quality of justice is significantly higher.

---

1. The President's Commission on Law Enforcement and Administration of Justice, *Task Force Report: The Courts* (1967)

5. Lower court judges may find their quality of justice hampered, however, because their courts are generally not **courts of record**, which means that the proceedings are not recorded by a court reporter. When a case is appealed from such a court, the case must be retried by a higher court. The appeal is then *de novo*, that is, the case is tried again.

The problem with a *de novo* appeal is that by the time the appeal is heard, witnesses may no longer be available, and the memory of those witnesses who are available may have faded. On the other hand, in a court of record, when a case is appealed, the court reporter records everything that was said in the trial court. This record is submitted to the appeals court, along with all the documents filed in the case. The appeals court then renders a decision after reviewing the lower court's record.

Experts agree that improvements at the lower level could have far-reaching effects. Because millions of individuals have contact only with these lower courts, their opinions of the entire American legal system, both criminal and civil, are strongly influenced by their personal experiences. Consequently, it is imperative that this level of the system perform effectively.

The Rights of the Accused

Although courts may from time to time render justice that is not always fair, in some cases what may be *perceived* as inefficient or unfair may in fact be due to the constant tension that exists between the public's demand for strict and quick administration of justice on the one hand and protection for the rights of defendants on the other. These protections stem primarily from Supreme Court interpretations of the United States Constitution.

Many of the basic concepts about criminal justice are stated in the first 10 amendments to the United States Constitution, called the Bill of Rights. Although the Bill of Rights was originally intended as a limitation on the actions of the federal government, the Supreme Court has now applied almost all of the Bill of Rights to the states. Each state is free to define what is a crime, and to create its own court system and criminal procedure for processing the crimes through its courts, but the state cannot go beyond the limits set out in the Bill of Rights.

Most rights and privileges of the criminal defendant that the Bill of Rights contains concern **procedural due process**. The Fourth Amendment states: "The right of the people to be secure in their persons, houses, papers and effects against unreasonable searches and seizures shall not be violated, and no Warrants shall issue, but upon probable cause . . ." The Supreme Court has interpreted the Fourth Amendment to mean that one is free from search unless the police have probable cause to believe that there is contraband or evidence of the suspected crime at the place to be searched.

Suspicion of a crime is inadequate for search or arrest: **probable cause**, that quantum of evidence that leads a reasonable person to believe that guilt is more than a possibility, is the essential element. Evidence that is obtained in violation of the standards set out in the Fourth Amendment must be excluded from court. This rule is known as the **exclusionary rule**.[2] The rule, however, does not prevent police from seizing evidence of unsuspected crimes during a legal search and using the evidence to bring additional charges.[3]

Among the Fifth Amendment's limitations on the government is a provision that all federal felony charges be brought in the form of a **grand jury indictment**. The states are not constitutionally required to have grand juries, but about half of them do so. A **grand jury** is an official body of citizens brought together to decide whether a person accused of a crime should be officially charged. If the grand jury decides to charge officially, it does so with an **indictment**. The purpose of the grand jury is to provide a barrier between the state—law enforcement agencies—and the individual. A grand jury indictment cannot be used by the prosecution as evidence or inference that a crime has been committed by the accused.

The Fifth Amendment protects a defendant from double jeopardy—i.e., being tried twice for the same offense. Once a person is acquitted of a

---

2. See *Mapp v. Ohio*, 367 U.S. 643 (1961).

3. See *Minnesota v. Dickerson*, 113 S.Ct. 2130 (1993).

charge, the prosecution cannot bring the same charge again. Nevertheless, the Supreme Court ruled in 1993 that a defendant can be charged with a *different* offense based on conduct for which he or she has already been prosecuted.[4]

Perhaps the most famous clause in the Fifth Amendment provides that a person shall not be compelled, in a criminal case, to be a witness against himself or herself. This is called the **privilege against self-incrimination**. The defendant does not have to prove that he or she did not commit a crime. The defendant does not even have to talk about it or take the witness stand. Instead, the prosecutor has the burden of proving that the defendant is guilty without the aid of the defendant's testimony. The defendant must, however, cooperate in the gathering of physical evidence such as fingerprints, samples of bodily fluids or examples of handwriting.

The United States Supreme Court has extended this privilege against self-incrimination to apply also to preliminary questioning by a police officer. Because this rule was established in a case called *Miranda v. Arizona*,[5] the rights enumerated in that case are called **Miranda warnings**. Under this rule, before any questioning, a person must be advised that he or she has the right to remain silent, that any statement the person does make may be used against the person, and that the person has the right to the presence of an attorney, to be provided by the government if the accused cannot afford one. Like evidence obtained in violation of the Fourth Amendment, evidence obtained in violation of *Miranda* under the Fifth Amendment must be excluded from court under the exclusionary rule.

This privilege against self-incrimination includes the protection of communications between a defendant and certain persons who have a protected relationship with the defendant, including a spouse, attorney, therapist, doctor, priest or minister. Generally unless the defendant consents, these persons may not volunteer or be forced to testify about confidential communications between them and the defendant. An exception occurs where the confidant is the victim of the defendant's

---

4. See *United States v. Dixon*, 113 S.Ct. 2849 (1993).

5. 384 U.S. 436 (1966).

crime. The defendant can waive the privilege, for example, to permit a therapist to testify that the defendant has been diagnosed as insane, or a minister can report that the defendant expressed deep remorse for the crime.

The Sixth Amendment provides that in all but the most minor criminal cases the trial must be by an impartial jury. The defendant may, however, waive his or her right to trial by jury and be tried instead by the judge. Another clause in the Sixth Amendment states that the defendant has the right "to be informed of the nature and cause of the accusation." An **indictment** or other charging instrument must contain precise technical language concerning the nature and cause of the accusation, because the defendant may only be tried for those offenses listed in the charging instrument. Therefore, evidence pertaining to any other offenses is usually not admissible during trial.

The Sixth Amendment also states that "in all criminal prosecutions the accused shall enjoy the right . . . to be confronted with the witnesses against him." This clause gives a criminal defendant the right to be present in the courtroom at every stage of the trial. It also ensures the defendant the right to cross-examine those who testify against him or her.

Finally, the Sixth Amendment gives a defendant the right to the assistance of counsel for his or her defense. Although anyone who can afford a lawyer may hire one at any stage of a criminal proceeding, the Supreme Court has interpreted this clause to mean that even those who cannot afford an attorney have the right to one. The Court has held that if a defendant is indigent, the judge must appoint an attorney to represent the defendant. Lying at the heart of this rule is the Court's realization that without an attorney, a defendant's chances of having a fair trial are slim. The Supreme Court has also ruled that the criminal defendant has the right to effective assistance of counsel. This means that if a defendant is convicted and the defense attorney's omissions or failures were sufficiently egregious, the conviction is not valid.

The right to be represented by counsel is not limited to defendants who are tried for serious offenses. The Supreme Court has ruled that "no person may be imprisoned for any offense; whether classified as petty, misdemeanor or felony, unless he was represented by counsel at his trial."[6] Therefore, if a person could go to prison—even for a day—as punishment for the offense with which he or she is charged, the person has the right to counsel. If, however, the maximum penalty is only a fine, the accused does not have the right to a court-appointed lawyer.

The Eighth Amendment forbids "cruel and unusual punishment." Courts have had great difficulty defining this elusive phrase. After many years of varying interpretations, it has come to mean punishment characterized by the unnecessary and wanton infliction of pain that is out of proportion to the crime. For example, in 1977 the Supreme Court ruled that the death penalty is out of proportion to the crime of rape where no life is taken.[7] In recent years the Eighth Amendment has been raised frequently by prisoners filing lawsuits in which they complain that prison conditions are so appalling as to constitute cruel and unusual punishment.

The Eighth Amendment also prohibits "excessive fines." In 1993, the Supreme Court ruled that forfeitures of property owned by defendants convicted under federal drug laws are subject to the Eighth Amendment test against excessive fines.[8]

The Lawyers

Prosecution

In a criminal case, the party that brings an action against a person accused of a crime is the government (e.g., federal, state, municipal) acting on behalf of its citizens. The lawyer who represents the government is called the **prosecutor**. The role of the prosecutor in a criminal case is complicated, but the prosecutor's most visible responsibility is as a representative of the government.

Because of the limited human and financial resources generally available to prosecutors, not all of the many cases presented to a

---

6. See *Argersinger v. Hamlin*, 407 U.S. 25 (1972).

7. See *Coker v. Georgia*, 433 U.S. 584 (1977).

8. See *Austin v. United States*, 113 S. Ct. 2801 (1993).

prosecutor will be prosecuted. Prosecutors have considerable discretion about which cases they prosecute, and a prosecutor will not take a case to trial unless he or she believes that a conviction is both warranted and achievable. To reach this conclusion, the prosecutor must rely on more evidence than may eventually be produced at trial. Like all attorneys, prosecutors want to win the cases they try and, unlike the defendant, they generally cannot appeal cases they lose. Therefore, they will usually prosecute their strongest cases. Some cases, however, will be prosecuted regardless of their strengths. For example, cases against defendants believed to be guilty of previous offenses and likely to commit future ones.

Contrary to common belief, the responsibility of the prosecutor is not merely to convict. The American Bar Association Code of Professional Responsibility requires the prosecutor to "seek justice." This special duty exists because:

- the prosecutor represents the sovereign and therefore should use restraint in the discretionary exercise of governmental powers, such as in the selection of cases to prosecute;

- during trial the prosecutor is not only an advocate, but he or she also may make decisions normally made by an individual client, and those affecting the public interest should be fair to all; and

- in our system of criminal justice, the accused is to be given the benefit of all reasonable doubt.

The prosecutorial decision to charge is based on complex factors. The most important is the seriousness of the crime, followed by the strength of the evidence. Also important is the criminal record of the accused. Obviously, if the crime is serious, the evidence strong, and the defendant a repeat offender, the prosecutor will bring charges. Conversely, if the accused is a first-time offender and acted in response to provocation from an undesirable victim, the prosecutor may bring a lesser charge, or even none at all.[9]

---

9. J. Kaplan, *Criminal Justice: Cases and Materials* (1986) (cited as *"Cases"*).

Political pressures also bear upon a prosecutor's decision to charge. Political pressures are greatest in the state courts where district attorneys are elected. They or their assistants may be persuaded not to prosecute politically unpopular cases. For instance, cases against community leaders or children of community leaders may never see the courtroom. Generally speaking, the more articulate or wealthy a defendant, the more public sympathy he or she will enjoy, which may compel a prosecutor to charge a lesser crime or recommend a more lenient punishment.[10]

Federal courts are less political. United States attorneys are appointed by the President with the advice and consent of the Senate and are less immune to local political pressure. Staff attorney positions at the Department of Justice, the Department of Labor and other departments with prosecutorial responsibilities are highly competitive and generally go to competent, well-trained individuals.

Defense

Prosecutors and defense counsel play significantly different roles, and so their ethical responsibilities vary accordingly. Defense counsel's obligations center around the constitutional right to counsel, the constitutional right against self-incrimination, the presumption of innocence and burden of proof, and confidentiality between attorney and client.[11]

Contrary to public belief, criminal defense lawyers make up only a small percentage of the practicing bar. Most lawyers advise clients about their business affairs. Few handle litigation, and the majority of those handle only civil litigation. Many lawyers handling criminal cases are not criminal lawyers at all but have been appointed by the court to represent indigent defendants because the vast majority of the people convicted of serious crimes are indigent.[12]

---

10. *Id.*

11. J. Kaplan, *Criminal Justice: Cases and Materials, Teacher's Manual* (1973).

12. J. Kaplan, *Cases, supra.*

Some states and most large urban areas have a public defender system. The quality of public defenders varies greatly from district to district. Public defenders are greatly overworked—they simply have too few resources and too many clients to defend. Most cases handled by public defenders end in plea bargains.[13]

The first question a criminal defense lawyer must ask is whether to represent a particular client. The American Bar Association says:

> A lawyer is under no obligation to act as adviser or advocate for every person who may wish to become his client; but in furtherance of the objective of the bar to make legal services available, a lawyer should not lightly decline proffered employment. The fulfillment of this objective requires acceptance by a lawyer of his share of tendered employment which may be unattractive both to him and the bar generally.[14]

> However, a lawyer should decline employment if the intensity of his personal feelings as distinguished from community attitudes may impair his effective representation of a prospective client.[15]

When a lawyer is appointed by the court to represent an indigent defendant, the ABA Code of Professional Responsibility imposes stricter standards. Only for compelling reasons should a lawyer decline such representation. "Compelling reasons do not include such factors as the repugnance of the subject matter of the proceeding, the identity or position of a person involved in the case, the belief of the lawyer that the defendant in a criminal proceeding is guilty . . . ."[16]

A lawyer should not withdraw from a case merely because the lawyer discovers that his or her client is guilty. In order for an adversarial

---

13. *Id.*

14. ABA *Code of Professional Responsibility*, EC 2-26.

15. EC 2-30.

16. EC 2-29.

system to work properly, it is necessary that the defendant have a spokesperson in court, just as the prosecutor is the spokesperson for society. Defense counsel should present the best defense he or she can in the best interest of the client. Defense counsel may, for example, decide to present nothing but try to put the prosecutor's case in the worst possible light. The prosecutor has the obligation to present the evidence and to prove the defendant guilty.

The Sixth Amendment, which guarantees the right to assistance of counsel, would be rendered meaningless if attorneys did not have a corresponding duty to represent all those who need representation, regardless of guilt or innocence and regardless of how distasteful the alleged crime may be. The late Edward Bennett Williams, an experienced criminal trial lawyer, explained that:

> Defending an unpopular client is an open invitation to
> be widely misunderstood . . . Every time I have
> assumed the defense of a case in which the crime
> charged is a heinous one, or the defendant is a social or
> political outcast, the criticism has come.[17]

Unfortunately, many Americans associate the lawyer with the person the lawyer is defending, rather than regarding the lawyer as an officer of the court who is the agent of the accused. This view reflects a misconception of the lawyer's role: as proposed ABA Model Rule of Professional Conduct 1.2(b) states, "(a) lawyer's representation of a client, including representation by appointment, does not constitute an endorsement of the client's political, economic, social or moral views or activities."

Since lawyers representing unpopular clients run the risk of identification with their clients in the public mind, they have a particularly heavy responsibility. The question that should be asked is not whether a lawyer can defend an unpopular client but, rather, what the lawyer can legally and ethically do for the client. The clash between two opposing sides presents the most effective way of determining the truth, and so

---

17. Glazer, *What Are the Limits of a Lawyer's Professional Conduct in Defending a Client?*, 54 Fla. B.J. 2 (1976).

the attorney's function in an adversarial system is to represent the client
to the best of his or her ability. The 1995 murder prosecution of O.J.
Simpson provides an example of lawyers vigorously defending a client
who many believed to be guilty. Although Simpson had supporters,
many people believed his guilt was obvious. Nevertheless, Simpson's
attorneys delivered a strong and effective defense that resulted in
Simpson's acquittal. In light of the terrorist attacks of September 11,
2001, the defense of people accused of terrorist acts will probably be
made more difficult by a widespread belief of their guilt.

To be able to fully represent the interest of the client, an attorney must
maintain uninhibited communication with the client. The ABA Standard
Relating to the Defense Function (3.2) states that as soon as practicable,
the lawyer should seek to determine all relevant facts known to the
accused: "In so doing, the lawyer should probe for all legally relevant
information without seeking to influence the direction of the client's
responses." To afford the lawyer free reign to take action, the ABA
Standard further indicates that it is unprofessional conduct for any
lawyer to instruct the client or to intimate to the client in any way that
the client should not be candid in revealing facts.

Pretrial Process

The criminal justice process consists of several different stages. As
individuals move through the stages of the pretrial process, their numbers decrease. The process may be viewed as a pyramid. On the bottom
are the number of individuals arrested; on a higher level, those charged
with an offense; and, on the very top, the very few who are convicted.
We will now examine the various stages of the criminal justice process
to determine how and where individuals drop from the system. The
discussion that follows describes a typical state law enforcement system
carried out at the local level. The federal law enforcement system
embodies a similar process but with some differences.

Investigation

The criminal justice process begins when the police are led to believe
that a crime has been committed. Investigation may be initiated in
several ways:

- when law enforcement personnel, whether federal, state, or local, observe a crime being committed or observe a person acting suspiciously

- when a victim or other affected person reports that a crime was committed

- when law enforcement officers decide to look for specific criminal activity that they believe is occurring or about to occur.

The latter usually results from accumulated law enforcement experience or from a tip from an informer.

Law enforcement may use investigating techniques such as examination of physical evidence left at the scene of a crime, interrogation of persons who act suspiciously, search of persons or premises, electronic eavesdropping, and various undercover activities.

Arrest

If, upon investigation, a law enforcement officer decides that enough evidence exists to believe with probable cause that a crime has been committed by a particular person, he or she may make an arrest, take a person into custody and, usually, transport the person arrested to the police station where the person is "booked" for the crime that the officer believes the person committed. Most arrests are made without warrants and are based on witnessing of offenses being committed, on reports of offenses having been committed, or on belief that persons are acting suspiciously.

The officer may use such force as is necessary to detain and hold a suspect, including deadly force in some situations and in some jurisdictions. In most jurisdictions, arrests for misdemeanors cannot be made without a warrant unless the officer witnessed the commission of the misdemeanor. In other words, since only minor crimes are involved, the right of an officer to make a warrantless arrest is limited. For minor violations, instead of taking the suspect into immediate physical custody, the officer may issue a **citation**, which is an order to appear before a judge at a later date. The officer may use reasonable force, but not deadly force, to detain and hold the suspect in a misdemeanor.

At bookings for felonies and some serious misdemeanors, the suspect is ordinarily fingerprinted. These prints are sent to the FBI to determine if the suspect is wanted elsewhere. As discussed earlier, in any interrogation the law enforcement officer must give the suspect his or her Miranda warnings, which advise the suspect of his or her rights to remain silent and to have immediate assistance of counsel.

Bail

Soon after the suspect is arrested, he or she is brought before a judge or magistrate for consideration of bail. The usual form of release pending trial is for the defendant to post a **bail bond**. A bail bond is a legal document containing a promise of the defendant to appear for the trial of the case or to forfeit a sum of money. The sum of money can be guaranteed by a deposit of cash (**cash bond**) or the guarantee of another to pay the amount of the bond if the defendant fails to appear (**surety bond**). Bail bonds, especially when they involve a minor offense or misdemeanor, are sometimes also referred to as **appearance bonds**.

The magistrate determines whether the defendant is bondable and the amount of the bond. These determinations are based primarily on the defendant's prior record and the seriousness of the offense. These criteria are weighed to determine the defendant's likelihood of appearing for trial. Should a defendant have "good standing" in the community (local job, residence, and family) and have no prior felony conviction, the defendant may be released on his or her **personal recognizance**. This simply means that the defendant agrees to appear at the trial without having to put up a sum of money to guarantee his or her appearance.

In areas that have a **pretrial release program**, a pretrial release officer checks out the defendant's background and, if the officer determines the defendant to be a good risk, recommends approval of a pretrial release bond. The defendant pays a small premium for the bond and is released until trial.

Charging

When bail is set, the evidence held by law enforcement is forwarded to the prosecutor to determine whether to charge the suspect. If the prosecutor agrees that there is probable cause to believe that a crime was committed and that the accused committed it, the prosecutor may decide to formalize the charge. In practice, only a fraction of the cases booked by law enforcement are charged at the same offense level recommended by the prosecutor,[18] who will often downgrade the booked offense to a lesser crime.

One way to charge a suspect formally is to seek an **indictment** from a grand jury. Grand juries are available in about half the states and in the federal system, but only a few jurisdictions use the grand jury exclusively in bringing felony charges. The number of individuals on the grand jury varies from state to state. Grand jury proceedings are secret, with neither the defendant nor defense counsel present. The prosecutor appears before the jury, presents the case, and asks for an indictment. Members of the grand jury may ask any questions they wish and can subpoena witnesses to ask them any questions. They may vote to issue an indictment on the charge requested or on some other charge, or they may decide not to indict at all. Although in the majority of cases grand juries follow the prosecutor's request, they are designed to serve as a check on the power of a prosecutor to go forward with a prosecution.[19]

An alternative to indictment by grand jury is by a charging document called an **information** or, sometimes, a **complaint**. This document is prepared by the prosecutor in lieu of going to the grand jury and generally occurs in misdemeanor cases. Complaints are usually presented at pretrial hearings where the judge can assess the evidence and decide whether or not to proceed with the case or dismiss it for lack of probable cause.[20]

---

18. J. Kaplan, *Cases, supra.*

19. *Id.*

20. *Id.*

Arraignment

After the indictment is returned or the information is filed, the
defendant is brought into court where the prosecutor reads the charge.
In some jurisdictions this appearance is called an **arraignment**. After
the charges are read, the defendant must plead to them. The defendant
may plead to the charges as "guilty," "not guilty," or "*nolo
contendere*" (Latin for "I will not contest it"). The latter plea may not
be used in another case as proof that the defendant committed the act,
although in all other respects it is a guilty plea.

Before accepting a plea of guilty, the judge must inquire of the
defendant if the defendant understands what he or she is doing and must
determine that the defendant voluntarily pleads. The judge must also
warn the defendant of the possible sentencing consequences and
determine that the defendant understands them. Many judges will also
inquire into the factual basis for the plea. In federal court the judge also
usually advises the defendant that he or she has the right to plead "not
guilty" and be tried by a jury, the right to confront and cross-examine
witnesses against the defendant, and the right not to be compelled to
testify against him or herself. If the court accepts a "guilty" plea, there
will be no trial, and the next stage will be sentencing.

Plea Bargaining

In most jurisdictions, the prosecutor and defense counsel may engage in
plea bargaining. This may take place at any stage of the proceeding
prior to trial; it may even occur during trial. Plea bargaining involves
negotiation between prosecutor and defense to enter a guilty plea in
exchange for the reduction of charges or some other benefit to the
defendant. The judge should not participate in such discussions, but the
judge should require the disclosure of the agreement in open court at
the time the plea is offered. A defense lawyer has the responsibility of
fully advising his or her client about whether a particular plea bargain
should be accepted.

Plea bargains were approved by the United States Supreme Court in the
case of *Santobello v. New York*.[21] Plea bargains are motivated by

---

21. 404 U.S. 257 (1971).

attorneys' concerns with what the jury will conclude from the evidence presented. If a defense counsel anticipates an adverse jury verdict, he or she may decide a guilty plea to lesser charges is in the client's best interest. Prosecutors are interested in obtaining plea bargains, usually because they have more cases than they can possibly try. Defense attorneys, on the other hand, will plea bargain a case because they believe that a trial will not achieve a better result for the defendant and may, in fact, result in a heavier sentence.[22]

Another consideration that enters into the plea bargain process is the fact that jails are unpleasant places. If a defendant pleads guilty, he or she is generally free to go until the day of sentencing. Therefore, a defendant who has not been able to make bail is highly motivated to plead guilty in order to expedite his or her release from jail. For those unable to make bail, the consolation is that pretrial jail time is usually credited toward the eventual sentence.

Pretrial Motions

Frequently, a defendant will plead "not guilty" in the initial stages of the process and, after pretrial motions are decided, change the plea to "guilty." A **motion** is a request to the court that it act in a certain way. For instance, a motion may request the court to dismiss the case, or to move the case to another jurisdiction, or perhaps to order that the government produce certain evidence for the defendant to examine before trial. Some of the more common pretrial motions are:

1. **Motion for Discovery and Inspection**. To prepare for trial, attorneys on both sides must gather information relevant to the case. This process of gathering information is called **discovery**. In most jurisdictions, the government must permit the defendant to inspect and copy relevant written or recorded statements made by the defendant that are within the possession of the government. A copy of a prior criminal record, if any, and other documents in the custody of the government that are material to the preparation of the defense should be provided to the defense attorney. If the government fails to provide

---

22. J. Kaplan, *Cases, supra.*

requested discovery, a defendant will file a motion for
discovery and inspection.

2. **Motion for Bill of Particulars**. A motion for bill of particulars
    asks the court to order the government to file a formal
    document giving details of the time, place, and manner in
    which the alleged crime was committed.

3. **Motion for Change of Venue**. A defendant is generally tried in
    the district in which the crime is alleged to have been
    committed. If there appears to be such prejudice that the
    defendant could not obtain a fair trial in that district, the court
    may grant a motion for change of **venue** (the geographical
    location where the case is tried).

4. **Motion to Sever**. In a case where two defendants are being
    tried together, one of them may feel that he or she will be
    prejudiced by the bad reputation of the other, by the strength of
    the evidence against the other, or by the confession of the
    other. If the court grants a motion to sever, the two will be
    tried separately.

5. **Motions to Suppress Evidence or to Dismiss the Indictment**.
    These motions are frequently based on alleged violations of a
    defendant's constitutional rights. For example, because all
    courts have interpreted the Constitution to require that the
    indictment precisely set forth the nature of the charges against
    the defendant, some defense counsel may file motions to
    dismiss the indictment on the ground that it is not sufficiently
    specific.

    Many motions are filed claiming that evidence the prosecution
    intends to introduce at trial was seized during a search that
    violated the Fourth Amendment. If the court finds that the evi-
    dence was illegally seized, it must suppress the evidence. This
    means that the evidence may not be introduced at the trial. If
    the evidence is crucial to the prosecution's case, the prosecutor
    may decide to abandon the case if the motion to suppress is
    granted.

Motions to suppress evidence, sometimes called **motions** *in limine* (Latin for "at the outset), are filed also on the grounds that the evidence is irrelevant or unduly prejudicial. This motion, usually filed shortly before trial, seeks to prevent any mention of the evidence in the presence of the jury. It is often filed to prevent introduction of the defendant's criminal record.

The public often criticizes courts for granting motions to dismiss or to suppress evidence, and claims that judges are letting defendants go free for things that are "minor technicalities." This attitude often results from ignorance about the nature and the importance of the constitutional rights at stake. Although a wrongdoer might have his or her case dismissed because a police officer did not have probable cause to arrest and search the individual, it would be much more unfortunate if police officers could arrest or search anyone without probable cause to believe that the person committed a crime. The constitutional probable cause requirement intentionally curbs police power so that innocent citizens will not be harassed, arrested, or jailed. The occasional freeing of a criminal is viewed as a small price to pay to preserve fundamental constitutional rights for all of us.

Trial

If the case survives the motion stage of the trial process and if the defendant persists in his or her "not guilty" plea, the case will be tried. The Sixth Amendment guarantees a defendant a trial by jury in all cases where imprisonment is a possible outcome. The defendant may, however, waive this right with the approval of the court and the consent of the government. In that event, the case will be decided by the judge.

Jury Selection

A jury trial begins with the selection of a **jury panel**. The panel usually consists of about thirty to forty members, depending upon the number of defendants involved in the case, chosen by some random process. In both federal and state courts, jurors who have reached this stage will have certain characteristics in common. They will be

- citizens of the United States and residents of the district for a specified term

- able to read, write, speak, and understand English

- able to fill out the juror questionnaire form.

They will be without mental or physical infirmities that would render their service unsatisfactory. And they must not have charges pending or convictions for a serious crime. Judges who check the qualifications of prospective jurors excuse those who do not meet these criteria. Because jurors are often selected from voter lists, jurors rarely form a truly representative cross section of the community. Young people, for example, are less likely to be registered voters than are older people. Poor people are much less likely to vote than the middle class. Professionals such as doctors, lawyers, and teachers often get excused.

The next step in the process is *voir dire* examination of the jury panel. *Voir dire* literally means "to speak the truth," and comes from Old French. The objective of the *voir dire* examination is to secure a fair and impartial jury. During this examination the prospective jurors are questioned by the judge or by the attorneys about their backgrounds, families, employment, views about crime and other aspects of their lives and opinions that may be considered relevant.

Although the stated objective is to select impartial jurors, in reality attorneys try to get jurors who will side with their clients. In the process of questioning jurors, the lawyers try to influence and persuade them, presenting themselves as the "good guys." Prosecutors and defense counsel naturally look for different types of jurors. Defense counsel prefers jurors who are like the defendant, while prosecutors seek jurors who are like the victim.[23]

The manner of jury selection varies greatly from state court to federal court and from judge to judge. In some state court systems, the attorneys ask the questions of prospective jurors. In addition to asking questions, state court prosecutors often explain the duties of jurors, define relevant terms, and question jurors about their attitudes on conviction, sentencing, and so on.

---

23. J. Kaplan, *Cases supra*.

In federal court, the judge generally asks the questions, although it is within the judge's discretion to allow the attorneys to do so (*Fed. R. Crim. P.* 24). In courts where the judge conducts the *voir dire*, attorneys may submit written questions they would like the judge to ask.

Parties on either side may ask that a member of the panel be excused if the examination indicates that the panel member is not qualified to be a juror or that the panel member may be prejudiced. This request is called a **challenge for cause**. The parties also have a right to a certain number of general challenges or strikes, called **preemptory challenges**, which may be exercised without giving any reason. It is not permissible to eliminate a juror due to race or gender. And a defendant may be able to challenge a conviction successfully if it can be proved that the jurisdiction in which he or she was convicted systematically discriminates against classes of jurors, especially on the basis of race.

The stated objective of the *voir dire* examination is to find a jury that will make a fair decision. A defense counsel representing a particularly unappealing client may decide, however, to waive the jury and instead have a trial before the judge, in hopes that the judge will be fairer than a jury.

Staging the Trial

After a jury has been selected, the jurors are seated together in the jury box. An oath is administered to them by the court, requiring them to render a true verdict. The attorneys then make their opening remarks, informing the judge and the jury what they believe the evidence will show.

The trial itself is somewhat like a stage performance, with the judge and lawyers writing the script. The courtroom is usually arranged with the judge's bench in the front, the jury box on one side, the prosecutor's table closest to the jury box and the defendant's table farthest from the jury box. The government or state agent who had responsibility for investigating the case may sit with the prosecutor, and the defendant will sit with his or her counsel. Spectators may sit on the benches in the back of the courtroom behind the "bar." Although the courtroom is open to the public and anyone may come and go, the atmosphere is formal, particularly in federal court, and appropriate dress is required. In most courts, when the judge enters or leaves the courtroom, everyone must rise, and when addressing the judge, attorneys and clients must stand.

The lawyers generally try to create maximum impact and maximum drama. The criminal trial has a greater importance, however, than simply drama. Beyond the public spectacle lies a fact-finding process bound by rules of evidence. The chief function of the judicial machinery is to learn the truth.

Publicity

If the objective is to find the truth, what about the public's right to know the truth? The First Amendment guarantees the right to freedom of the press, but what if that freedom comes in conflict with the fact-finding mission of the judicial process? This conflict is obviously a serious one. Much has been written by justices of the Supreme Court and others weighing the relative importance of these two interests.

The great majority of cases have no press coverage at all. In cases that receive newspaper coverage, however, the judge usually instructs the jury not to read any newspaper articles about the case because jurors must make their decisions based on evidence presented in court, not from a newspaper. Moreover, newspaper accounts are often inaccurate. Reporters are usually not lawyers, and their exposure to the legal system is often infrequent and haphazard. Discussions about whether to allow or not to allow certain evidence are often conducted in court after the jury has been excused or before the jury is brought into the court-room.

Certain information of interest to the general public may be excluded from a jury's consideration because it is unreliable and may mislead them or because the evidence is obtained in unauthorized ways. Perhaps the defendant has confessed, but the confession is not admissible. If such information is included in newspaper accounts, a very misleading interpretation could be drawn. Jurors must render a verdict based only on admissible evidence developed during the trial.

If newspaper reporters are allowed in the courtroom, could television
camera operators be excluded? In 1965, at a time when television
equipment was bulky and obtrusive, the Supreme Court held that
television coverage of a criminal trial was so physically disruptive that
the defendant was denied due process of law. *Estes v. Texas*, 381 U.S.
532 (1965).

In 1981, however, the Supreme Court revisited the issue. After
reviewing the advances in television technology made in recent years,
the court explained that the *Estes* case did not establish a *per se* rule
barring television coverage, but instead meant only that the particular
television coverage in that case had deprived the defendant of his rights.
Chandler v. Florida, 449 U.S. 560 (1981). The Court held that
allowing television coverage was neither constitutionally required nor
constitutionally prohibited, but was a matter for each state to decide. It
left the door open for a defendant to show that television coverage had
disrupted his or her particular trial, or had prejudiced his or her
particular judge or jury, but refused to presume that this type of injury
would occur in all cases. Today, many years after *Chandler*, television
cameras are widely accepted in the courtroom, although usually within
the discretion of the trial judge.

The American Bar Association's Code of Professional Responsibility
restricts an attorney from revealing information to the press or to
someone who may reasonably be expected to reveal it to the press.
Only the following statements may be made:

- information that is in a public record

- the fact that an investigation is ongoing and the general scope of
  the investigation

- a request for assistance in apprehending a suspect.

An attorney is not supposed to make statements that could be expected
to be disseminated to the press regarding a party's

- character, reputation, or prior criminal record

- the existence of a confession, admission, or statement by the accused or the failure of the accused to give the same

- the performance or result of a test

- the identity, testimony, or credibility of a prospective witness

- any opinions as to guilt or innocence of the accused or the merits of the case against the accused.

The judge assigned to a case may fine an attorney for making prohibited statements, and may even issue a gag order to prevent inappropriate and possibly damaging revelations. If violations have significantly prejudiced either side in a case, the judge can declare a mistrial.

Basic facts, such as the name, age, residence, occupation, and family status of the accused, the nature of the charge, and the status of the judicial proceedings may, however, be revealed. After completion of the trial, extrajudicial statements that might affect the imposition of sentence are prohibited. In cases where there has been too much pretrial publicity, the judge may grant a motion for change of venue, transferring the case to another area where the publicity may have been less. Of course, some cases have received national press attention, and the defendant will not be given a fair trial anywhere. In that event, the defendant will get a trial that is only as "fair a trial as we can give him."[24]

Presenting Evidence

After the jury is seated in a case and sworn, the charging instrument is read to the jury, and the defendant enters a plea. Then the prosecutor begins presentation of his or her case by calling the first prosecution witness to testify. Each witness will be questioned first by the prosecuting attorney. This process is called **direct examination**. Attorneys often try to question witnesses in such a way that the witness' answer will be to that side's greatest benefit. Documents that pertain to

---

24. *Id.*

the witness' testimony may also be presented in evidence at that time. Such documents must be marked as **exhibits** and must carry exhibit numbers. All documents must be shown to the opposing counsel, the judge, and the jury. When the prosecuting attorney has completed interrogation of the witness, the defendant's attorney has an opportunity to ask that witness questions. This process is called **cross-examination**.

After the prosecutor has completed questioning all of his or her witnesses and the defense counsel has cross-examined them, the prosecutor rests. Defense counsel may then start his or her case by calling the defense witnesses and presenting documents. If the defense counsel believes that the prosecutor has not proved the prosecutor's case, defense counsel may rest without putting on any witnesses. Or, the defense counsel may decide to call some witnesses but not to put the defendant on the stand. By law, the fact that the defendant does not testify may not be considered as evidence against the defendant—to allow this would violate the defendant's Fifth Amendment right against self-incrimination. Any witnesses the defense does produce will be cross-examined by the prosecutor. The defense counsel's objective is to raise reasonable doubts about the prosecutor's case, often by discrediting the prosecutor's witnesses. An alternative strategy is to establish some affirmative defense such as self-defense or insanity.

Jury Instructions

After all the evidence is presented, attorneys on both sides usually meet with the judge in chambers to determine what the judge's **jury charge** will be. Both sides may present specific instructions that they want the judge to make. Objections to instructions should be recorded by the court reporter.

In addition to the judge's instructions to the jury, the lawyers have an opportunity to present closing arguments to the jury. In their arguments, they will attempt to summarize the evidence and interpret to the jury what they believe the evidence showed. Each side will try to appear more believable than the other. After both sides have presented closing arguments, the prosecutor, who has the burden of proof, has a final opportunity to argue.

Closing arguments may be offered either before or after the judge
instructs the jury, depending upon the local rule. The judge will instruct
the jury on the elements of the crime and other rules of law that they
must follow and apply in arriving at a decision in the case. The judge
will state that it is his or her duty to preside over the trial to determine
what testimony and evidence is relevant under the law for their
consideration and that they must follow his or her instructions. Some
judges use standard jury instructions. Standard jury instructions in
federal court include the following:

> . . . Upon retiring to the jury room you should first
> select one of your number to act as your foreman or
> forewoman who will preside over your deliberations
> and will be your spokesperson in court.

> . . . Any verdict must represent the considered
> judgment of each juror. In order to return a verdict, it
> is necessary that each jury agree thereto. In other
> words, your verdict must be unanimous.

> . . . It is your duty as jurors, to consult with one
> another, and to deliberate in an effort to reach
> agreement if you can do so without violence to indi-
> vidual judgment. Each of you must decide the case for
> yourself, but only after an impartial consideration of the
> evidence in the case with your fellow jurors. In the
> course of your deliberations, do not hesitate to
> reexamine your own views and change your opinion if
> convinced it is erroneous. But do not surrender your
> honest conviction as to the weight or effect of the
> evidence solely because of the opinion of your fellow
> jurors, or for the mere purpose of returning a verdict.

> Remember at all times, you are not partisans. You are
> judges – judges of the facts. Your sole interest is to
> seek the truth from the evidence in the case.[25]

---

25. U.S. Fifth Circuit District Judges Association, *Pattern Jury Instructions,*
     Criminal Cases (1979).

Standard jury instructions have been adopted by many trial courts in an effort to balance the sometimes conflicting objectives of keeping instructions simple and intelligible for a lay audience and yet technically precise enough to pass an appellate court's scrutiny.[26] Whenever a case is appealed, the appellate court will examine the court reporter's transcript of the trial court proceedings, including instructions that were given to the jury. Errors in instruction may cause the reversal of the trial court's decision.

A jury is allowed to deliberate as long as is necessary to reach a unanimous verdict. Some juries may reach a verdict in a couple of hours. Other juries deliberate for days or even weeks. On occasion, a jury will report that it is hopelessly deadlocked and unable to reach a verdict. This is called a **hung jury**. The judge then declares a mistrial, and the case may be tried again to a different jury before the same or a different judge.

In addition to the obvious service a jury performs in rendering a verdict, a jury serves another important function: that of bringing societal values into the courtroom. The jury, in effect, serves as a check upon the legislature, and by a process known as jury nullification, it acts to limit the force of any unpopular laws the legislature may have passed. Marijuana laws, for example, are unpopular in some areas, and juries sometimes bring in verdicts of innocence in marijuana cases in those areas. If juries continually fail to convict, they may force legislatures to change the laws. During the liquor prohibition era, the legislature did exactly that.

Sentencing

In some state courts, a jury that finds the defendant guilty may be sent back to the jury room to deliberate about the defendant's sentence. In other state courts and in the federal courts, the judge decides the sentence. In federal court, when a jury renders a guilty verdict, the judge usually sets a date for sentencing several weeks hence. During the interim, a United States Probation Officer will prepare a background

---

26. ABA Commission on Standards of Judicial Administration, *Trial Courts* (1976).

investigation of the defendant. The result of this investigation is compiled in a document called a **presentence report**. A presentence report will also be prepared on defendants who have pled guilty and waived their right to trial. The presentence report includes the defendant's version of the criminal event as well as the government version, personal and family data, the defendant's employment record, health and military history, the defendant's financial condition, and so forth. The report also includes the defendant's prior criminal record, if any, and any charges against the defendant that are currently pending.

In the final paragraph of the report, the probation officer usually recommends a sentence that he or she believes appropriate in the case, within the legally established maximum and minimum for each offense. The judge may or may not follow this recommendation. Most judges require defense counsel to examine the presentence report and to review it with the defendant.

Many judges consider the task of sentencing a heavy burden. In spite of guidelines and recommendations from the prosecutor, at the state level the weight of sentencing responsibility generally falls on the judge. However, in an effort to prevent crime and segregate criminals, California and several other states have passed "**3-strike**" laws that impose a mandatory life sentence without parole on any person convicted of a third felony. These laws tend to dilute judicial discretion in sentencing. Due to sentencing guidelines for all federal crimes, this is especially true at the federal level. Designed to ensure greater uniformity of sentencing across the federal system, the guidelines have, some argue, replaced the power of the judge to determine a sentence with the power of a prosecutor to determine what severity of crime to charge.

A judge may begin his or her sentencing duty with the question: "What am I trying to do?"[27] **Deterrence, protection of the public, rehabilitation**, and **retribution** are common objectives. One or more of these four objectives generally becomes the focus of the judge's consideration. If deterrence of similar crimes by potential new offenders is the judge's primary consideration, he or she may consider not only the

---

27. Higginbotham, *The Philosophy of Sentencing*, 42 Tex. B.J. 497, 499 (1979).

type of sentence that will best accomplish that function but also how that sentence will be communicated to potential offenders.

Deterrence is often the primary objective in "white collar" crimes. For more violent crimes, such as rape, protection of the public may be the primary consideration. Rehabilitation may be the most difficult objective, given the low level of achievement and educability of most prisoners.[23] Retribution is also a complicated objective. Historically it has been assumed that for every crime there would be retribution. Community feelings of guilt or vengeance often play a part. United States Circuit Judge Patrick E. Higginbotham finds that the criminal sentence is "laced with release of community guilt feelings and atonement."[29]

In spite of the different objectives in sentencing, authorities seem to agree that if laws are to have any power, failure to obey the laws must be accompanied by punishment. In other words, a commitment to law as a specific form of government is already logically a commitment to the policy of punishing violators. The very concept of law itself embodies the concept of retributive punishment.[30]

The concept of sentencing is firmly rooted in society, and judges will continue to struggle with sentencing objectives and the types of sentences to impose. Although a judge has considerable latitude in the sentence he or she imposes, minimum and maximum sentences for types of offenses are fixed by law.

The most common sentences are **probation** or a term of **imprisonment**. A combination of the two is referred to as a **split sentence**.

Imprisonment involves sentencing a convicted defendant to jail for a fixed length of time that is defined by law. Frequently, however, prisoners do not have to serve out the entire term of their sentences in

---

28. J. Kaplan, *Cases, supra.*

29. Higginbotham, *supra* note 27.

30. Fingarette, *Law and Punishment*, 50 Proc. and Addresses Am. Philosophical A.

prison. Instead, they receive **parole**, which is a conditional release from prison that entitles them to serve out the remainder of their sentences in the community.

Not to be confused with imprisonment and parole, the split sentence requires the defendant to serve all of a fixed term in prison followed by a fixed term on probation. Generally, however, the fixed term of a split sentence is short, such as six months. An alternative to imprisonment is the **suspended sentence**, where the defendant is permitted to serve the entire prison sentence on probation.

General conditions of probation include a requirement that the probationer report to the probation office on a regular basis, usually once a month, at which time the probation officer makes sure the probationer is employed and that his or her current address is known. Most felony probationers are not permitted to travel outside the state. More and more defendants are being required to perform **supervised community service** as a condition of probation or a suspended sentence, such as cleaning up parks, refurbishing public buildings, tutoring underprivileged children and other similar efforts. A community service sentence embodies goals of punishment, restitution to society, and rehabilitation.

If a defendant violates the terms of probation, the judge can send the defendant (back) to prison, especially if the probation violation is serious. The probationer will be called before the court to determine if probation privileges should be revoked. Such a hearing is called a **probation revocation hearing**, at which the defendant is guaranteed the right to be represented by counsel under the Sixth Amendment to the Constitution. In contrast, if a parolee violates the terms of his or her release on parole, no hearing is generally required. He or she can be arrested and, in most cases, summarily returned to prison.

Another sentencing alternative is the **fine**. A fine may be imposed by itself, or in association with probation or imprisonment. Confiscation of a felon's assets, including cars, jewelry, and real estate, is a type of fine often imposed on violators of drug laws. The money and property received from the fines goes to the government.

The court may also order **restitution**, which is the payment of monetary damages to the victim, such as the value of property taken or destroyed as a result of the crime. Restitution, which can be a term of probation or imprisonment, recognizes that crime victims are often overlooked in the pursuit of justice. Sentencing an offender to probation or prison may satisfy and protect society, but it does little to help the victim heal and get on with his or her life. Restitution seeks to mitigate this need.

The philosophy and mechanics of sentencing are the subject of much ongoing debate. New proposals are continually being advanced in an effort to accommodate the often-conflicting interests of society, victims, and criminals.

Appeal

Individuals convicted of criminal offenses have the right to appeal their convictions. Those convicted in state courts can generally appeal through their state's highest court. Likewise, those convicted in federal courts ultimately can seek a hearing before the Supreme Court. In most cases, appeals courts have discretion whether or not to hear an appeal based on some alleged error in the lower court's proceedings. State defendants have access to federal courts for the purpose of appealing only if they assert that the state failed to observe a federally imposed procedural guarantee. These include

- the right to a jury trial for serious offenses
- the assistance of counsel if a jail sentence may be imposed
- the privilege against self-incrimination
- establishing guilt beyond a reasonable doubt
- the right to refuse to take part in a police interrogation or to have an attorney present
- freedom from racial and sexual discrimination.[31]

Many people think of the criminal justice system as the process by which a criminal defendant is tried in a courtroom before a jury. This chapter has illustrated the narrowness of that point of view: the process

---

31. J. Kaplan, *Cases, supra.*

is an ongoing one, from the time a person arouses the suspicion of the police officer·on the beat to the time the criminal has served out his or her term of imprisonment, parole, or probation. Many individuals enter the system only once, at the lowest level, and are never charged with or convicted of a crime. Others pass through the entire length of the system time and time again, returning to a life of crime as soon as they gain their freedom. For this reason, the presumption of innocence, which is critical to our system of criminal justice, is often difficult to put into practice.

TERMS TO KNOW

crime
criminal justice system
misdemeanors
felon
United States Supreme Court
jurisdiction
- subject matter
- personal
court of record
defendant
de novo
procedural due process
probable cause
exclusionary rule
grand jury indictment
grand jury
privilege against self-
  incrimination
Miranda warnings
indictment
citation
bail bond
cash bond
surety bond
appearance bond
personal recognizance
pretrial release program

indictment
information
complaint
arraignment
nolo contendere
plea bargaining
motion
discovery
venue
voir dire examination
jury panel
challenge for cause
peremptory challenge
in limine
direct examination
cross-examination
jury charge
hung jury
presentence report
deterrence
protection of the public
prosecutor
rehabilitation
retribution
probation
imprisonment
split sentence

suspended sentence
time
restriction
probation revocation
 hearing
sentencing guidelines
parole
restitution

Chapter Three

SUBSTANTIVE CIVIL LAW

In contrast to criminal law, which regulates the conduct of individuals who threaten the peace and order of society, civil law defines the responsibility of individuals to one another and regulates that conduct through **injunctions,** the award of money **damages** and, in some cases, government fines.

The topics covered by substantive civil law are as varied as the conduct that the law attempts to regulate. Many types of civil laws are created by statute. State statutes are the greatest source of civil liability and cover a wide range of commercial and personal activity. Federal civil statutes also create liability for such matters as securities fraud, antitrust conspiracies, or patent, trademark, and copyright infringement that involve people and transactions in more than one state. One of the better known and most widely applicable bodies of federal civil law, for example, is the Internal Revenue Code that deals with federal taxation.

Civil statutes may also define the legal consequences of certain acts or conditions, such as statutes that provide for the distribution of the property of people who die without a will, or statutes that define the effectiveness of a deed that has not been properly recorded with the county clerk.

Beyond the statutes passed by Congress and the state legislatures (and, of course, the administrative regulations adopted under those statutes) is the common law, which sets forth the standards of conduct applicable in most day-to-day situations and establishes the rules of liability in many civil lawsuits. Often, a lawsuit will contain claims based on both the common law and on statutes.

The remainder of this chapter will discuss four of the most fundamental areas of the common law: torts, contracts, the law of real property, and the law of wills and descent of property. An understanding of the basic principles of these fundamental areas is essential to an understanding of more complex areas of civil law. The chapter concludes with a brief discussion of legislation as a source of statutes, administrative regulations, and procedure, including the increasing use of alternative methods of resolving disputes outside the courtroom.

Torts

A **tort** may be broadly defined as an act or omission to act that causes legal harm to another, committed under circumstances where the law imposes a duty to refrain from causing such harm. Although some torts, such as **fraud**, may be connected with a contractual relationship, the obligation to refrain from committing a tort is usually one imposed by law and not by any agreement between the parties.

Torts fall into three broad categories: intentional torts, such as **battery**; negligent torts; and so-called "**strict liability torts**," such as the marketing of an unreasonably dangerous product.

Intentional Torts

Apart from torts such as fraud, discussed later, there are six principal intentional torts:

- battery
- assault
- false imprisonment
- intentional infliction of emotional distress
- trespass
- conversion.

Most of these torts are derived from the old English **writ of trespass**, which in medieval times was a quasi-criminal remedy for redress of a direct and usually intentional injury. As their labels imply, each of these modern torts must be committed intentionally. This does not mean, however, that the person who commits the tort (referred to in legal parlance as the **tortfeasor**) must have wanted the resulting harm to occur; it is sufficient that the tortfeasor be aware that harm is substantially certain to occur. Thus, for example, someone who blows up a plane in order to kill one passenger has committed an intentional tort against all the passengers who are injured, even if he or she had no desire to harm any of the other passengers.

It is not necessary that the tortfeasor anticipate all of the harmful consequences that actually follow from the commission of the tort: he or she will be held liable for all results that are reasonably foreseeable. For example, a robber who clubs a victim, intending only to incapacitate the victim, but who "unintentionally" kills the victim, is liable for all the resulting harm because it is foreseeable that clubbing someone may cause death. It is not even necessary that the tortfeasor intend that the harmed individual be the one to suffer harm: under the **doctrine of transferred intent**, the intent to harm one person is "transferred" to the person actually harmed. Thus a tortfeasor who attempts to strike A, but misses and instead strikes B, has committed an intentional tort against B, even if the tortfeasor had no intention to strike B.

Battery is defined as the harmful or offensive touching of another, such as striking another with one's fist. It is not necessary that the contact be directly with the victim's body; any harmful or offensive touching of the clothing, or of an object closely associated with the body, such as a plate held in the hand, is sufficient to constitute a battery. The harm need not be caused directly; thus one who digs a hole into which he or she knows a victim will fall is guilty of a battery. And the contact need not be physically harmful—any contact that a person of reasonable sensibilities would find offensive is a battery. It is not even necessary that the victim be aware of the contact at the time of its occurrence; hence someone who is kissed by a stranger while asleep has a valid claim for battery.

The tort of **assault** consists of placing someone in the apprehension of an immediate battery. The actual battery need not occur for there to be an assault; all that is necessary is that the victim reasonably expect that a battery is about to follow. A prime example would be raising one's fist to strike. Nor does "apprehension" refer to fear on the part of the victim: a ninety-pound weakling may assault a heavyweight prize fighter if the latter is led to expect that an immediate battery, that is, an immediate harmful or offensive touching, will occur. It is not necessary that a battery be actually physically possible. Hence pointing an unloaded gun at someone may constitute an assault if the victim does not know the gun is unloaded. The apprehension must be of an immediate battery: a threat to commit a battery in the future is not sufficient.

False imprisonment consists of restraining someone within a bounded area against that person's will: the tort commonly referred to as "false arrest" is a good example. It is not necessary that the victim be confined to a small area, but it is essential that the area be bounded. Thus, confining someone to a city would be false imprisonment, but preventing someone from entering a building would not. The restraint may be by actual physical force or may consist of the expressed or implied threat of physical force. The force or threat of force may be directed toward the victim, the victim's immediate family, or the victim's property. In cases where the restraint causes actual physical harm, the victim need not be aware of the restraint at the time; thus a sleeping person who is confined and suffers harm may recover for false imprisonment.

Finally, false imprisonment, like many other torts, may occur through an act or through a failure to act where there is a duty to act. Thus, for example, a jailer who fails to release a prisoner at the appropriate time is liable for false imprisonment.[1]

The **intentional infliction of emotional distress** is sometimes a tort. In order for recovery to be allowed, the defendant's conduct must be extreme and outrageous, transcending all bounds of common decency. Except in special situations, such as the conduct of a common transportation carrier or innkeeper toward a customer, or conduct directed toward a child or other person of special sensibilities, offensive or insulting language is not ordinarily sufficient to constitute the tort of intentional infliction of emotional distress.

In most cases, the severe emotional distress must result in physical consequences or symptoms before a recovery will be permitted. Under some limited circumstances, a person who causes another to witness an injury to a third party (usually a member of the victim's family) and thereby causes the victim to suffer severe emotional distress, will be held liable.[2]

---

1. See *Weigel v. McCloskey*, 113 Ark. 1, 166 S.W. 944 (1914).

2. For an example of such a case, see *Hill v. Kimball*, 76 Tex. 210, 13 S.W. 59 (1890).

The predecessor of most modern intentional torts is the tort of **trespass**. A trespass is an intentional interference with an individual's right to exclusive and complete possession of land or tangible goods. The right to possession of land includes the right to use a reasonable amount of air space above the land as well as the space beneath the surface. Thus one may commit a trespass by throwing or shooting a projectile over someone's land or by mining underneath it.

In the case of trespass to land, it is not necessary to prove any physical damage in order to recover. For trespass to physical objects (**chattels**), however, it is necessary to show damage to the chattel, injury to its owner, or deprivation of its use for a substantial period of time.

The law of **conversion** is complex and detailed. The *Second Restatement of Torts*, §222A, however, provides a summary definition: "an intentional exercise of dominion or control over a chattel which so seriously interferes with the right of another to control it that the actor may justly be required to pay the other the full value of the chattel."

Negligence Torts

By far the majority of modern tort lawsuits are not concerned with intentional torts, but with **negligence**. Negligence consists of four basic elements:

1. a duty to conform to a certain standard established by law
2. a failure to meet the standard
3. a cause-and-effect relationship between that failure and the resulting injury
4. damages resulting from the injury.

All four of these elements must be present before there can be a recovery for negligence.

Duty

The standard of conduct established by law is expressed with reference to the conduct of a hypothetical "reasonable person of ordinary prudence, acting under the same or similar circumstances." Negligence consists of doing what a reasonable person would not do under the circumstances or of not doing what a reasonable person would do under the circumstances. Thus, it is no defense that the tortfeasor is as careful as he or she knows how to be if the tortfeasor does not exercise so-called "ordinary care."

One who is incapable of ordinary care due to insanity, mental deficiency, or simple stupidity is nonetheless liable for negligence if his or her actions do not measure up to this hypothetical standard. Only children are permitted a lesser standard: the conduct of a child is judged by the conduct of a typical child of the same age, intelligence, and experience.

The ordinary rules of negligence are applicable in the case of alleged malpractice by professionals such as doctors, lawyers, accountants, architects, and the like. Thus, for example, a physician is liable who does not conform to the standard of knowledge and skill of medical practitioners in good standing in the physician's community. This does not mean that the physician will be liable for any error of judgment: there is negligence only where the error is one that a competent practitioner would not make.

While general practitioners are governed by the standards of other general practitioners in the community, a specialist is held to the standard of others practicing the same specialty, and the comparison is not limited to those in the specialist's community. Except where the medical implications of the defendant's conduct are obvious to a layperson (such as where a surgeon mistakenly removes the wrong kidney), expert testimony is required to establish the appropriate medical standard of care.

Liability for malpractice is not limited to direct negligence by the physician: the physician who fails to obtain the "informed consent" of the patient before performing a procedure may also be liable. Malpractice liability is not limited to physicians: in this regard you may wish to review Wade, *Tort Liability of Paralegals and Lawyers Who Utilize Their Services.*[3]

---

3. 24 Vand. L. Rev. 1133 (1971).

Where a statute prohibits certain conduct, courts often hold that a violation of the statute is itself negligence. This doctrine is known as **negligence per se**. In order for a plaintiff to rely on negligence per se, the plaintiff must establish that he or she is a member of the class of people for whose benefit the statute was enacted and that the harm that he or she suffered is the kind of harm the statute was enacted to prevent. Thus, a motorist who is struck at night by a car that has no headlights may recover for negligence, since nighttime accidents are one of the dangers that the headlight law was designed to prevent, and nighttime motorists are the group to be protected.[4] It is necessary, however, that the violation of the law play a part in causing the injury; thus one who is speeding is not automatically liable for any accidents that may occur, but only for those in which excessive speed played a part.

A specialized form of proof of negligence goes by the imposing name of *res ipsa loquitur*. This phrase is Latin for "the thing speaks for itself." Where an accident occurs that is of a type that does not ordinarily take place in the absence of negligence, where the object or instrumentality that causes the accident was in the exclusive control of the defendant, and where the accident cannot have been due to any action of the plaintiff, the judge or jury is permitted to infer that the accident occurred as a result of the defendant's negligence. Thus, for example, in an old English case, a barrel of flour fell out of the second floor of the defendant's warehouse and struck the plaintiff. Since such a circumstance does not ordinarily come about unless someone is negligent, since the barrel was in the exclusive control of the defendant, and since the plaintiff could not have been at fault, *res ipsa loquitur* was applied.[5]

Causation

In order for there to be liability for negligence, two types of **causation** must be present. These are commonly known as **causation in fact**, on the one hand, and "legal" or **proximate causation** on the other.

---

4. See *Martin v. Herzog*, 228 N.Y. 164, 126 N.E. 814 (1920).

5. See *Byrne v. Boadle*, 2 H. & C. 722, 159 Eng. Rep. 299 (1863).

Causation in fact is relatively straightforward: the negligent conduct causes the resulting injury if the injury would not have occurred unless the negligent conduct had occurred. Where there are two or more causes for a single injury, as where fires negligently set by two individuals combine and burn down a house, a tortfeasor is liable if the tortfeasor's conduct was a substantial factor in causing the injury.

The concept of legal or proximate causation is harder to understand. The law does not impose liability for every injury that is caused in fact by tortious conduct, but only for those injuries that are sufficiently direct. Thus in a case where a ship was negligently moored, broke loose, floated downstream, struck another ship and caused it to break loose, following which the two ships struck a bridge and caused the bridge to collapse and dam up a river, flooding the land upstream, the tortfeasor was forced to pay for the flood damage, because such damage was regarded as sufficiently direct. But the tortfeasor was not liable for damages to the owner of a ship whose path was blocked by the collapsed bridge, because that injury was determined to be too remote.[6]

The problem of determining which injuries are sufficiently direct is one of the most difficult problems in tort law. A good rule of thumb is that a defendant will be held liable for all the injuries that the defendant might have reasonably foreseen would result from his or her conduct. If a second cause intervenes to produce the injuries, the defendant will be held liable if that cause was reasonably foreseeable, but not otherwise. For example, if a roof blows off in a high wind and injures someone, the defendant may be liable if the area often gets high winds that cause significant property damage, because the danger was foreseeable. But the defendant will likely not be liable if the wind was much stronger than might reasonably have been expected.[7]

Not all negligent actions or inactions that proximately cause injuries are the subject of tort liability. In addition to these elements, there must be a duty to act or not to act that is imposed by law. While one ordinarily has a duty to prevent harm to others, this is not always the case. For

---

6. Compare *In re Kinsman Transit Co.*, 338 F.2d 708 (2d Cir. 1964) with *In re Kinsman Transit Co.*, 388 F.2d 821 (2d Cir. 1968).

7. See *Kimble v. Mackintosh Hemphill Co.*, 359 Pa. 461, 59 A.2d 68 (1948).

example, a person is ordinarily under no duty to save someone from a danger that the person has not created. While it may be morally reprehensible to stand by and watch someone suffer injury, one who does so is not liable for damages. If, however, aid is given, it must be given in a reasonable manner. One who begins to aid a person and then abandons the person may have caused others not to come to the person's assistance, while one who gives aid in a negligent manner may cause further injury.

Torts Involving Landowners

The duty of a landowner with respect to dangerous conditions on his or her land is governed by special rules. A landowner is ordinarily not liable for injuries to someone outside the landowner's land caused by dangerous natural conditions of the land, such as a rotten tree on the edge of the land that falls and injures a passerby.[8] The landowner *is* generally liable, however, for injuries caused by artificial conditions that the landowner negligently fails to correct.

In most states, persons on a defendant's land are divided into three categories for purposes of analyzing the landowner's duty toward them. First are those who are on the land without express or implied permission; that is, **trespassers**. A landowner's sole duty to a trespasser is to refrain from willfully or wantonly injuring the trespasser. Thus, observed trespassers must be warned of known dangerous conditions on the land, and the landowner must exercise reasonable care in not injuring the trespasser once the trespasser is discovered.

There is ordinarily no duty, however, toward undiscovered trespassers, except to avoid wanton conduct in disregard of the danger to any trespasser who might be on the premises. Thus, for example, a landowner would not be liable if an undiscovered trespasser falls into a pit on the land, but the landowner might be liable if he or she shoots a gun recklessly without regard for whether there are any trespassers on the premises. A special exception to this rule, known as **attractive nuisance,** exists in the case of trespassing children. If the landowner knows or should know that children are likely to trespass but

---

8. See *Lemon v. Edwards*, 344 S.W. 2d 822 (Ky. 1961).

negligently allows an unreasonably dangerous condition to exist the landowner will be held liable for injuries suffered by the children because they cannot learn of or appreciate the danger. Despite the name of this doctrine, it is not necessary that the child be "attracted" onto the premises by the dangerous condition; it is only necessary that the presence of children can be reasonably anticipated.

The second category of visitors on a defendant's land is that of **licensees**. Licensees are those persons who are on the land with permission and for a legitimate purpose but who are not there as ordinary members of the public or for a business purpose of the landowner. Common examples of licensees include members of the landowner's family and household or social guests. The duty of a landowner toward a licensee is one of ordinary care; in other words, the general negligence standard applies. This means that the landowner must exercise ordinary care to refrain from injuring the licensee and must warn a licensee of hidden dangers that he or she is likely to encounter.

The final category is that of **invitees**, those who are on land as members of the public or to further the business interests of the landowner. Examples include passengers in public conveyances or customers in a store. The term "invitee" is misleading: the fact that someone has received an invitation to come onto the land does not necessarily make that person an invitee. Social guests, discussed above, are a prime example. A person is an invitee only so long as he or she remains on the property for the business purpose of the owner. Thus, a customer who loiters in a store for an unreasonable time after making a purchase, or who travels to areas of the store not open to the public, will lose invitee status. The owner owes a duty to an invitee to maintain the premises in a reasonably safe condition and must take all reasonable steps to avoid injury to an invitee.

In some states the distinctions among the duties owed to trespassers, licensees, and invitees have been abolished, and all landowners owe the ordinary duty of reasonable care to those on their premises.

Ordinarily, a landlord owes no duty with respect to premises that the landlord has leased to someone else. There are, however, a number of important exceptions.

First, a landlord must exercise reasonable care to inspect and repair parts of the premises that are not exclusively leased to one tenant, such as hallways, stairways, sidewalks, and the like.

Second, a landlord must use ordinary care to see that the premises are safe at the time possession is transferred with respect to persons outside the land and in situations where the premises are leased for the purpose of allowing the public to enter, such as the lease of a theater or store.

A landlord will also be liable if he or she fails to disclose any unreasonably dangerous condition that exists at the time possession is delivered, fails to comply with a contractual obligation to make repairs; or negligently makes repairs (whether required to do so or not).

The Negligent Victim

Until recent years, almost all states followed a contributory negligence rule under which a plaintiff whose own negligence was a contributing cause of his or her injuries was barred from any recovery. This harsh rule sometimes had the effect of barring a plaintiff whose negligence was slight when compared to the negligence of the defendant, and the rule has gradually been abandoned.

The usual rule is now one of **comparative negligence**: The plaintiff is permitted to recover so long as the plaintiff's negligence is not greater than that of the defendant. The judge or jury is asked to apportion the total negligence between the parties in percentage terms, and the plaintiff's damages are reduced accordingly. Thus, if the plaintiff's fault is determined to represent 30% of the total fault that caused the injury, his or her damages will be reduced by 30%, and the defendant will be liable only for the remaining 70%. This system ensures that a plaintiff is penalized for his or her own negligence, yet it prevents the defendant from escaping without liability due to the plaintiff's slight negligence.

Strict-Liability Torts

Up to this point our discussion has focused on torts in which the tortfeasor possesses some degree of fault. Are there situations in which someone may be held liable in tort despite having acted with the utmost care? The answer is that there are **strict-liability torts**, the three leading examples of which are discussed in the following paragraphs.

Ultrahazardous Activities

While most activities result in liability only if the actor is negligent, certain "ultrahazardous" activities may be undertaken only at the actor's own risk. These activities include dangerous conduct such as blasting, use of poisons, and the flying of especially dangerous aircraft. Among the factors to be considered in determining whether an activity is abnormally dangerous are whether it involves a high likelihood of harm, whether the harm is likely to be great, whether the activity can be made safe through reasonable care, whether it is a matter of common usage, whether it is inappropriate for the place where it is carried on, and whether it is valuable to the community. Thus an activity may be abnormally dangerous under some circumstances, but not under others.

Animals

The owners of wild animals are generally held to be strictly liable to those who are injured by the animals. The status of domesticated animals, such as pets or barnyard animals, is slightly more complicated. Such an animal is treated as a "wild" animal if its owner has reason to know that it has a vicious disposition, but not otherwise. This has given rise to what is sometimes known as the "one-bite" rule; that is, that the owner of a cat or dog is not liable on the first occasion on which the pet bites a person. Such a rule is misleading, since the true test is whether the owner should know of the animal's nature, rather than whether it has been vicious in the past.

Product Liability

By far the most important of the strict liability torts is the liability that a manufacturer or seller bears for defects in products. This is known as

products liability, and in recent years it has come to represent a substantial percentage of all tort litigation. While at one time products liability existed only under theories of negligence or breach of warranty and was subject to difficult burdens of proof and broad defenses, most states have made products liability a strict-liability tort.

In the *Second Restatement of Torts*, Section 402A discusses liability for physical harm to persons or property caused by any defective product that is unreasonably dangerous at the time it leaves the defendant's hands. This rule applies whether or not the user or consumer who is injured dealt directly with the defendant. Thus, a manufacturer is liable even if its product was sold and resold several times before reaching the consumer.

The products-liability rule, as adopted by the courts, has two important aspects:

1. The product in question must be defective
2. It must be unreasonably dangerous.

Both of these elements are required before liability exists.

A "defective" product is one that does not meet the reasonable safety expectations of the ordinary consumer.[9] The defect may be inherent in the product, (that is, the product may be improperly designed) or, it may be properly designed but improperly manufactured, packaged, or labeled. Alternatively, the defect may consist of a failure to provide an adequate warning as to the limitations or dangers of the product or a failure to provide proper instructions for its safe use.

It is immaterial whether the manufacturer or seller knew of the defect, or even whether it was negligent in not knowing of the defect. As with other strict-liability torts, liability is imposed without regard to fault. While the defect must be one that existed at the time the product left the defendant's hands, the failure to provide a safeguard against future defects that the defendant knows are likely to occur may itself be a defect.

---

9. See *McCullough v. Beech Aircraft Corp.*, 587 F.2d 754 (5th Cir. 1979).

The second aspect of products liability is that the defect must cause the product to be unreasonably dangerous. It is not enough to show that a product could have been made without the defect; the plaintiff must show that it was unreasonable not to do so. Thus, while products liability is technically a strict-liability tort, one of the elements of negligence—reasonableness—comes in "through the back door," so to speak, because the jury must hear evidence and decide if the product was unreasonably dangerous. In making the determination of reasonableness, the judge or jury must weigh the utility of the product against the risk involved in its use.[10]

In determining whether a product is unreasonably dangerous, the feasibility and cost of eliminating the danger must be compared with the danger itself and the risk of injury that it presents. Some products, such as certain prescription drugs, may be "unavoidably unsafe"; that is, the products may be so useful that they should be marketed despite the fact that there is no way to make them completely safe. In such a case, the manufacturer or seller will not be held liable. The manufacturer or seller may, however, be required to include a warning of the danger if a warning will help to minimize the risk.

A manufacturer or seller is ordinarily not liable if its product is put to an improper use in a manner not contemplated when the product was designed. This defense is, however, subject to an important qualification: the misuse must be of a kind that the defendant could not reasonably expect. Thus, while automobiles need not be built to withstand every type of crash, it is to be expected that automobiles will be involved in accidents, and hence the manufacturer must make them as "crashworthy" as is reasonably possible. A defense of misuse of the products by the plaintiff may also be unavailable if an adequate warning might have prevented the misuse.

While contributory and comparative negligence have no place in products liability cases, a few states have an unusual doctrine known as **comparative causation**. Under this doctrine, a manufacturer's liability may be reduced by a percentage that represents the degree to which the plaintiff's misconduct participated in causing the injury, much like a

---

10. See *Foster v. Ford Motor Co.*, 621 F.2d 715 (5th Cir. 1980).

negligent tortfeasor's liability is reduced under comparative negligence.[11]

Nuisance

Two very different types of torts fall under the general heading of nuisance. A **private nuisance** is an interference with a landowner's right to possession and enjoyment of his or her land, while a **public nuisance** is an interference with the rights of the public generally. Nuisance is not, strictly speaking, a separate tort; it is instead a label applied to a variety of torts. Thus, there may be negligent nuisances, intentional nuisances, or nuisances for which strict liability is imposed. Public nuisances include such things as "houses of prostitution, gambling dens, hog pens, illegal liquor establishments, indecent exhibitions, bullfights, unauthorized prize fights and the illegal practice of law and medicine."[12] To be permitted to sue to stop such things, the plaintiff cannot sue simply as a member of the general public but must instead have suffered a specific injury.

A private nuisance, on the other hand, involves conduct that interferes with a specific individual's right to enjoyment of a specific piece of land by interfering with access to the land or with its habitability, by reducing its value, or by otherwise unreasonably depriving its owner of its full use. A nuisance may be one that is a nuisance under all circumstances (a **nuisance per se**) or one that is a nuisance only by virtue of the particular circumstances in which it is conducted (a **nuisance per accidents**). As the United States Supreme Court has stated, "A nuisance may be merely a right thing in the wrong place, like a pig in the parlor instead of the barnyard."[13] Many nuisance suits involve adjacent landowners quarreling about barking dogs, loud music, and other disruptive activity.

---

11. See *Signal Oil & Gas Co. v. Universal Oil Products*, 572 S.W.2d 320 (Tex. 1978).

12. See *Culwell v. Abbott Construction Co.*, 211 Kan. 359, 506 P.2d 119 (1973).

13. See *Village of Euclid v. Ambler Realty Co.*, 272 U.S. 365. 388 (1926).

Other Torts

A variety of torts do not involve bodily injury or property damage. Chief among these is the tort of **deceit**, or **fraud**, which consists of making a knowingly false representation upon which someone reasonably relies to his or her detriment in deciding to enter into a transaction. Other so-called **"business torts"** include **negligent misrepresentation**, **interference with business relations**, and **unfair competition**. A number of business torts, such as securities fraud, antitrust torts, and the use of deceptive trade practices, are created by statute.

Another group of torts involves interference with personal rights. Examples of these include **defamation** (**libel** and **slander**), **invasion of privacy**, and **malicious prosecution** (sometimes called abuse of process where a civil case is involved). Other torts involve a combination of personal and financial rights, such as the torts created by Title VII of the Civil Rights Act of 1964 and the Age Discrimination in Employment Act for employment discrimination on grounds of race, sex, religion, national origin, or age.

Damages and Remedies for Tort

Two principal types of damages are awarded in tort lawsuits: **compensatory** (or actual) damages and **punitive** (or **exemplary**) damages. The purpose of compensatory damages is to restore the tort victim to the place the victim would have occupied had the tort not occurred, to the extent that this may be done by a monetary payment. In some cases, a tort may technically have been committed, but the victim may have suffered no loss. In such cases, an award of **nominal damages**, usually $1, is made.

Punitive damages, on the other hand, are designed to punish the tortfeasor and are awarded only in the case of intentional torts or cases involving so-called "gross" negligence or "willful and wanton misconduct." Some statutory torts have their own damage scheme; for example, damages for antitrust violations are trebled as a way of punishing the wrongdoer. Some statutes also require that a losing defendant pay the plaintiff's attorneys' fees.

Finally, in appropriate cases an **injunction** may be granted to bring a halt to a continuing tort, such as a nuisance or ongoing pattern of harassment.

It is impossible to discuss all of tort law in a few short pages. Entire volumes are written on the subject and, indeed, entire volumes have been written on each of the many topics that have been discussed. The discussion presented in this section is designed to provide a background understanding of the most important aspects of tort law. Many topics have been omitted, while others have been explained in general but not in detail. For a more detailed understanding of particular topics, consult the *Second Restatement of Torts*, published by the American Law Institute, or a good treatise on the subject, such as W. Prosser's *The Law of Torts*.

Contracts

The second of the three principal branches of the common law is the law of contracts. Like modern tort law, much of modern contract law is derived from an old English writ – this time the **writ of assumpsit**. The principal difference between contract and tort liability is that, with limited exceptions to be discussed below, no contractual liability can be created except by means of an agreement.

Contractual liability is as infinitely varied as the types of agreements into which individuals may enter. All that is required is that there be an offer and an acceptance, that the contract be of a type that the law will recognize and enforce, and that it be breached by one party with damage resulting to the other. In the pages that follow, we will explore each of these elements. In addition, we will examine the **Uniform Commercial Code**, a statutory codification of many aspects of the common law of contracts that has been enacted in every state and that sets forth rules for business transactions.

Types of Contracts

Contracts may be broadly grouped into three categories. First, an agreement may be an **express contract,** where the parties have expressly agreed, orally or in writing, that each is to be bound to do certain things. Common examples include real estate leases, bills of sale, and formal employment contracts.

Secondly, a contract may be **implied in fact**. In this type of contract the parties have not formally agreed to be bound, but a mutual intention to make a contract can be inferred from their conduct. For example, a patient who visits a doctor's office usually does not agree with the doctor in advance that he or she will pay a specific fee in exchange for certain specific acts by the doctor. Rather, there is an implied contract by which the doctor agrees to use his or her best efforts to cure the patient, while the patient agrees to pay the doctor's usual and reasonable fee for that service.

A contract can be both express and implied. Where the parties have made an express contract but have omitted one or more terms, it is possible that their intentions with respect to those terms may be inferred from their conduct. Thus, if a customer has bought widgets from the Acme Widget Company for twenty years, and on each occasion the widgets have been shipped by rail, a "shipment by rail" term may be implied in a sales contract that does not discuss the method of shipment.[14]

Finally, a contract may be **implied in law**. These contracts differ from implied-in-fact contracts in that the parties never reached any kind of agreement, express or implied. This makes the expression "implied-in-law contract" somewhat misleading, since there is really no contract; indeed, this type of liability is sometimes called **quasi-contractual liability**.

In an implied-in-law contract, the law imposes requirements on the parties even though they have not agreed to be bound by those requirements, usually because it would be unfair (or, in legal parlance, would produce **unjust enrichment**) to allow one party to receive a benefit conferred upon him or her by the other without paying for that benefit. For example, in an old Arkansas case a man suffered injuries in a streetcar wreck and was found by a doctor, who treated the man in an unsuccessful attempt to save his life. Despite the fact that the victim

---

14. Uniform Commercial Code, §2-305.

had been unconscious and so could not possibly have agreed, expressly or by implication from his conduct, to pay for the doctor's services, the court permitted the doctor to recover the reasonable value of his services from the victim's estate.[15]

Elements of a Contract

In order for a binding contract to be formed, there must be an **offer** and an **acceptance**. An offer is no more than a communication by one party to the other that reasonably leads the receiving party to believe that the offering party is willing to enter into a contract. The intention must be to enter into an immediate contract, not merely to set forth the terms under which further negotiations can occur. Thus a statement such as "I will sell you this for $50" is an offer, while a statement such as "My usual price for this is $50" would not be construed as an offer. All the surrounding circumstances, including the language used, the method of communication, the specificity of the terms, and the custom between the parties and in the industry, must be examined to determine if an offer has been made.

An offer remains open until it expires, is withdrawn, is rejected, or is accepted. Some offers, especially those in writing, contain an express expiration date, such as "This offer will expire at noon on January 15, 1999, unless accepted before that time." Whether or not an offer contains such a term, the offering party may ordinarily withdraw the offer at any time by communicating that fact to the receiving party.

Exceptions exist where the offering party has been paid something in exchange for making the offer. If the offer states, "For a fee of $1,000, I hereby offer to sell you 1,000 widgets for $10 each at any time during the next six months," it is irrevocable. When a merchant makes a "firm" offer, the merchant promises to keep the offer open for a reasonable time.[16]

An offer also terminates when it is rejected by the receiving party. A rejection may be express, as by stating "I reject your offer." Or the

---

15. See *Cotnam v. Wisdom*, 83 Ark. 601, 104 S.W. 164 (1907).

16. Uniform Commercial Code, §2-205.

rejection may occur by lapse of a reasonable time. In addition, any counteroffer that varies the terms of the original offer is a rejection: the exchanges "I will buy that for $50," followed by "I will sell it for $100," show that the original $50 offer from the buyer is rejected and replaced by a new $100 offer from the seller.

Once an offer is terminated by expiration, withdrawal, or rejection, it cannot be accepted to form a binding contract. If not terminated, however, an offer may be accepted in any reasonable manner. Acceptance creates a binding contract and terminates the right to withdraw the offer.

Offers may be divided into two broad categories: those which contemplate a promise in exchange for a promise, called offers for **bilateral contracts** ("I promise to pay you $1,000 if you will promise to deliver 1,000 widgets") and those which contemplate actual performance as an acceptance, called offers for **unilateral contracts** ("I promise to pay you $1,000 if you will deliver 1,000 widgets").

Where an offer makes plain that only acceptance by performance is contemplated, an acceptance by promise is insufficient; on the other hand, acceptance of an offer for a bilateral contract may be by promise or by performance. Most offers do not make clear which type of acceptance they seek; in such circumstances Section 2-206 of the Uniform Commercial Code permits any reasonable form of acceptance. The ordinary rule is that an acceptance may not vary any of the terms of the offer: that is, an offer is a "take it or leave it" proposition.

Section 2-207 of the Uniform Commercial Code creates an exception to this rule, designed to cover the so-called "battle-of-the-forms" situation where the offer and the acceptance contain differing "boilerplate" (i.e., standard, often preprinted) language, as often happens in dealings between large companies. In such a situation, additional terms in the acceptance become part of the contract unless objected to by the offering party, and those terms plus the terms on which the parties can agree become the contract.

In order for a contract to be binding, it must be sufficiently specific. Thus it must identify the parties and the subject matter; a contract to sell "a piece of land" or "some corn" is not specific enough to be enforced. But it is not necessary that all items be spelled out: In the absence of terms dealing with these subjects, the law will imply a reasonable price, a delivery of goods in one lot, a place for delivery, shipment within a reasonable time, payment within a reasonable time, a requirement that a choice of options under the contract be made in good faith, and sometimes even a reasonable quantity.

If the contract deals with these subjects, however, it must be sufficiently specific to identify the intentions of the parties. A contract to sell goods at a price of "$10 to $20 each" is too vague, since the parties have given some indication of their intent but have not given enough information to allow a court to determine what they meant. Similarly, an agreement to sell "at a price to be negotiated later" is not binding unless and until a price is agreed upon.

In addition to an offer and acceptance, a contract may not ordinarily be enforced unless the party seeking enforcement has given some legal **consideration** in exchange for the promise or performance of the other party.

Consideration is something of value such as money, or an act that a party performs or promises to perform, even though the party has no legal duty to do so. Consideration can also be **forbearance** or a promise to forbear from an act that the party has a legal right to do.

A famous example concerns a case in which an uncle promises his nephew $5,000 if the nephew would refrain from drinking, smoking, swearing, and gambling until he reached age 21. The nephew complied and received $5,000 when he turned 21. However, a dispute arose over whether the nephew had given sufficient consideration for the $5,000, since his health and morals had benefited from his forbearance. The court determined that because he had refrained from doing things that he had a legal right to do, the consideration was sufficient regardless of its beneficial effect.[17]

Note, however, that had the promise been only to refrain from smoking marijuana, there would have been no consideration, since in that case

---

17. See *Hamer v. Sidway*, 124 N.Y. 538, 27 N.E. 256 (1891).

the nephew would not be refraining from doing that which he had a legal right to do. Similarly, a promise to do something, such as pay a debt that the party is already under a legal obligation to do will not serve as sufficient consideration (absent a *bona fide* dispute about the existence of a legal obligation).

Consideration must be bargained for. Thus, a promise to a homeless person that "I will give you a new coat if you will come to my store and pick it up" is not binding, because even though the homeless person walks a long distance to retrieve the coat, he or she has no legal obligation to do so.

Equitable Contracts

Under the doctrine of **promissory estoppel** or **detrimental reliance**, a promise that the promising party should reasonably expect to cause definite and substantial reliance by the other party, and that does cause such reliance, is binding even if the other party furnishes no consideration.

A classic example is a case where the defendant promised to make a contribution to a charitable organization. In reliance on the promised contribution, the charity contracted for a new building, at which point the erstwhile donor reneged on his promise. Even though the charity had given no consideration for the gift, it was permitted to enforce the promise against the donor.

Intention of the Parties

Once a contract is created, it must be interpreted—that is, the words and phrases in the contract must be examined to determine what the parties intended. Under the **parol evidence rule**, statements – usually oral – made before the contract was reduced to writing may not be used to contradict the terms of the written contract.

Likewise, typewritten or handwritten modifications of an otherwise typeset contract generally must be signed by the party or parties to be bound by the modification in order to be effective. For example, a line drawn through "$1,000" on a standard real estate earnest money contract and the substitution of "$2,000," handwritten by the real estate agent, must at least be initialed by both buyer and seller.

When the parties intend that the written contract is to be a full and complete expression of their agreement, no additional terms, oral or written, are admissible. In other circumstances, however, additional terms are admissible so long as they are consistent with the written terms.[18]

Unenforceable Terms and Contracts

For a variety of reasons, a contract or an individual term in a contract may be held to be unenforceable.

Oral Contracts

Contracts can be both oral and written. However, the **Statute of Frauds,** a 1677 English statute that has been adopted throughout the United States, requires certain types of contracts to be in writing. Many categories of contracts are subject to this requirement, but the most important ones for our purposes are:

- contracts for the sale of an interest in land
- contracts that cannot be performed within one year
- contracts for the sale of goods worth $500 or more.

The last category is governed by §2-201 of the Uniform Commercial Code. Note that for the second category the Statute of Frauds does not come into play whenever a contract might take more than one year to perform, but only when it *must* take that long. For example, a lease for two years is covered by the Statute of Frauds, but a lease for two years or until the tenant dies, whichever is earlier, is not, since the tenant might die during the first year.

A formal written contract signed by both parties is not necessary under the Statute, but there must be at least a memorandum of the transaction signed by the party against whom the contract is to be enforced.

---

18. Uniform Commercial Code, §2-202.

Illegal Contracts

Some contracts are unenforceable because they are illegal. This may
mean that the making of the contract is itself a crime, as in the case of
contracts for criminal acts, gambling contracts, or antitrust price-fixing
agreements. The most famous case along these lines is *Everet v.
Williams*, decided by the English Court of Exchequer in 1725. In that
case, one highwayman sued another for breach of a partnership
agreement to divide the profits of their endeavors. Not only did the
court dismiss the case, but it fined the plaintiffs' lawyers, and both
plaintiff and defendant were later caught and hanged!

A contract may be unenforceable for "illegality" even if its making was
not a crime. Examples of this type of contract are agreements involving
usurious interest rates or leases of property that violate health or
building codes.

Unconscionable Contracts

Some contracts do not involve any direct illegality but are nevertheless
unenforceable because the bargain is so one-sided that enforcement
would be unjust. As the United States Supreme Court stated in *Scott v.
United States*,[19] "[i]f a contract be unreasonable and unconscionable,
but not void for fraud, a court of law will give to the party who sues for
its breach damages, not according to its letter, but only such as he is
equitably entitled to."[20]

Only where there is a gross imbalance of bargaining power resulting in
extremely unfavorable terms to the weaker party will a contract be
voided as unconscionable. These cases usually involve a contract of
adhesion; that is, a standardized contract, usually preprinted, to which
the weaker party – often the buyer – must agree if the weaker party
wishes to do business with the stronger party.

---

19. 79 U.S. (12 Wall.) 443, 445 (1870).

20. See also Uniform Commercial Code, §2-302.

Incapacity to Contract

A contract entered into by a minor, an insane person, or one so intoxicated that he or she does not understand what he or she is doing is ordinarily not enforceable against that person. An exception is created for contracts involving necessities such as food and shelter. While no express or implied contract is created due to the contracting party's incapacity, the law implies a quasi-contract to pay the reasonable value of the necessary goods or services.

Note that the contract may be unenforceable against the person without capacity, but it is not unenforceable against the other party. Minors, for example, can enforce their contracts like anyone else.

A contract entered into by one who does not have capacity to contract may be ratified once the incapacity is removed. Thus, if an adult ratifies a contract made by him or her while a minor, it becomes fully enforceable.

Fraud and Inducement

Contracts may also be avoided for fraud, misrepresentation, **duress**, or **undue influence**. Fraud consists of the making of a knowingly false representation that is reasonably relied upon by the other contracting party in entering into a contract he or she would not otherwise have made. There are two types of fraud: **intrinsic fraud** (sometimes called **fraud in the factum**) and **extrinsic fraud** (sometimes called **fraud in the inducement**).

Intrinsic fraud occurs when the party is not aware of the nature of the agreement into which he or she is entering, as where a person signs a release, having been told that it is not a release but something else. Extrinsic fraud occurs when the party is aware of the bargain he or she is making but has been induced to make the agreement by a deliberately false representation.

Duress and undue influence, on the other hand, consist of pressure that is so severe that the contracting party's will and freedom of choice are overcome. For example, a contract signed at gunpoint would be voidable for duress. Duress need not be physical and may consist of an economic threat that, under the circumstances, operates to deprive someone of free choice.[21]   Undue influence consists of similar pressure of a moral rather than a physical or economic kind.[22]

Discharge of a Contract

A contractual duty may be discharged in a variety of ways. The most obvious of these is by performance of the duty. A duty is also discharged when it becomes illegal or impossible to perform, as, for example, where a concert pianist contracts to give a recital but becomes ill and cannot do so.

Sometimes a duty is discharged by the fact that an event upon which the duty is conditioned never comes to pass, as where a house is insured against fire, but no fire occurs.

A duty may be modified or discharged by contract in a variety of ways:

- The contract giving rise to the duty may be modified or cancelled by agreement of the parties.

- A dispute over the rights and obligations of the parties may be compromised (called an **accord and satisfaction**).

- The parties may agree with a third party that the third party will take over some or all of the contractual obligations (called a **novation**).

A contract may also be **rescinded** by a court due to illegality, incapacity, fraud, or other reasons.

---

21. See *Mitchell v. C.C. Sanitation Co.*, 430 S.W.2d 933 (Tex Civ. App.— Houston [14th Dist.] 1968, writ ref'd n.r.e.)

22. See *Methodist Mission Home v. B.,* 451 S.W.2d 539 (Tex. Civ. App. — San Antonio 1970, no writ).

Contractual Damages

Contractual damages are substantially different from tort damages. Tort damages are based on the notion of restitution; that is, that a party should be put in the position he or she would have occupied if the tort had not occurred. Contractual recovery, on the other hand, is based on an **expectation theory**: that is, that the injured party should be placed in the position he or she would have occupied if the contract had been fully performed. In other words, the contracting party gets the benefit of the bargain it made.

Thus, one who pays $50 in exchange for an item worth $75, but does not receive the item, is entitled not only to restitution of the $50 paid, but also to recovery of the $25 profit that would have been made had there been no breach.

As with tort damages, injunctive relief is sometimes called for where damages are inadequate to restore a party to the party's rightful place. As in contracts for the sale of land or unique goods, **specific performance** may be ordered. The breaching party is in effect forced by court order to comply with the terms of the contract. Where a contract is avoided due to fraud, incapacity, or the like, the court may order rescission of the contract, whereby each party returns to the other that which the party has received and the contract is treated as void.

Contracts Governed by the Uniform Commercial Code

The Uniform Commercial Code deals with most of the topics discussed above in connection with sales of goods. An important aspect of the UCC is its treatment of warranties. The UCC covers express warranties, such as the limited warranties that come with most household goods. It also covers implied warranties, including those made to buyers by merchants or sellers of goods. So, for example, when a buyer goes to a hardware store to purchase a lawn mower, the merchant warrants to the buyer that the merchant has title to the inventory of lawn mowers on display, that the lawn mowers are at least of average quality and adequately labeled, and that they are fit for doing what the buyer intends, to cut grass. In other words, the merchant warrants title, merchantability and fitness for a particular purpose. The

UCC also contains provisions governing the extent and manner in which these warranties may be disclaimed.

An important variety of specialized contract, governed by Article Three of the UCC, is known as **commercial paper**. Commercial paper exists in two forms:

- **promissory notes**, which are written contracts to pay a sum of money to a specified individual or to a person designated by the individual ("to the order")

- **drafts**, which are written orders to a third party directing the third party to pay a sum of money to the order of a specified person.

Checks are an important form of draft; a check is merely a draft that is drawn on a bank and payable on demand. The most important feature of notes and drafts is that they are **negotiable**. This means that a person or company to whom a note or a draft is transferred ordinarily obtains it free of any claims that he or she was unaware of when the note or draft was acquired. This important aspect of commercial paper renders it especially useful in a commercial setting: checks, certificates of deposit, and most corporate and governmental bonds flow freely back and forth from owner to owner with little risk on the part of the purchaser.

A note or draft (sometimes referred to as a **negotiable instrument**) may be negotiated from one owner to another by **endorsement**, which consists of the signature of the holder, sometimes with language such as "Pay to the order of John Smith." An endorsement makes the endorser liable to pay the instrument if the maker or the party against whom it is drawn does not. In this manner a "bounced" check is returned from one endorser to another farther up the chain, until finally the check comes to rest in the hands of the party to whom the check is made payable. This party must bear the loss unless he or she can obtain payment from the signer.

Article Nine of the Uniform Commercial Code deals with **secured transactions**. This branch of the law is a marriage between contract law and property law. A secured transaction is one in which a party obtains or retains a **security interest** in goods or other personal property. A security interest is a **lien** or **mortgage** (such as a mortgage on real property) that gives the owner a right to sell or take possession of the property in the event that the secured debt is not paid.

In order to be perfected, a security interest must ordinarily be recorded in the office of the secretary of state or county clerk, just as a real estate mortgage must ordinarily be recorded. The Uniform Commercial Code sets up an elaborate system of priorities among the owner of the property, the various parties holding security interests, and unsecured creditors. If the debtor goes into bankruptcy, these priorities are further affected by the federal Bankruptcy Code.

Other Sources of Contract Law

In recent years, statutes other than the Uniform Commercial Code have come to play an important role in contract law. These include the

- Uniform Consumer Credit Code
- Consumer Credit Protection Act, which includes the Truth-in-Lending Act
- Fair Credit Reporting Act
- Equal Credit Opportunity Act
- Uniform Fraudulent Conveyance Act
- Magnuson-Moss Warranty Act
- Bankruptcy Code.

Consumer protection statutes, passed by every state, deal with contractual relationships between consumers and merchants. Also important are various regulations adopted pursuant to these statutes, including the Truth-in-Lending regulations adopted by the Federal Reserve Board and other regulations adopted by the Federal Trade Commission under the Federal Trade Commission Act.

For more detailed information on contract law, you should consult the Uniform Commercial Code, the American Law Institute's *Restatement (Second) of Contracts*, or any good treatise on the law of contracts, such as those by Williston or Corbin on general contract law or by White and Summers on the Uniform Commercial Code.

Real Property

The law of real property is by far the most ancient of our inheritances from the common law of England, where it began to develop shortly after the Norman Conquest in 1066. Real property encompasses land and things associated with the land, such as buildings, timber, minerals, water, and even the air above. The common law of real property owes its origin to the feudal system in medieval England. Under this system, the ultimate title to all lands in England, and some other places as well, was vested in the king. The king would make grants of land to nobles of various ranks in exchange for their agreements of support, both financial and military. These nobles, called tenants-in-chief, in turn made grants to squires, knights, and other intermediate-level landholders called mesne lords, again in exchange for their support. Those to whom grants were made in turn made grants of their own, and so on down to the level of the lowest peasants.

Each landholder or tenant swore an oath of homage to the landlord and agreed to perform certain services in exchange for the right to hold the land. The landlords, on the other hand, possessed certain rights, such as the right to a payment by a tenant's heir upon the tenant's death (called "relief") and the right to choose whom the tenant would marry. Most early real property law developed as a means of thwarting various legal devices by which the landlords would otherwise have been deprived of their feudal rights.

Freehold Estates

Under modern property law, as under the feudal system, the owner of land may grant to another some or all of the rights in the land which the owner possesses. The various types of ownership interests which may be created are known as **estates in land**. These interests may be as varied as the imagination of the granting party (the **grantor**) permits. Thus, estates in land may be conveyed that entitle the receiving party (the **grantee**) to possession and use of the land in perpetuity, or for the next tenth of a second, or until such time, if ever, as Liechtenstein invades Monaco.

Nevertheless, certain types of estates in land represent the bundles of ownership rights that are most commonly conveyed. The most common estate in land is known as the **fee simple**, representing complete ownership of the land. The grant of a fee simple is commonly made by deeding the property "to A and his or her heirs," but any words that indicate an intent to give A the total ownership rights in the property will suffice. A fee simple estate may be subject to certain conditions such as a promise always to use the premises as a residence (a **fee simple determinable**) or never to allow gambling (**fee simple subject to a condition subsequent**.) Or, the grant may be a **fee simple absolute**, where the grantee has the maximum possible ownership rights subject to no conditions whatsoever.

An estate in land of great importance in early England but of only marginal relevance today is the **fee tail**, by which land was granted to an individual and passed to his lineal descendants until such time, if any, as the line of descendants ran out.

An estate in land whereby the land is granted to an individual for the duration of his or her lifetime is known, not surprisingly, as a **life estate**. A life estate—ordinarily created by using words such as "to A for life"—may be created in one person with reference to the life of another ("to A for the life of B"). This is known by the old French name of an *estate pur autre vie* ("for the life of another").

The fee simple, fee tail, and life estate are known as **freehold estates**, and it is these estates to which we normally refer when we say that an individual "owns" a piece of land. There are, however, several other types of estates in land, as anyone who has ever rented an apartment knows well. These are known as **leasehold estates**.

Leasehold Estates

The most important leasehold estate is the **term of years**. A term of years gives the grantee the right to the possession and use of the property for a specified period of time, which, despite the name of the estate, need not be for one year or more. Thus, any fixed-term lease, whether it is for six months or 99 years, creates a term of years.

The other common leasehold estate is the **periodic tenancy**. This estate is a leasehold estate for a given period of time that automatically renews itself unless one party notifies the other that renewal is not desired. A periodic tenancy may be from day to day, week to week, month to month, year to year, or may have any other fixed renewal period. Many leases for a fixed period, which thus create a term of years, contain provisions for continuation beyond the expiration date of the lease on a year-to-year or month-to-month basis, thereby creating a periodic tenancy following the initial term of years. The notice required to terminate a year-to-year tenancy must be given six months in advance of the termination date, while other periodic tenancies may be terminated on notice equal to the period of the tenancy. The notice must terminate the tenancy at the end of a period and not in the middle of the period.

The final leasehold estate is the **tenancy at will**. This estate in land is terminable without advance notice by either party and is thus the most fragile estate in land that can be imagined. True tenancies at will are rare, because the periodic payment of rent for a tenancy at will usually converts the tenancy into a periodic tenancy. A tenancy at will terminates automatically if either party dies or if the landlord sells the property.

Nonestate Interests in Land

In addition to the freehold and leasehold estates described above, there are a variety of interests in land that do not rise to the level of estates. There are four main categories of such interests, the most important of which is the **easement**. An easement is a right to make some specified use of the land of another. The most common easements are the **utility easements**, where the utility company is granted the right to erect poles or bury underground cables or pipes, and the **right-of-way easement**, where a landowner is granted the right to pass over land of his or her neighbor to reach the landowner's own property.

Some easements, especially right-of-way easements, may be created by implication; thus, where a grantor conveys an inaccessible portion of his or her land, the grantee receives not only that land but an implied easement (known as an **easement appurtenant**) entitling the grantee to travel over the rest of the grantor's land to reach the conveyed property.

Other nonestate interests in land include:

- profits (sometimes called **profits a prendre**), which are rights to sever minerals or crops from the land

- **licenses**, which create a limited right to use the land for a specific purpose, such as a theater ticket

- **restrictive covenants**, which are placed in a deed to limit the uses to which the land may be put or the individuals to whom it may be conveyed.

These limited interests may assume major importance in a particular transaction or type of transaction. Restrictive covenants prohibiting the sale of real estate to ethnic groups constituted a major source of housing discrimination until they were struck down in 1948 by the United States Supreme Court in *Shelley v. Kraemer*.[23]

In addition to the above, there are other limited property interests that affect land ownership. These include:

- **mineral rights**, which give title to minerals, oil, gas, precious metals, gravel, soil, timber, and other substances below the surface of the land. Title conveys the right to extract these substances and to profit from their sale. The person or entity holding title can lease these rights to others. Thus, the actual land can be owned by one party and the minerals by another;

- **water rights** that determine who can use water that crosses property boundaries, whether a flowing stream, a lake, or an underground aquifer;

- **air rights** that determine who and what can occupy the air above the land.

The right to extract minerals is almost sacrosanct, and even today it can justify the destruction of whole neighborhoods and towns that are in the way. Water has embroiled many arid western states in lawsuits with one another over rights to water that originates as snow runoff in one

---

23. See *Shelley v. Kraemer*, 334 U.S. 1, 68 S.Ct. 836 (1948).

state but flows into and through several others. The outcome of these disputes threaten entire cities who are unable to get their "fair share" of the dwindling supply of precious water. International disputes have arisen between the U.S. and Canada and the U.S. and Mexico concerning rights to water that commences in one country and flows into another.

Air rights involve everything from noise to overhanging trees and from power lines to airport flight patterns. They also involve the even more arcane rights to air waves, an area of law that has heated up in recent years due to the growth of cellular and digital technology. As with water rights, air rights litigants often include governmental entities seeking to protect the interests of their respective residents. The ultimate issue involving air rights concerns the right to explore, use, inhabit and even pollute outer space.

Environmental law, a legal specialty that has emerged and developed in the latter half of the twentieth century, also embodies issues involving rights in land. Environmental law seeks to answer the question, "To what extent is the public entitled to breathe clean air, drink clean water, and enjoy the environment in its natural state as compared with the rights of property owners to exploit the commercial and economic value of their holdings?" Thus, it combines important civic notions inherent in the American legal system such as equality of all persons before the law and the right to life, liberty, and the pursuit of happiness with issues of property ownership and rights.

Co-Ownership

Two or more persons may concurrently own a single piece of land in a variety of ways. First among these is the **tenancy in common**, in which the owners hold undivided interests in the land. By this is meant that each has the right to full and complete possession and use of all the land, subject only to the same right as to all the other tenants in common. If land held by tenancy in common is leased or put to productive use, the tenants in common all share in the profits.

Note that it is not necessary that each tenant in common be entitled to the same undivided interest in the land; a tenancy in common may be created, for instance, where A owns two-thirds and B owns one-third.

Any tenant in common may demand a partition of the land—that is, that he or she receive exclusive title to a portion of the land representing his or her fair share. If the parties are unable to agree on a satisfactory partition, a lawsuit seeking a partition may be brought, and the court will divide the land equitably.

An important form of concurrent ownership, similar in most respects to the tenancy in common, is the **joint tenancy**. The owners of a joint tenancy bear the same relationship to one another as do tenants in common, with one important exception: each joint tenant has a **right of survivorship**. This means that upon the death of one joint tenant, that tenant's interest automatically passes by operation of law to the other joint tenant or tenants. Joint tenants may demand a partition or may convey their interests to a third party. Such an act, however, operates to destroy the right of survivorship, leaving the new owner in possession of only a tenancy in common and eliminating the right of the owner who has demanded partition to any of his or her former co-tenant's interests on the co-tenant's death.

A specialized form of the joint tenancy that is important in most states is the **tenancy by the entireties** between a husband and wife. In states that follow the common-law system of marital property, a conveyance to a husband and wife as joint tenants creates a special type of joint tenancy. The parties may not convey their separate interests or demand a partition. Traditionally the husband was entitled to sole possession and control of the property and the rents and profits from it.

In states that follow the community property system, all property acquired with funds earned during the marriage is community property belonging equally to both husband and wife. In some community property states, it is not possible to create a joint tenancy between a husband and wife.

The tenancy in common, joint tenancy, and tenancy by the entireties are, of course, not the only means by which more than one person may hold an interest in the same piece of land. Any conveyance of an estate less than a fee simple absolute necessarily involves a second owner who owns the remaining property interest (called a **reversion** if owned by the grantor and a **remainder** if owned by a third party). Thus, if a

grantor who owns a fee simple conveys "to A for life," the owners of
the property are A and the grantor. A is entitled to use and possession
during A's lifetime, and the grantor regains the property thereafter.

Liens

An important form of co-ownership is created through **mortgages**
(sometimes termed **deeds of trust**) and other forms of **liens**. A
mortgage is an interest in land created when one party lends money to
another to purchase property. The lender who owns the mortgage (the
mortgagee) may seize and sell the property if the debt owed to the
lender by the buyer of the property (the **mortgagor**) is not paid when
due. In many states, the mortgagee owns a lien on the property and can
seize it for nonpayment only through a formal process called
foreclosure. In some states, however, the mortgagee has the legal right
to seize and possess the property in the event of nonpayment of the lien
with little or no notice to the mortgagor. A few states provide a
procedure that is a hybrid of foreclosure and summary seizure.

A transaction involving the construction of a large office building may
involve several mortgages, including one to pay for the land, another
for interim construction costs, and a third for permanent financing. In
some states a mortgage transaction is accomplished by conveying the
property to a **trustee**, usually a representative of the mortgagee. The
trustee holds the property on behalf of the mortgagee, allows the
mortgagor to use the land, and releases the property to the mortgagor
when the mortgage indebtedness is fully paid.

A mortgage is one form of **lien**, or security interest, in land, arising
from the consent of the owner. Other forms of lien arise by operation
of law, irrespective of the owner's consent. Among these is the
vendor's lien, which is a lien in favor of the property seller to ensure
that the seller receives the full purchase price. Where construction work
is performed on property, **mechanic's liens** in favor of contractors or
workmen and **materialmen's liens** in favor of suppliers of construction
materials may arise to secure the payment of those individuals' charges.

Tax liens may arise to secure payment of unpaid taxes, while a
judgment lien is awarded to the winner of a lawsuit against the lands of

the loser to secure payment of the judgment. There are also other liens, such as hospital liens, that secure other types of payments.

Deeds

A conveyance of land is generally accomplished by means of a **deed**, which is a written record of the fact that land has been transferred from one party to another. (In medieval England, transfer was accomplished by the parties' going to the land and the grantor's giving the grantee a clod of earth or twig to symbolize transfer of the land; this ceremony, known as **livery of seisin**, has long ago given way to more formal methods of transfer.)

In the typical real estate transaction, delivery of a deed is usually preceded by the signing of a contract of sale that sets out the terms of the agreement, including the price to be paid, the method of financing the purchase, the date and procedures for the **closing**, and where the deeds, mortgages, and money are transferred. Under the Statute of Frauds, discussed briefly above with reference to contract law, all contracts for the transfer of an estate in land (except for leases of property for one year or less) must be in writing.

Three types of deeds are commonly used today. The first is the **general warranty deed**, which includes a warranty (i.e., a promise) that the grantor holds good title to the land (that is, that he or she owns an estate at least as big as the one he or she is conveying). A **special warranty deed** promises only that the grantor is giving the grantee as good a title as the grantor originally received from his or her grantor; or, in other words, that the grantor has done nothing to impair the title to the property during the grantor's ownership of it.

Finally, a **quitclaim deed** contains no warranties, and simply gives the grantee whatever interest in the property (if any) that his or her grantor had at the time of the deed. A contract of sale typically states the type of deed to be delivered, and ordinarily requires the grantor to have "good and marketable title," that is, a title free of liens and other actual or potential ownership interests in third parties (these are known as **clouds on the title**).

Since there is ordinarily no reliable way to learn the identity of the owner from the appearance of the land itself, a system of deed recording has been developed to make this information readily available. Under this system, every deed and deed of trust, together with records of certain other interests (such as some liens), is recorded in the county clerk's office in the county where the land is located. (Leases may be, but are not often, recorded.) Each document is indexed under the name of the grantor and under the name of the grantee. By means of these indices, the chain of grantors and grantees of a particular piece of land may be traced: this is known as a **title search**.

Beginning with the most recent owner, the searcher goes back through the grantee index until he or she finds the deed by which that person received the property, doing the same for each previous owner until the researcher has traced the title as far back as he or she wishes to go. The researcher can then go forward through the grantor index to be sure that no previous owner tried to sell the property to two different purchasers, or created any other cloud on the title.

The researcher might then prepare an **abstract of title**, which is a summary of the transactions by which title to the property has changed hands over the years, and a **title opinion** confirming that the seller holds good title. This will give the current purchaser a guarantee that the seller holds the property in an unbroken chain of title. The purchaser might also want to obtain a policy of **title insurance** from an insurance company that will make good any losses if it is later discovered that the title is defective.

In order to make the recording system work, the purchasers must be protected from the effects of deeds that are not properly recorded. Hence by statute a *bona fide* **purchaser**, that is, one who is unaware of any ownership interests not reflected in the deed records, takes title to property irrespective of any unrecorded deeds and other interests. Thus, it is extremely dangerous to fail to record a deed; the third party will receive full title and the holder of the unrecorded deed will receive nothing. While this may seem harsh, it is the only means by which someone who has searched the deed records can be sure that he or she is getting full title to the property.

Law casebooks are full of lawsuits brought by the holder of an
unrecorded deed against a subsequent *bona fide* purchaser. A typical
scenario might involve the sale of timber land to Buyer X who fails to
record the deed, and who seldom visits the property. The seller dies.
Her heirs offer the land to Buyer Z, who searches the county records
and finds a clear chain of title back through the seller and her heirs.
Buyer Z purchases the property and records his deed. Subsequently,
Buyer X finds out about Buyer Z and files a lawsuit to regain either the
property or its full value. Even if Buyer X can prove that the seller's
heirs were aware of the original sale, it is highly unlikely that Buyer Z
will be forced to relinquish the land or pay damages to Buyer X.

Restrictions on Ownership

In addition to the so-called "record interests," which one may find
recorded in the deed records, there are certain non-recorded interests.
Chief among these is **adverse possession**. Under this doctrine, a party
who remains in open, continuous, and adverse possession of a tract of
land for a specified time (twenty years in most states) acquires title to
the land. In order for a claim of adverse possession to be made, the
party must possess the land without the permission of the true owner
and must claim openly that he or she has a right to be on the land.
Adverse possessors may add together the periods of their possession of
the land; thus if one adverse possessor remains on the land for ten years
and then sells to another, the second party need remain only another ten
years to acquire complete title.

One of the most frequent applications of adverse possession today is the
situation where land has been incorrectly surveyed and a fence or
building encroaches on a neighbor's land. Unless the neighbor takes
legal action within twenty years, the owner of the fence or building
acquires by adverse possession the land on which the office or building
is located.

Ownership of land, even in the case of a fee simple "absolute," is never
truly absolute. A variety of governmental regulations control the use to
which land may be put. Chief among these are **zoning ordinances**,
which in most cities regulate the use to which land may be put and the

structures that may be erected on it.[24] When property is first brought under a zoning ordinance, structures and uses that are inconsistent with the zoning classification are permitted to remain as **nonconforming uses**, but such uses may not be changed or expanded. Hence, the property eventually comes under the zoning law.

Another important governmental interference with the unfettered use and possession of land is the right of **eminent domain**. Where a specific tract of land is needed for a governmental purpose, such as the construction of a road, park, or governmental building, a governmental entity having the right of eminent domain may force the owner to sell it by bringing a **condemnation** proceeding in court. The court will order the land to be transferred and will determine a fair price that the owner must be paid. The Fifth Amendment of the United States Constitution provides that private property shall not "be taken for public use, without just compensation," and the constitutions of many states contain similar prohibitions. Some state constitutions also prohibit the use of the eminent domain power for private uses of the condemned land.

The assessment of real estate taxes and assessments for improvements to streets, sewers, sidewalks, and the like, are yet other examples of limitations on the complete ownership of land.

Equitable Ownership

In addition to the legal ownership of land is its **equitable ownership**. Equitable interests in land are the product of the old English courts of chancery, which developed new remedies and legal institutions in an attempt to compete with the common law courts. Today, although law courts and equity courts have been merged in the federal system and in almost every state, these equitable interests survive and play an important role in real property law.

Two equitable devices are especially important. The first is the doctrine of **equitable conversion**, under which a contract for the sale of land creates not only a legal contractual obligation for the seller to deliver a

---

24. See *Village of Euclid v. Ambler Realty Co.*, 272 U.S. 365 (1926) (which sustained the constitutionality of so-called "Euclidean" zoning, whereby zones of land with fixed boundaries are designated for specific uses.

deed (which in turn delivers the legal title to the land) but an equitable title to the land, which arises on behalf of the buyer as soon as the contract is signed. This permits the buyer to make use of the equitable remedy of specific performance (see the section on contract law) to force the seller to deliver the deed, thus completing the sale. It also means, however, that the buyer becomes responsible in the interim for such items as fire insurance (absent a contractual provision to the contrary). Likewise, it enables the seller to force the buyer to pay the purchase price.

The **trust** is another institution developed by the equity courts. In a trust transaction, real or personal property is conveyed by one individual (the **settlor** or **trustor**) to another (the **trustee**), who receives legal title to the property but holds it for the benefit of a third party (the **beneficiary** or *cestui que* **trust**), who holds the equitable title. While the settlor, trustee, and beneficiary are usually different individuals, it is possible for two of these to be the same person. A trust may be **revocable** or **irrevocable** and may be created by a deed (an ***inter vivos* trust**) or by will (a **testamentary trust**). A typical trust instrument contains provisions describing the interests of the various beneficiaries, the powers of the trustee, and the way in which the trust will terminate.

An important pitfall for the drafter of a trust or other instrument conveying property is the common-law **rule against perpetuities**. Any thorough discussion of the rule against perpetuities would occupy an entire chapter and is beyond the scope of this book. Even experienced attorneys sometimes have difficulty with this concept. Indeed, one court has held the rule to be so complex that an attorney is sometimes not liable for malpractice for drafting an instrument that violates the rule.[25]

Suffice it to say that the rule establishes a time limit — the lifetimes of those who are alive at the time the instrument takes effect, plus 21 years — beyond which no interest may vest under the instrument. Any interest that might theoretically take effect after this time is void, no matter how remote the possibility that this will occur and without regard for whether it does in fact occur. Some states have enacted so-

---

25. See *Lucas v. Hamm*, 15 Cal. Rptr. 821, 364 P.2d 685 (1961).

called "wait-and-see" statutes, under which an interest is not void
unless it does in fact take effect too late.

Landlord-Tenant Law

Although no discussion of real property law would be complete without
some mention of **landlord-tenant law**, few generalizations can be made
for the simple reason that most obligations of landlord and tenant are
created by the lease contract that they make, and hence those
obligations vary considerably depending on their agreement. There are,
however, a few rules that apply to virtually every lease.

A lease creates rights and obligations in each party. The landlord is
obliged to provide possession of the premises, together with **quiet
enjoyment** (this does not refer to noise, but to possession without
interference). Some leases also impose an obligation to make repairs, to
provide hot water or other utilities, or perhaps to provide security
services, but the landlord ordinarily has no obligation to provide these
items unless the lease so specifies.

Where the landlord so interferes with the tenant's right to possession
that the interference is equivalent to a forcible eviction, there is a
constructive eviction and the tenant is relieved of any further
obligations. Thus, where the landlord is obligated to provide water but
fails to do so, the tenant may vacate the premises and stop paying rent.
Of course, the tenant has the right to use all other available legal
remedies for breach of contract, which may include money damages or
an injunction.

When the landlord transfers ownership of the premises, the new owner
is subject to all the obligations under the lease that "touch and concern"
the land, including obligations to repair, to provide utilities, and the
like.

The tenant's primary obligation under a lease is to pay rent, but this is
not the tenant's only obligation. The premises must be kept free from
waste, that is, significant negligent or intentional destruction or
damage. If the tenant alters the premises without the landlord's consent,
the tenant must restore them to their previous condition before the end
of the tenancy. A tenant is ordinarily under no obligation to make

repairs (except for repairs that are necessary to prevent damage to the property, such as replacing broken windows), but the tenant may agree to do so in the lease.

The tenant may transfer his or her rights and obligations to another tenant unless the lease prohibits this. A transfer of all the tenant's interests is known as an **assignment of the lease**, whereby the new tenant becomes responsible to the landlord for all of the obligations under the lease. A transfer of fewer than all rights is a **sublease**, under which the tenant becomes a junior landlord and the new tenant owes his or her obligations to the original tenant, who in turn owes obligations to the landlord. In neither case is the old tenant excused from his or her obligations to the landlord.

A tenant who "holds over" on the premises after a lease has expired may be forced by the landlord into a new periodic tenancy. Thus a tenant who leases from January to December of 1999 but holds over into January of 2000 may be forced by the landlord to pay rent through December of 2000, due to the creation of an implied year-to-year tenancy. At common law a landlord could also use force to evict a tenant in wrongful possession of the premises, but modern statutes prohibit so-called **forcible entry**.

On the other hand, the common law gave the landlord no remedy other than a suit for breach of contract where the tenant was not in wrongful possession but had unjustifiably defaulted on his or her obligations. Modern statutes create a new action of **ejectment** (sometimes misleadingly referred to as **forcible entry and detainer**) that permits the landlord to regain the premises and force the tenant to vacate with a minimum of delay and legal red tape.

Personal Property

Many of the principles of real property apply to personal property as well, including lease law, deeds, titles, liens, trusts, recording statutes, and equitable principles. Unlike land, however, personal property can be lost, hidden, stolen, consumed and completely destroyed. Law students study 200-year-old cases involving the rightful ownership to sperm whales harpooned by one crew and boat, only to escape and be captured by another. These cases are amusing to us today but were deadly serious to the people who risked their lives to capture wild animals in order to earn a livelihood. Thus, property law has had to develop legal concepts especially designed to deal with the ephemeral nature of nonreal property.

Personal property includes things such as vehicles, equipment, animals, household goods and personal effects. It also encompasses money, securities, checks, and other "paper," including title documents to depository accounts and personal property. Just as individuals own personal property, businesses can also own personal property. For example, inventory is considered a type of personal business property.

One branch of personal business property that has grown into a legal specialty of enormous importance is **intellectual property**, involving patents, copyrights, trademarks, trade names and other intangible "property of the mind." Subspecialties of intellectual property that have developed recently include computer software law and Internet law.

Important reference works on the law of property include A. Casner, *American Law of Property* (1952), and the American Law Institute's *Restatement of Property*. The original *Restatement of Property* was published in five volumes from 1938 to 1944. *The Restatement of the Law, Second, Property 2nd*, has added a volume on landlord and tenant and four volumes on donative transfers. The *Third Restatement* contains new information on mortgages and servitudes and additional material on donative transfers.

Wills and Intestate Succession

Wills were not generally recognized by the common law before enactment of the Statute of Wills in 1540. Prior to that time, land, which in early days constituted the bulk of all wealth, passed by operation of law to a feudal tenant's **heirs**, that is, his closest surviving descendants or other relatives. The heirs made a payment (known as "relief") to the landlord. In the event that there were no heirs, the property returned to the lord by **escheat**.

Since the Statute of Wills, property ordinarily descends by will to those designated by the maker of the will, the **testator**. Nevertheless, feudal heirship still survives in the form of modern statutes that define the distribution of the property of a person who dies without a will, termed **intestate succession**, and property continues to escheat to the state in cases where no heir can be found.

Intestate Succession

The statutes that govern the intestate succession of property employ two main systems for distribution. When property passes **per capita**, each person who is entitled to shares takes an equal share. Imagine a decedent who leaves three surviving children, two surviving grandchildren, and two surviving great-grandchildren, as seen in the following diagram. If the decedent's property passes per capita, each of the seven surviving descendants will take a one-seventh share.

Property may also pass **per stirpes**, whereby each descendant takes a share that represents a proportionate distribution of the property at each succeeding generation. In the example given, each living child would take one-fourth of any property passing per stirpes, since there were four children altogether. Each surviving grandchild would take one-third of his or her parent's one-fourth share (that is, one-twelfth), since the deceased child had a total of three children. The two great-grandchildren would each take one-half of their parent's one-twelfth share (that is, one-twenty-fourth). The total of these shares (1/4 + 1/4 + 1/4 + 1/12 + 1/12 + 1/24 + 1/24) adds up, as it must, to 100% of the property.

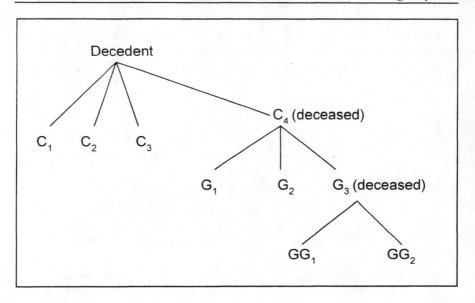

Intestate succession often depends on the type of property involved (real or personal, marital or separate), as well as the identity of the survivors. The distribution scheme is summarized in the accompanying table.

Note that spouses generally get at least one-half of the marital property. In most community property states, this represents the spouse's share of community property. In other words, the surviving spouse already owns one-half of the marital (community) property, and he or she inherits some or all of the remainder from the deceased spouse. In common law property jurisdictions, which accounts for most of the states, the first spouse to die is presumed to own all of the marital property and, therefore, all of it passes according to the state's intestate succession laws.

A child born out of wedlock inherits from his or her mother and inherits from the father if the father has later married the mother or if the father has acknowledged paternity in writing. The Supreme Court held in *Trimble v. Gordon*[26] that certain statutes limiting inheritance by illegitimate children are unconstitutionally discriminatory. Half-brothers

---

26. 430 U.S. 672 (1977).

and half-sisters inherit half as much as would full-blooded siblings, while stepchildren have no inheritance rights unless adopted.

The intestate succession laws attempt to make the distribution of property that, it is assumed, most people would want to make. If, however, the scheme set up by those laws is not to an individual's liking, he or she is free to alter the dispositive scheme by making a will.

Distribution by Will

There are only two limitations on the class of persons who may make a will. First, a testator must be at least eighteen years of age unless he or she is married or a member of the armed forces. Second, the testator must be of sound mind. The latter requirement does not refer to mental health or illness as a psychiatrist might classify it, but to testamentary capacity as defined by law. The testator must:

- understand the nature of the act of making a will
- know the nature and character of his or her property
- understand to whom he or she is giving his or her property
- understand the gifts he or she is making.

If these requirements are satisfied, it does not matter whether the testator is, medically speaking, suffering from mental illness, or whether he or she has been declared legally incompetent. One who suffers from such disabilities can execute a will during a "lucid interval" in which he or she meets the four-part test above.

Example of Intestate Succession

		Survived By		
Type of Property	**Spouse Only**	**Spouse and Descendants**	**Descendants Only**	**Neither Spouse Nor Descendants**
Marital Property	all to spouse	½ to spouse ½ to descendants (*per stirpes*)	There can be no marital property where the spouse does not survive, since the death of both spouses destroys the community.	
Separate Real Property	½ to spouse ½ to parents or collateral relatives	⅓ life estate to spouse ⅓ remainder + ⅔ outright to descendants	all to descendants	½ to each parent *or* ½ to surviving parents and ½ to brothers & sisters or their descendants *or* all to brothers & sisters or their descendants *or* all to other collateral relatives
Separate Personal Property	all to spouse	⅓ to spouse ⅔ to descendants	all to descendants	

There are three very different ways to make a valid will.

1. The most usual form of will is a document signed by the
    testator and two witnesses. The witnesses must be of sound
    mind, must be more than 14 years old, and must sign in the
    presence of the testator. Their job is to attest to the signature of
    the testator. In many states, the witnesses need not, however,
    sign in each other's presence, nor need they be aware that they
    are witnessing a will.

2. A second form of valid will is the **holographic will**, which is a
    will written in the testator's handwriting and signed by the
    testator. All writing that is an essential part of the will must be
    in the testator's handwriting, but writing by others may be
    disregarded if it is not necessary to complete the will.

3. Finally, under very limited circumstances an oral (or **nuncupa-
    tive)** will is valid. Such a will may apply only to personal
    property, must have been made during the testator's last
    sickness, must ordinarily be witnessed by three witnesses, and
    generally must be probated within six months of the maker's
    death.

With limited exceptions, there are no restrictions on the manner in
which property may be distributed by will. Among the few limitations
is the **rule against perpetuities**, which has been previously discussed in
connection with real property. In most jurisdictions that follow the
common-law system of marital property, a person cannot disinherit his
or her spouse. If the will does so, **forced heirship statutes** provide that
a surviving spouse may elect to take the share (if any) given him or her
by the will or the share specified in the statute.

In addition, common-law states give the widow **dower rights** in her
husband's lands and the widower **curtesy rights** in his wife's lands.
Community property states have no such provisions, and there is
nothing to prevent one spouse from completely disinheriting the other.
This is because half of the community property belongs to the spouse
regardless of what the testator may do. A will that attempts to dispose
of all of the community property, sometimes called a **widow's election
will**, gives the survivor the option to take what the will gives him or

her, or alternatively to take his or her own half share of the community property irrespective of the will.

Problems may arise when the persons designated in the will to receive property (**devisees**, with respect to real property, and **legatees**, with respect to personal property) do not survive the testator. The common-law rule is that a testamentary gift to a person who is dead when the will takes effect "lapses"—that is, disappears. But this has been modified by statute in most states: If a child or other descendant predeceases the testator but leaves behind children or descendants, the gift to the beneficiary does not lapse but instead passes to the deceased beneficiary's children or descendants according to the rules of intestate succession.

The **Uniform Simultaneous Death Act** governs the situation in which the testator and beneficiary die so close in time that it cannot be determined who died first, as in a plane crash or auto accident. In such a situation, half the property passes as though the testator had died first, and half as though the beneficiary had died first.

There are four basic classifications of legacies under a will. First is the **specific legacy** (or devise, when referring to real property). This is a testamentary gift of a specific object or tract of land, as "I give my gold watch to my son Bill."

Next is the **demonstrative legacy**, which is a gift of a specified sum to be taken from a particular source, as "I give $10,000, to be taken from my Swiss bank account, to my wife Mary."

A **general legacy** is a gift out of the estate in general and not out of any specified fund or source, as "I give $500 to my servant Tom."

Finally, a **residuary legacy** is a gift of the balance of the testator's estate after all debts and other legacies have been paid, as "I give the balance of my estate, real and personal, to my husband George."

The importance of this classification is that certain priorities apply where the estate is not large enough to satisfy all debts and legacies. Debts are satisfied first, followed by specific, demonstrative, general, and residuary legacies, in that order. A specific legacy may also be

adeemed, that is, destroyed, if the specific property in question is destroyed or sold before the testator's death. Thus in the example given, Bill would get nothing if the gold watch had been sold before the testator's death, while Mary would get $10,000 from other sources even if the Swiss bank account had been closed.

Finally, estate taxes are taken out of the residuary estate unless the will specifies otherwise, which may mean that most or all of the residuary legatees' share disappears in the payment of those taxes.

A will ordinarily remains in effect until revoked by the testator or by operation of law. While the making of a new will does not automatically revoke the old will (unless the two wills are inconsistent), it is the usual practice to include in a new will a statement that the old will is revoked. Any document executed with the same formalities as are necessary to make a will may serve as a valid revocation.

A will may also be revoked by its physical mutilation or destruction by the testator or at the testator's direction and in his or her presence. Where a will is produced for probate, it is presumed until proven otherwise that it was not revoked. On the other hand, if a will was last seen in the testator's possession but cannot be found after the testator's death, or if it is found in a mutilated condition, it is presumed until proven otherwise that the testator revoked the will.

A will may also be revoked or partially revoked by operation of law. While a will is not revoked when the testator marries, it is revoked so far as the testator's spouse is concerned when the testator is divorced. The gift that would have been made to the divorced spouse passes instead as though the spouse had died before the testator.

The **pretermitted child statute** operates with limited exceptions to revoke a will that was executed at a time when the testator had no living children if the testator later has a child who survives for one year after the testator's death. The statute also governs the case where a testator has children living at the time he or she makes a will but later has additional children; again, with limited exceptions, the new child is entitled to the share that the child would take by the intestate succession laws if the child is not otherwise provided for in the will.

A will that has been revoked can be revived only by reexecuting it just as though a new will were being made.

When a testator dies, his or her will must be **admitted to probate**, that is, filed in the probate court. A witnessed will may be admitted to probate upon the testimony of one of the attesting witnesses. If both witnesses are dead, the will may be proved by the testimony of two persons that the handwriting of the testator, or of either witness, is genuine.

Most modern wills contain a **self-proving affidavit**. If the self-proving affidavit is executed in a statutorily specified form by the testator and witnesses before a notary and is produced for probate, the valid execution of the will can be proved by the affidavit. No live testimony is required. A holographic will may be proved either by the testimony of two witnesses that the will is in the testator's handwriting or by a self-proving affidavit by the testator (executed before a notary public) that is attached to the will.

Once a will is admitted to probate, an **executor** is appointed to manage the estate. The will usually designates the executor, but if the will names no one, or if the executor dies or resigns, a statute provides priority for certain relatives or beneficiaries.

More and more states permit wills to contain a clause providing for **independent administration**, whereby the executor may take charge of the estate on his or her own without court supervision. Independent administration is also available in limited circumstances where the testator has made no provision for it. Unless independent administration is obtained, all decisions relating to the estate (such as the sale of property, payment of debts, and distribution to the beneficiaries) must take place under the supervision and prior approval of the probate court, which is very costly and time-consuming.

Taxes

No discussion of the law of wills would be complete without some reference to estate and inheritance taxes. A federal estate tax is imposed on all property remaining in an estate after debts have been paid, together with other property such as certain trust funds, property held in joint tenancy with right of survivorship and insurance benefits. A deduction is allowed for property transferred to the decedent's spouse or to charity. The estate tax rates, like income tax rates, are graduated and depend on the size of the estate and the amount of property that has been transferred during the decedent's lifetime.

Estates valued below a threshold amount are assessed no federal estate tax. The threshold is set from time to time by Congress at an amount high enough to exempt most estates.

It is the responsibility of the executor (called an administrator when the decedent dies without a will) to file the estate tax return within nine months of the decedent's death. Most states also impose an estate tax.

Some states also impose inheritance taxes, which are taxes on the beneficiaries. They are determined by the amount of the inheritance and, in some cases, the relationship of the beneficiary to the deceased.

Gift taxes are also imposed in order to prevent evasion of estate taxes through lifetime gifts.

For more detailed information on wills and intestate succession, consult the Probate Code of your state or a treatise such as A. Casner, *Estate Planning*.

Legislation

The common law, which we have seen is the product of a line of court cases decided by judges, is only part of the substantive law of the United States. Statutes, administrative regulations and administrative procedures comprise most of the remainder. In fact, the average attorney is more likely to deal with matters that are directly governed by legislation and rules made by administrative agencies rather than by purely common law.

Constitutional Law

No discussion of statutory law can begin without first considering the United States Constitution and the constitutions of the sovereign states. The U.S. Constitution is the fundamental source of law in the United

States. In addition to setting forth the framework for government and allocating duties and responsibilities among the three branches (executive, legislative, and judicial), it also spells out fundamental human rights. All other laws, including the common law, that violate its principles are unconstitutional.

Most attorneys and paralegals may work their entire careers without encountering a matter that directly challenges a constitutional principle. Nevertheless, every law is built on a constitutional foundation and, if not, is unenforceable. For example, federal statutes and regulations that govern the transportation of goods across state lines are based on the Commerce Clause that grants to Congress the right to regulate interstate commerce. Laws, such as the Americans with Disabilities Act, that prohibit discrimination based on physical ability, race, gender, religion and other protected categories, are constitutional under the Fourteenth Amendment.

Statutes, rules, and court decisions that seek to regulate the flow of published information must withstand the scrutiny of the First Amendment's guarantee of free speech. At the local level, laws and ordinances promulgated within the boundaries of each sovereign state must not conflict with the constitution of the state or the United States Constitution.

Statutory Law

Statutes are laws made by legislative bodies including Congress, the legislatures of the various states and territories, county commissioners, city councils and other similar bodies. As compared with the common law, which begins as a response to a particular dispute between two real parties, statutory laws are intended to solve general, and often hypothetical, problems and usually apply to most if not all citizens. Statutory law attempts to reduce principles of law to rules that mean exactly what they say. Hundreds of hours of committee discussion, dozens of speeches from the floor of the legislature and thousands of pages of transcripts may have preceded the final rule. But what counts is the rule itself.

Principles of law that are codified in the form of statutes come from several sources. The Constitution is the most important source for residents of the United States, but another important source for statutes is the common law. For example, some states have passed laws holding a bar owner liable if a patron becomes visibly intoxicated and later injures someone in an accident. The idea for this law emerged from a pattern of decisions in hundreds of personal injury and wrongful death suits in which judges came to agree with plaintiffs that sellers of liquor by the drink should be held responsible for the damage caused by their drunken patrons. States passing these laws hoped to reduce accidents, lower court case loads and achieve consistent results at trial by imposing responsibility on all bar owners.

Statutes are published in statute books that can be found in law libraries and most public libraries, as well as law offices throughout each community. Federal statutes are published in the United States Code, a set of volumes that fills several shelves. Statute books are often annotated, meaning that they contain helpful references to the discussions that preceded the rule (called legislative history) to court cases in which the law has been applied, to related laws, and to other useful material that will help the reader understand and apply the statute.

Administrative Regulation

Once a law is passed, it is the responsibility of the executive branch of government to enforce it. In fact, most laws will state which department and agency of the executive branch is to have responsibility for enforcement. At the national level, federal criminal laws are referred to the Department of Justice, tax laws go to the Department of the Treasury, treaties are the responsibility of the State Department, and laws dealing with highways are sent to the Department of Transportation.

In order to enforce the law effectively, the enforcing agency must write regulations that break the law down into manageable parts. For example, environmental regulations describe in detail to whom the law applies and what numerical measurements constitute legally clean air and water. Medicare regulations define the medical procedures that the government will pay for and how many days a patient can be hospitalized for a particular diagnosis and receive reimbursement.

Transportation regulations prescribe the size and weight of trucks that are permitted on federal highways.

Each agency of the federal government has penned dozens of volumes of regulations to help it enforce the laws that have been consigned to it. These regulations are often criticized as lawmaking by unelected employees of the executive branch. Debate has raged for nearly a century over the question of whether Congress can delegate its authority to make law to another branch of the government. The answer that has emerged is that Congress may delegate such authority provided appropriate safeguards are in place. Those safeguards are the foundation of administrative procedure.

Administrative Procedure

Administrative procedure deals with how regulations are created, challenged, and reviewed. The purpose of administrative procedure is to protect individuals from unnecessary and unconstitutional governmental interference into their lives, and it is based on the constitutional guarantee that neither rights nor property will be taken without due process of law.

The Administrative Procedure Act—a federal statute—sets forth the rules that govern the process of regulatory activity. This Act applies across the board to all agencies that generate administrative regulations. When a federal agency writes regulations, it is required to publish them in the *Federal Register* to permit interested persons to submit written responses, and to publish finalized rules in the *Federal Register* no fewer than 30 days before the effective date.[27] Regulations are subject to judicial review and may be challenged in court, unless the underlying statute passed by Congress specifically states that it is not reviewable.[28] This is rare, however. A citizen who has a dispute with an agency over its decision in a particular case must generally exhaust all of the grievance procedures within that agency before he or she can bring a suit in court against the government. Sometimes these procedures, usually involving one or more hearings, can include dozens of steps,

---

27. Administrative Procedure Act, §553. Rule Making

28. *Id.* at §701.

pages of forms and can take months and even years to conclude.
Citizens often have legal representation, especially at administrative
hearings. If the citizen emerges from this process dissatisfied with the
results, he or she can institute a suit against the agency and ask a court
to review the case. Generally, the court will consider whether or not
agency actions and procedures conformed with the purpose of the
underlying statute. Every year, thousands of such cases are brought
against the government at both the federal and state levels.

Alternative Dispute Resolution

Administrative hearings represent an important method available to
citizens to resolve disputes with various government agencies. In the
private sector, people are increasingly using alternative means to
resolve their disputes with one another rather than using the courts.
These include mediation, arbitration, summary jury trials, minitrials,
and a host of other techniques designed to promote settlement of
disputes both before and after a suit is filed, but in either event before
the case goes to trial.

Alternative dispute resolution, known as ADR, has become an integral
part of the American system of justice, and its role is expected to grow
in the future. The growth of ADR is fueled by a variety of forces,
including the strain on the courts caused by the increasing number of
cases filed each year and the inability of a large portion of the
population to afford traditional litigation to resolve their disputes. Also,
there is a growing recognition that the adversarial nature of the
American legal system may not provide the best atmosphere for solving
certain types of disputes. Litigation and trial tend to destroy any
relationship the parties enjoyed before the lawsuit. Thus, where the
parties hope to continue their relationship after the dispute is settled,
ADR can offer resolution methods that are less adversarial and that, in
some situations, can promote better cooperation in the future. Some
examples of disputes where an ongoing relationship between the parties
is important include divorce and child custody matters, disputes
between businesses and their suppliers or customers, and labor disputes
between employers and their employees. ADR can help to resolve the
current problem and also preserve the relationship for the future.

ADR techniques can be characterized in one of three ways. First, there are those methods that enable the parties to resolve the dispute among themselves rather than asking a judge, jury, or other third party to make the decision for them.

- *Direct negotiation* between the parties and their attorneys is the most commonly used form of ADR and occurs at some point in almost every lawsuit. Diplomats also use negotiation to settle disputes between countries.

- *Mediation* uses a neutral third party to act as a referee while the parties negotiate. Often, the mediator will separate the parties into different offices or conference rooms and then shuttle back and forth between them conveying messages, offering insights into how the opposite side is thinking and feeling, and other communications designed to bring the parties to a negotiated settlement. If the mediator is successful, the parties will reach an agreement they can both accept. If not, at least they will each have gained insight into how the other side views the dispute, which is information that may enable them to settle the matter at a later time.

- *Minitrial*, which is well suited to business cases involving highly complex and technical issues, employs a trial-like procedure presided over by a neutral moderator hired by the parties. Executives from each of the companies involved in the dispute attend the minitrial and listen to the lawyers for each side present an abbreviated version of their cases. Afterwards, the executives get together and attempt to settle the dispute based on the strengths and weaknesses of the evidence and arguments they heard.

A second type of ADR includes those techniques that provide litigants with an expert opinion on the strengths and weaknesses of their cases.

- *Summary jury trial* uses a mock jury that hears evidence and arguments from each side and then issues an advisory verdict, including the reasoning behind the decision. In this manner, the parties learn how a real jury might decide the case, which can put pressure on both sides to settle.

- *Moderated settlement conference* is similar to minitrial, except that it uses a panel of experienced attorneys rather than a single moderator. The lawyers for each side present the factual and legal arguments of their clients' cases, and then the panel questions them and their clients. The panel then deliberates and provides an evaluation of the legal strengths and weaknesses of each side's case, including a dollar or percentage range for settlement.

The third type of ADR involves a neutral third party who renders a binding decision.

- *Arbitration* is the best known form of third-party ADR, and has been used for most of the twentieth century to resolve disputes between employers and unions. Arbitration is similar to trial, but less formal. Like most ADR, the proceedings and outcome are confidential. An arbitrator, or panel of three arbitrators, who often are experts in the type of dispute involved, listen to evidence and arguments from each side and render a decision, called an award.

- *Administrative hearings*, which are discussed above, is another example of third-party dispute resolution. Administrative hearings are used not only by government agencies but by private groups as well. For example, many major employers provide internal administrative forums for airing employee disputes, while colleges and universities use hearings to deal with rule violations by students.

ADR is not universally suitable to all legal disputes, such as those involving violent crimes or where a large corporation has endangered the public in a significant way. Situations such as these need the full authority of a court to punish the offending party. ADR is also not appropriate in those situations where some social condition needs correction. For example, the 1954 U. S. Supreme Court decision in *Brown v. Topeka Board of Education* desegregated public schools nationwide. If the case had been decided privately using ADR, its impact would have been confined to Topeka, Kansas, and would not have had such a far-reaching effect. Despite its weaknesses, ADR is expected to be used to resolve many more disputes in the future.

Having discussed the two principal branches of the law—civil and criminal—we now turn to topics of importance to all legal practitioners, regardless of their field of specialty. These include the rules of conduct by which all legal professionals must abide (Chapter IV on Legal Ethics), the mechanics of determining the state of the law on a particular subject (Chapter V on Legal Research), and the jurisdiction, personnel, and procedure of the federal court system (Chapter VI).

TERMS TO KNOW

injunctions
common law
tort
battery
strict-liability torts
writ of trespass
tortfeasor
doctrine of transferred
 intent
assault
false imprisonment
intentional infliction of
 emotional distress
trespass
chattels
conversion
negligence
negligence per se
res ipsa loquitur
causation in fact
proximate causation
trespassers
attractive nuisance
licensees

invitees
comparative negligence
"one-bite" rule
products liability
comparative causation
private nuisance
public nuisance
nuisance per se
deceit
fraud
business torts
negligent misrepresentation
interference with business
 relations
unfair competition
defamation
libel
slander
invasion of privacy
malicious prosecution
compensatory damages
punitive damages
exemplary damages
nominal damages

writ of assumpsit
Uniform Commercial Code
express contract
implied in fact
implied in law
quasi-contract liability
unjust enrichment
offer
acceptance
bilateral contract
unilateral contract
consideration
forbearance
promissory estoppel
detrimental reliance
parol evidence rule
Statute of Frauds
adhesion
duress
undue influence
intrinsic fraud
fraud in the *factum*
extrinsic fraud
fraud in the inducement
accord and satisfaction
novation
rescinded
specific performance
commercial paper
promissory notes
negotiable
negotiable instrument
secured transactions
security interest
lien
mortgage
tenant
estates in land
grantor

grantee
fee simple
fee simple subject to a
  condition subsequent
fee simple determinable
fee simple absolute
fee tail
life estate
estate *pur autre vie*
freehold estates
leasehold estates
term of years
periodic tenancy
tenancy at will
easement
utility easement
right of way easement
easement appurtenant
profits *a prendre*
licenses
restrictive covenants
tenancy in common
joint tenancy with right of
  survivorship
right of survivorship
tenancy by the entireties
remainder
mortgages
deeds of trust
liens
mortgagee
foreclosure
mortgagor
trustee
vendor's lien
mechanic's lien
materialmen's lien
tax liens
judgment lien

deed
livery of seisin
closing
general warranty deed
special warranty deed
quitclaim deed
clouds on the title
title search
abstract of title
title opinion
title insurance
bona fide purchaser
adverse possession
zoning ordinances
nonconforming uses
eminent domain
condemnation
equitable ownership
equitable conversion
trust
settlor
trustor
trustee
beneficiary
cestui que trust
revocable trust
irrevocable trust
inter vivos trust
testamentary trust
rule against perpetuities
quiet enjoyment

constructive eviction
assignment of the lease
sublease
forcible entry
ejectment
forcible entry and detainer
heirs
escheat
testator
intestate succession
per capita
per stirpes
holographic will
nuncupative will
forced heirship statutes
dower rights
curtesy rights
widow's election will
devisees
legatees
Uniform Simultaneous
 Death Act
specific legacy
demonstrative legacy
general legacy
residuary legacy
adeemed
pretermitted child statute
self-proving affidavit
executor
independent administration

Chapter Four

LEGAL ETHICS

The practice of law, like the practice of medicine and other learned professions, is regulated by each of the 50 states. This regulation takes two principal forms: restrictions on who may practice law and restrictions on the manner in which it may be practiced. Each of these types of regulation is important to the student.

Nonlawyers and the Practice of Law

In a 1967 American Bar Association Formal Opinion, the Standing Committee on Professional Ethics stated:

> A lawyer can employ lay secretaries, lay investigators, lay detectives, lay researchers, and lay scriveners. In fact, he may employ nonlawyers to do any task for him except counsel clients about law matters, engage directly in the practice of law, appear in court or appear in formal proceedings . . . so long as it is he who takes the work and vouches for it to the client and becomes responsible for it to the client. In other words, we do not limit the kind of assistance that a lawyer can acquire in any way . . . so long as the nonlawyers do not do things that lawyers may not do or do the things that lawyers only may do.[1]

This opinion forms the basis of current guidelines formulated by the **National Association of Legal Assistants** (NALA), the **National Federation of Paralegal Associations** (NFPA), the **American Association for Paralegal Education** (AAfPE) and the **Legal Assistant Management Association** (LAMA).

---

1. ABA Formal Opinion 316 (1967).

Nonlawyers must refrain from activities that constitute the actual practice of law and must be careful to observe the same standards of ethical conduct that are applicable to the lawyers for whom they work.

Admission to the bar is controlled in each state by the legislature or supreme court of that state, often through a board of bar examiners composed of lawyers from throughout the state. With rare exceptions, all applicants for the bar must be graduates of a law school accredited by the American Bar Association. Most states also require at least some college-level training. Applicants must pass a bar examination consisting of multiple-choice questions in areas of the law common to all states and essay questions on the law of the state in which they seek to be licensed. Applicants who pass the bar exam must take an oath and, in many states, must pay annual dues to the state bar association as a condition of retaining their licenses.

What, then, are the activities in which only lawyers may engage? The answer to this question is not a simple one: one court has referred to "the line of demarcation, often shadowy and wavering, which defines the limits of the functions of the legal adviser from those of the layman."[2] Nevertheless, it is possible to identify a number of activities that most or all states agree constitute the practice of law in most or all circumstances.

Some of these are suggested by the above-quoted ABA Opinion. A nonlawyer may not

- give advice to clients concerning their legal rights and responsibilities
- hold himself or herself out to the public as a lawyer
- appear as the legal representative of a client before a court.

Other, less obvious prohibitions are also present. For example, a nonlawyer may not use a lawyer's professional stationery without in some manner identifying himself or herself as a nonlawyer (*e.g.*, "Dana

---

2. *State ex re. Johnson v. Childe*, 139 Neb. 91, 95, 295 N.W. 381, 384 (1941).

Doe, Paralegal"). To do otherwise might mislead the recipient as to the nonlawyer's status.[3]

Finally, except as part of a retirement plan, a nonlawyer may not share in the profits of a lawyer's practice.

With these principal exceptions, a nonlawyer may do anything that a lawyer may do. A paralegal's activities are undertaken as the agent of the lawyer and under the lawyer's supervision.[4] The lawyer must maintain a direct relationship with the client, supervise the delegated work, and have complete responsibility for the work product. This includes both the accuracy of the paralegal's work and the propriety of the paralegal's conduct.

According to the **Model Rules of Professional Conduct** promulgated by the American Bar Association in 1969, a law firm must have measures in place to ensure that the behavior of nonlawyer assistants is compatible with the professional obligations of lawyers. A lawyer who supervises an assistant and who either orders the assistant to violate a rule of professional conduct or ratifies such conduct is responsible for the violation. The supervising attorney, or any partner in the firm, who learns of the conduct but fails to prevent any further damages from being done will also be held responsible.[5] Thus, the supervising attorney, and the firm itself, through its principals, have joint responsibility to ensure that the assistant's job is performed competently and ethically.

If paralegals may assume a wide range of responsibilities, what are the ethical obligations that accompany those responsibilities? At a minimum, the paralegal must bear the same ethical responsibilities as the lawyer for whom he or she works. In the words of the ABA Formal Ethics Opinion 316 (1967) "nonlawyers may not do things that lawyers may not do."

---

3. ABA Informal Opinion 660.

4. ABA Formal Opinion 85 (1932).

5. Model Rule 5.3

The Ethical Practice of Law

The ethical responsibilities of attorneys are established in each state by the legislature or supreme court of the state. The ethical codes of most states are based, sometimes with minor modifications, on the Code of Professional Responsibility of the American Bar Association, referred to above. The standards of legal ethics are the subject of constant reevaluation. The 1969 Code was based in large part on 32 Canons of Professional Ethics adopted by the ABA in 1908 and on 15 additional Canons adopted between 1928 and 1937.

The ABA has adopted Model Rules of Professional Conduct as the standard of professional conduct for attorneys throughout the country. Through its Standing Committee on Ethics and Professional Responsibility, the ABA also issues formal and informal opinions on questions of legal ethics submitted to it by attorneys. State and local bar associations often issue similar opinions.

The **ABA Code of Professional Responsibility** consists of:

- Canons that express "in general terms the standards of professional conduct expected of lawyers in their relationships with the public, with the legal system and with the legal profession."

- Ethical Considerations (ECs), aspirational in character, which "represent the objectives toward which every lawyer should strive" and which "constitute a body of principles upon which the lawyer can rely for guidance in many specific situations."

- Disciplinary Rules (DRs), mandatory in character, which "state the minimum level of conduct below which no lawyer can fall without being subject to disciplinary action."

Some aspects of the Code have little applicability to paralegals. What follows is a discussion of some the features that paralegals should be aware of in their day-to-day work. Paralegals should also become familiar with the **Model Standards and Guidelines for Utilization of Legal Assistants** issued by the National Association of Legal Assistants (NALA), and the **Model Code of Ethics and Professional Respon-**

sibility and **Guidelines for Enforcement** promulgated by the National Federation of Paralegal Associations (NFPA), both of which are based on standards set by the ABA Code of Professional Responsibility and Model Rules of Professional Conduct.

The chart on pages 124-126 cross-references the various ABA codes and rules with those promulgated by NALA and NFPA. However, the paralegal codes and rules address several issues that are specific to the profession, including paralegal education and training, disclosure of one's paralegal status, relationship with clients, conduct before courts and other authorities, *pro bono* activity, and much more. Paralegals should also be familiar with—and encourage their employers to become familiar with—the **ABA Guidelines for the Utilization of Legal Assistants**.

Canon 1: Maintain the Integrity and Competence of the Legal Profession.

Canon 1 states that "[a] lawyer should assist in maintaining the integrity and competence of the legal profession." In particular, attorneys must not engage in

- illegal conduct
- conduct involving dishonesty, fraud, deceit, or misrepresentation
- conduct that is prejudicial to the administration of justice
- conduct that adversely reflects on their fitness to practice law.

Lawyers must not violate the disciplinary rules, nor may they circumvent the disciplinary rules through the actions of others. An attorney should not advise or sanction an act by his or her client that the attorney should not do.[6]

An attorney who becomes aware of improper conduct by another attorney must report such conduct to the appropriate authorities. Likewise, attorneys must cooperate with disciplinary investigations of other attorneys.

---

6. ABA Formal Opinion 75 (1932).

Canon 2: Make Legal Counsel Available.

Canon 2 states that "[a] lawyer should assist the legal profession in fulfilling its duty to make legal counsel available." Topics under this Canon include publicity and advertising by lawyers, solicitation of legal business, specialization, fees and fee-splitting, and acceptance of and withdrawal from legal employment. While the paralegal is not directly concerned with these topics, the paralegal should be aware of the basic guidelines in these areas as part of a general understanding of legal ethics.

The rules concerning lawyer advertising are at present in a state of flux. Before 1977, virtually all publicity and advertising by lawyers was prohibited. In that year, however, the United States Supreme Court held in the case of *Bates v. State Bar of Arizona*[7] that lawyer advertising was protected in large part by the First Amendment.

In contrast, the ABA Model Rules of Professional Conduct place few restrictions on lawyer advertising, so long as it is not false, fraudulent, or misleading. Future rules in this area are likely to fall somewhere between these two extremes.

Solicitations of clients to obtain their legal business is also regulated by state and ABA rules. The ABA Model Rules permit solicitation only under limited circumstances, and they prohibit coercion, duress, harassment, and taking advantage of the client's physical, emotional, or mental state.[8]

With the exception of patent, trademark, and admiralty attorneys, lawyers may not refer to themselves as specialists in a particular field of law unless they are certified as specialists by their state board of legal specialization, or by an organization recognized by the state bar association. In some states, lawyers who meet certain experience and education requirements and who pass an examination may be certified as specialists in areas offered by their state's board of legal specialization.

---

7. 433 U.S. 350 (1977).

8. Model Rule 7.3.

The fees charged by a lawyer must be reasonable and should be explained to the client in advance. Some of the factors that should be considered in determining a reasonable fee include

- the time, labor, and skill required to perform the legal service properly
- the novelty and difficulty of the questions involved
- the customary fee of other lawyers for the same services
- the amount involved and the results obtained
- the experience, reputation, and ability of the lawyer involved.

In most civil cases, lawyers may charge a **contingency fee**; that is, a fee (usually a percentage of the amount recovered) that is to be paid by the client only if the outcome is successful.

A fee may be divided among lawyers who are not part of the same firm only where the client consents and where the total fee is reasonable. A few states permit a lawyer who "forwards" a case to another lawyer to collect a fee for that service.

It has been a longstanding tradition of the bar that lawyers often represent charitable organizations or those who are unable to afford necessary legal services at no charge or at a reduced charge. This service, together with participation in activities for improving the law, the legal system, or the legal profession, is referred to as *pro bono publico* or *pro bono* service.

The issue of mandatory *pro bono* is an ongoing topic of discussion.

More paralegals are accepting the responsibility for *pro bono* services by volunteering in legal clinics, courts, and mediation services. *Pro bono* offers paralegals the opportunity to learn a field of law in which they do not work on a daily basis.

While the standards governing acceptance of employment are very broad, the circumstances under which a lawyer may discontinue representation are carefully regulated. A lawyer must withdraw if:

- the client insists that the lawyer pursue a course of action solely for purposes of harassment

- the lawyer will be forced to violate a Disciplinary Rule
- the lawyer is unable to continue effective representation
- the lawyer is discharged by the client.

A lawyer may withdraw under a variety of other circumstances, so long as he or she takes all reasonable steps to avoid prejudice to the rights of the client. The lawyer must give due notice to the client, allowing time for employment of other counsel, and must deliver to the client all papers and property to which the client is entitled, including a refund of any unearned fees. In most circumstances, permission of the court is required for a lawyer to withdraw from a pending lawsuit, and the lawyer must continue representation if ordered to do so by the court.

Canon 3: Prevent the Unauthorized Practice of Law.

Under Canon 3, "[a] lawyer should assist in preventing the unauthorized practice of law." There is a fine line between those activities that constitute the practice of law and those that do not, and this aspect of Canon 3 has been discussed in general terms above. Canon 3 also prohibits a lawyer from sharing legal fees with nonlawyers, except through retirement plans or through payments to the estate of a deceased lawyer. A law partnership may not include a nonlawyer as a partner.

Canon 4: Preserve Client Confidentiality.

Canon 4 states that "[a] lawyer should preserve the confidences and secrets of a client." The information covered by this Canon falls into two categories:

1. information protected by the attorney/client privilege, that is, information that may be legally withheld from evidence in a court of law ("**confidences**").

2. other information gained in the professional relationship that the client has requested to be kept secret, the disclosure of which would be embarrassing or potentially detrimental to the client ("**secrets**").

The attorney/client privilege is governed by state and federal law and not by standards of legal ethics. In order to be privileged, however, a statement must be made outside the presence of anyone except the attorney and the attorney's paralegals, secretaries, investigators, or other agents. The client may, of course, waive this right if he or she so chooses, thereby permitting the lawyer to make the disclosure. Federal Rule of Evidence 501 makes a state's rule applicable in federal cases with respect to questions governed by state law.

Confidential information may be revealed with the consent of the client (or all the clients, if the information relates to more than one client), but only after a full disclosure of all the relevant factors. Confidential information may also be revealed when required by law or court order or when necessary to prevent the client from committing a crime. The Model Rules limit such disclosure to crimes involving death or serious bodily harm.

Finally, lawyers may reveal confidential information to establish or collect their fees or to defend themselves or their employees or associates against an accusation of wrongful conduct, but only when it is necessary to do so.[9]

The obligation of confidentiality is especially important for paralegals. The operation of a successful law practice requires that clients' confidential information be shared among lawyers within the firm and with paralegals and other support personnel—there is nothing unethical about such disclosure. It is extremely important, however, that those to whom confidential information is revealed treat that information in the same manner as is required of the attorney handling the case.

An attorney is responsible for improper disclosure by the attorney's employees. ABA Disciplinary Rule 4-101 (D) states that "[a] lawyer shall exercise reasonable care to prevent his employees, associates, and others whose services are utilized by him from disclosing or using confidences or secrets of a client . . . ."

---

9. ABA Formal Opinion 19 (1930).

Canon 5: Avoid Conflicts of Interest.

Clients are protected from conflicts of interest on the part of their lawyers by Canon 5, which states that "[a] lawyer should exercise independent professional judgment on behalf of a client." Under this Canon, a lawyer must not accept employment in cases where the lawyer's judgment may be affected by his or her own financial, business, property, or personal interests, except with the consent of the client after full disclosure. Thus, for example, a lawyer may not prepare an instrument, such as a will, giving the lawyer or a member of the lawyer's family a gift.

By the same token, a lawyer must not obtain any ownership interest in a client's case (except for a contingent fee arrangement or a lien to secure the lawyer's fee and expenses), because doing so might affect the lawyer's judgment as to the client's best interests. A lawyer should not make loans to a client in connection with litigation, except that the lawyer may prepay expenses on behalf of the client.

Finally, a lawyer must not enter into a business transaction with a client except under limited circumstances designed to ensure that the transaction is fair and equitable to the client. In this regard, a lawyer may not acquire publication rights with respect to a client's case until that case is concluded.

Conflicts of interest may also arise due to a lawyer's representation of other clients. For this reason, a lawyer must not accept employment from a client if the lawyer's professional judgment on behalf of other clients will be impaired. A lawyer may represent clients with conflicting interests only if *both* clients, after disclosure of all the facts and circumstances, consent. If a conflict arises between two clients in the course of their representation, the lawyer must resolve the conflict by withdrawing from one or both cases. Examples of potential conflict for a lawyer include defending a husband and wife who are accused of filing a fraudulent joint tax return, drafting a man's will at the request of his children, or representing a corporation and its president on the same matter.

A lawyer may not make an aggregate settlement of the claims for or against two or more clients unless the terms are fully disclosed to the clients and each consents.

A lawyer is often asked to serve as an intermediary between clients. For example, a lawyer may be asked by a husband and wife who have been previous clients to arrange the terms of an uncontested divorce settlement. Under the Model Rules, a lawyer may participate in such an arrangement only under limited circumstances. Each client must be able to make informed decisions; the lawyer must be able to act impartially and without prejudice to the clients' interests; and each client must consent after an understanding of the advantages and risks of such an arrangement. A lawyer must withdraw from such representation on the request of either client or if it becomes apparent that genuine conflict has arisen.

Under limited circumstances, a lawyer may accept compensation for his or her services from someone other than the client. Thus, for example, a lawyer may be paid by a liability insurance carrier to represent a customer of the carrier who is being sued. Full disclosure to the client must be made, and an arrangement must be provided that ensures that the lawyer can exercise independent professional judgment on behalf of the client.

A lawyer must not accept or continue representation where

- it is apparent that the lawyer will be a witness, except where the testimony relates to an uncontested matter or formality

- the testimony relates to the lawyer's fee and

- refusal or withdrawal would work a substantial hardship on the client.

Under the Model Rules, members of a lawyer's firm may testify if no conflict of interest is created.

Canon 6: Represent Clients Competently.

Canon 6 states that "[a] lawyer should represent a client competently."
The requirements of this Canon are simple: a lawyer must not handle a
matter that he or she is not competent to handle, unless the lawyer
undertakes the work and study necessary to become competent. A
lawyer must not handle a matter without adequate preparation and must
not neglect a matter entrusted to him or her. These obligations include

- prompt attention to legal matters
- adequate communication with clients
- punctuality in appearances before courts
- adequate continuing legal education.

While the requirement that a lawyer be competent ought to be self-
evident, neglect and inadequate representation are a major disciplinary
problem. Federal Judge Jerry Buchmeyer has estimated that over one
third of all grievances filed against Texas attorneys relate to such
problems.[10]

Canon 7: Represent Clients Zealously.

Canon 7, which provides that "[a] lawyer should represent a client
zealously within the bounds of the law," is by far the most complex of
the Canons. The Ethical Considerations and Disciplinary Rules under
this Canon attempt to balance the lawyer's duty to be a vigorous
advocate for a client's interests with the lawyer's duty to be fair and
honest with the legal system and with opposing parties and counsel.

A lawyer must seek the lawful objectives of the client through all
reasonably available means permitted by law and the standards of legal
ethics. A lawyer's personal distaste for a client, or disagreement with
the client's conduct or legal position, does not affect the lawyer's
obligation to represent the client to the best of the lawyer's ability.
Under our legal system, individuals are generally permitted, within the
bounds of the law, to decide for themselves whether their conduct is
appropriate or inappropriate, and it is for the courts and not for

---

10. Buchmeyer, *How to Avoid Grievance Complaints,* 43 Tex B.J. 113 (1980).

attorneys to decide whether a particular course of conduct is legally permissible. This does not mean that the lawyer may not urge a client to do what the lawyer thinks is right, but the final decision must be the client's.[11]

The lawyer's obligation to represent a client zealously is not absolute and must yield to a duty of fairness, honesty, and courtesy. A lawyer must always be courteous to the courts and to opposing parties and counsel and should agree to reasonable requests regarding court proceedings, settings, continuances, waiver of procedural formalities, and similar matters that do not prejudice the rights of the lawyer's client. The lawyer should generally comply with local customs of courtesy or practice of the bar or of a particular court. A lawyer must not take any action solely for purposes of harassment or delay, make any frivolous legal argument, make any misrepresentation of law or fact, or create, preserve, or use false evidence.

A lawyer who becomes aware of fraud committed by a person who is not the lawyer's client must promptly reveal the fraud. The duty of the lawyer to reveal a client's fraud is an area of legal ethics that is undergoing continuing debate. The Model Rules contain a requirement applicable in civil cases that the lawyer must call upon the client to rectify the fraud. If the client fails to do so, the lawyer must reveal the fraud.

The area of greatest concern involves a lawyer whose client wishes to commit perjury in the course of a criminal trial. Special standards adopted by the American Bar Association in 1969 require that the lawyer in such a situation withdraw if possible. If withdrawal is impossible, the lawyer must allow the client to tell the client's perjurious story without benefit of direct questioning by the lawyer and without the lawyer's referring to the false testimony in closing argument.[12]

---

11. Model Rule 2.1.

12. *ABA Project on Standards of Criminal Justice: The Defense Function* §7.7 (1969).

The Model Rules take the position that a lawyer may not participate in perjurious testimony and must reveal perjury when it occurs.[13]

A lawyer may not communicate directly with an opposing party whom the lawyer knows to be represented by counsel without the permission of that person's lawyer, nor may the lawyer cause another person to make such contact. In particular, a lawyer may not engage in settlement negotiations with an opposing party without the consent of that party's counsel.[14] A lawyer may not give legal advice to an opposing party who is not represented by a lawyer, except for the advice to secure a lawyer.

A lawyer may not make or threaten to make a criminal charge against someone solely to obtain an advantage in a civil case.

In presenting a case, a lawyer may not

- refer to irrelevant matters or matters not supported by evidence
- ask degrading questions that are not relevant to the case
- state his or her personal knowledge of the facts or his or her personal opinion regarding the matters in question.

The Model Rules provide elaborate guidelines concerning public statements that a lawyer may make concerning pending litigation. These guidelines are designed to ensure that civil or criminal proceedings are not influenced by reports in the press. ABA Disciplinary Rule 7-107(J) requires a lawyer to exercise reasonable care to prevent the lawyer's employees from making statements that the lawyer is prohibited from making.

A lawyer may not contact prospective or actual jurors or their families before or during the course of a lawsuit or criminal trial. After the case is concluded and the jury is discharged, the ethical standards prohibit a lawyer from contacting a juror or the juror's family solely for purposes of harassment or embarrassment. It should be noted that the rules of some courts prohibit all contact with jurors after a trial except by permission of the court. Finally, a lawyer must report improper

---

13. Model Rule 3.3.

14. ABA Formal Opinion 124 (1934).

conduct by jurors or improper contact by anyone with a juror or member of the juror's family.

A lawyer may not advise or cause a person to hide himself or herself or to leave the jurisdiction for the purpose of making himself or herself unavailable as a witness.

A lawyer may pay an expert witness a reasonable fee for the expert witness' services but may pay a nonexpert witness only for the expenses and loss of time incurred by the nonexpert witness in attending or testifying. In no case may a witness be paid a contingency fee.

A lawyer must not make gifts or loans to any judge or judicial employee, although campaign contributions are permitted. A lawyer may not communicate with a judge about a particular case except during the course of court proceedings or when the opposing party or attorney is present. The opposing party or attorney must be furnished with a copy of any written communications to the judge.

Canon 8: Improve the Legal System.

Canon 8, which states that "[a] lawyer should assist in improving the legal system," regulates the conduct of lawyers who are public officials or judicial candidates. The Canon prohibits lawyers from making false accusations against a judge.

Canon 9: Avoid Professional Impropriety.

Canon 9 states that "[a] lawyer should avoid even the appearance of professional impropriety." This Canon governs conduct that is not necessarily improper by itself but that is likely to create the appearance of impropriety and hence to reflect badly on the lawyer and the legal system.

In addition to this general standard, there are some specific prohibitions under Canon 9. Lawyers are prohibited from accepting private employment in matters they have dealt with as a judge or public employee. A lawyer may not state or imply that he or she is able to improperly influence any tribunal, legislative body, or public official.

ABA Disciplinary Rule 9-102 governs a lawyer's handling of the funds
and property of the lawyer's clients. These funds must be placed in a
separate bank account or accounts and may not be commingled with the
lawyer's funds. A lawyer must promptly notify a client of the receipt
of funds or other property, must maintain complete records of such
funds or property, and must promptly deliver the funds to the client
upon request.

Many of the foregoing standards of legal ethics will have little
relevance to the legal assistant. Some, however, are of crucial
importance. The paralegal should particularly be aware of ABA
Disciplinary Rule 5.3, which clearly obligates the attorney to supervise
all work by a nonattorney.

In addition, the following topics will play a significant role in the
day-to-day work of the legal assistant:

- Publicity, Advertising, and Solicitation
    - Old ABA Canon 27
    - New ABA Canon 2
    - Disciplinary Rules 2-101 through 2-104
    - Model Rules 7.1 through 7.5

- Unauthorized Practice of Law
    - Old ABA Canon 47
    - New ABA Canon 3
    - Disciplinary Rule 3-101
    - Model Rule 7.4(c)
    - NALA Canons 1,3,4, and 6
    - NFPA EC 1.8

- Sharing Fees with Nonlawyers
    - Old ABA Canon 34
    - New ABA Canon 3
    - Disciplinary Rule 3-102

- Confidential Communications
    - Old ABA Canon 37
    - New ABA Canon 4

- ◆ Disciplinary Rule 4-101
- ◆ Model Rule 1.6
- ◆ NALA Canon 7
- ◆ NFPA EC 1.5

- Competence
  - ◆ Old ABA Canon 21
  - ◆ New ABA Canon 6
  - ◆ Disciplinary Rule 6-101
  - ◆ Model Rule 1.1
  - ◆ NALA Canon 7
  - ◆ NFPA EC 1.1

- Communication with Adverse Party
  - ◆ Old ABA Canon 9
  - ◆ New ABA Canon 7
  - ◆ Disciplinary Rule 7-104
  - ◆ Model Rules 4.2 and 4.3
  - ◆ NFPA EC 1.2

- Trial Publicity
  - ◆ Old ABA Canon 20
  - ◆ New ABA Canon 7
  - ◆ Disciplinary Rule 7-108
  - ◆ Model Rule 3.6
  - ◆ NFPA EC 1.5

- Contact with Jurors
  - ◆ Old ABA Canon 23
  - ◆ New ABA Canon 7
  - ◆ Disciplinary Rule 7-108
  - ◆ Model Rule 3.5
  - ◆ NFPA EC 1.2

- Contact with Witnesses
  - ◆ Old ABA Canons 18 and 39
  - ◆ New ABA Canon 7
  - ◆ Disciplinary Rule 7-109

      ◆   Model Rule 3.4

      ◆   NFPA EC 1.2

- Contact with Officials
  - ◆ Old ABA Canon 3
  - ◆ New ABA Canon 7
  - ◆ Disciplinary Rule 7-110
  - ◆ Model Rule 3.5
  - ◆ NFPA EC 1.2

While these are the topics most directly relevant to the work of a paralegal, he or she must be generally familiar with all the standards of legal ethics.

There are at least two reasons why this is the case:

1. The paralegal must be careful to avoid deliberately or accidentally violating any of these standards or causing his or her employer to violate the standards.

2. It is the paralegal's obligation, just as it is the lawyer's, to report any substantial violation of the standards.

The descriptions of ethical standards in this chapter are only summaries. Most of the standards have been oversimplified, and many of the more detailed points have been omitted. A person who is in need of the precise ethical standards applicable in a particular situation should directly consult the state's Rules of Professional Conduct.

A copy of the Model Rules of Professional Conduct and other codes and rules promulgated by the American Bar Association may be obtained by calling 312-988-5522, or by checking the ABA home page on the Internet at http://www.abanet.org. NALA and NFPA sites can be found at nala.org and paralegals.org. Summaries of current opinions of the ABA Standing Committee on Ethics and Professional Responsibility are published from time to time in the American Bar Association *Journal*. Other publications on the subject of legal ethics may be found in any good law library.

TERMS TO KNOW

confidences
secrets
pro bono

Chapter Five

LEGAL RESEARCH

The public often imagines that a lawyer has an immediate answer to every legal question—or at least every legal question within the lawyer's area of specialization. When confronted with a legal problem, a lawyer is expected to think back to his or her law school training and immediately arrive at the correct and complete answer.

Unfortunately for members of the legal profession, matters are seldom that simple. The amount of substantive and procedural law in any given jurisdiction is far beyond the capacity of any lawyer to learn and remember. Even in a given specialty, the most that can be expected is that a lawyer will master the basic rules and be familiar with the most fundamental cases and statutes that govern the lawyer's practice.

The lawyer may face a question involving the law of a foreign country or of a state other than the lawyer's own. Not even the most brilliant legal scholar can be familiar with such a vast body of material.

Finally, new cases are being decided and new statutes, regulations, and rulings passed every day. It is impossible to keep up with this influx of new law in its entirety.

For all these reasons, **legal research**, the process of looking up the law on a particular topic, is a basic part of the training of every legal professional.

Even if one could somehow find the mythical lawyer who knew all the answers to all the questions, legal research would still be necessary. Successful legal argument, both oral and written, depends not only on knowing the answers, but on being able to convince the judge or judges that the answers put forth by the lawyer are indeed correct. This is accomplished by the **citation** of relevant legal materials in support of the lawyer's contentions. The judge or the judge's staff can then refer to these materials to learn whether or not the lawyer has correctly interpreted and stated the rules of law that the materials contain.

Knowing the relevant law is important, but being able to demonstrate the state of the law is often equally important. Only lawyers can argue in court and provide legal advice to clients, but a properly trained paralegal can be an invaluable aid in helping the lawyer learn and demonstrate the law.

The questions that must be answered can range from the simple and straightforward ("What is the statute of limitations for burglary?") to the complex, difficult, and sometimes unanswerable. ("How have the courts interpreted the phrase 'actual cash value' as used in insurance policies in connection with the loss of men's clothing samples?")

Regardless of the nature of the problem, however, or its degree of difficulty, there are certain fundamental techniques of legal research that will lead the researcher to the correct answer. Sometimes legal research will demonstrate that the problem is one that has never before been addressed by the law. Mastery of legal research requires three types of knowledge:

1. an understanding of the sources from which various types of law are derived

2. familiarity with the legal materials in which law from each of these sources is embodied

3. a systematic way of using these materials to locate the answer to a given question.

Sources of the Law

The three main sources of law in the United States correspond to our three branches of government: executive, legislative, and judicial.

Since the courts are the ultimate arbiters of the law, the law made by the judicial branch is often of greatest importance to the legal researcher. The decisions rendered by judges over the years are relevant to current legal problems through the doctrine of *stare decisis* (Latin for "let the decision stand"). In order to maintain consistency, fairness, and economy of effort, a rule of law established in one case (a **precedent**) is followed in similar cases as they arise, unless the court is firmly convinced that the rule is incorrect or unless changing circumstances have rendered the rule no longer equitable.

Although most judicial decisions, especially at the trial court level, are announced orally, these decisions lack permanence and widespread availability and are therefore seldom of much use to the legal researcher. Of far greater value are the written opinions of appellate courts (and some trial courts) that are reported and published nation-wide.

A judicial opinion will not only state the outcome of the case before the court but will explain the facts of the case, the court's reasoning, and the precedent on which the court relies in reaching its decision. This gives the opinion particular value to the legal researcher. The facts stated in the opinion can be compared to the facts of the problem at hand; the court's reasoning can be examined to determine whether it is persuasive and logical; and the precedents cited by the court can be checked to determine whether they are themselves of assistance.

Reported judicial decisions form by far the largest body of written law. There are presently over 3,000,000 reported cases from federal and state courts, and dozens of volumes of new opinions are issued every year.

The role of the legislative branch in the establishment of law has grown enormously in modern times. In ancient England and in colonial America, **statutes** were the exception rather than the rule, and were enacted only where the **common law** failed to supply the answer or reached an unsatisfactory result.

Today the tables have been turned. Most modern judicial decisions "fill in the gaps" in the text of statutory enactments. Indeed, it is becoming increasingly difficult to find a legal subject on which the federal or state legislatures, or both, have not passed legislation.

Where a statute is plain and specific, its text is often the only legislative source to which the researcher need refer. There can be little doubt about the meaning of a statute that states, for example, that "Rhode Island constitutes one judicial district. Court shall be held at

Providence."[1] Other statutes, however, can be considerably more vague. How, for example, should the courts interpret a statute which states that "[e]very contract, combination in the form of trust or otherwise, or conspiracy in restraint of trade or commerce . . . is declared illegal?"[2]

Where the text of a statute is vague or ambiguous, its **legislative history** can sometimes furnish the necessary clarification. The legislative history of a statute includes

- the record of its passage through the legislature

- prior drafts of the statute

- transcripts of the hearings of committees to which the proposed statute was referred

- reports of those committees recommending that the statute be passed, often proposing amendments

- the debates about the statute on the floor of the legislature

- (sometimes) the speeches made by the chief executive signing the statute into law.

Of increasing importance in recent years is the law made by the executive branch of government. Administrative agencies and officers of the executive branch often exercise a quasi-legislative function, adopting regulations that have the force of law. These regulations, issued pursuant to authority delegated by the legislature, may interpret a statute, providing answers to detailed questions where the statute speaks only in generalities, or may establish rules of procedure for implementing the statute.

Some regulations affect only the conduct of the agency itself (such as a regulation establishing an agency's hours of business), while others

---

1. 28 U.S.C. §120.

2. 15 U.S.C. §1.

require affirmative conduct by private individuals or corporations (such as regulations requiring certain safety devices or warnings in hazardous places of employment).

Executive agencies and officers may also perform a quasi-judicial function. Each year agencies such as the Federal Trade Commission and the Federal Energy Regulatory Commission issue thousands of rulings in administrative proceedings that come before them, often issuing written opinions that resemble judicial opinions. Officials such as attorneys general, state comptrollers, and representatives of the Internal Revenue Service also issue opinions on matters referred to them by other officials and by private parties.

Finally, strange as it may seem, some sources of law are not associated with government. While the statement or action of an individual or group with the power to make the law, such as a judge, legislature, agency, or official, provides direct guidance to the legal researcher, the opinion of someone particularly qualified to analyze, predict, or recommend the law is also of value in answering legal questions. Such a person may be a distinguished lawyer, a law professor, a retired or active judge, or simply an author in a prestigious legal periodical or other well-regarded legal publication.

Where an opinion is put forth by such a person, it often carries the weight of law, since it is likely to be followed by courts, legislators, and other lawmakers. These so-called **secondary sources** include legal encyclopedias, law reviews, legal treatises, and form books.

Legal Materials

Having identified the sources of the law, we must now explore the variety of legal materials in which that law is located. Each source of law is associated with several types of legal materials in which its output is published. In addition, some types of legal materials do not directly present the law but operate as research aids to facilitate the use of other materials.

Judicial Decisions

Judicial decisions are collected and published in volumes known as
reporters. Some state courts and the United States Supreme Court have
official reporters issued by the government, in which those courts'
decisions are published.

Most federal courts and an increasing number of state courts have no
official reporter. For these courts, **unofficial reporters**, published by a
private legal publishing company, are the means by which opinions are
disseminated. The unofficial reporters also provide a handy reprint of
officially reported decisions.

The accompanying chart summarizes the reporters that publish the
decisions of the various American courts. Each type of federal court
has its own reporter system. Selected decisions of the United States
District Courts are published in the *Federal Supplement* or the *Federal
Rules Decisions*. Opinions of the United States Courts of Appeals are
reported in the *Federal Reporter*. The United States Supreme Court has
an official reporter (the *United States Reports*) and two permanent
unofficial reporters (the *Supreme Court Reporter* and *United States
Supreme Court Reports – Lawyers' Edition*).

While a few states still publish official reporters for their courts, most
states have eliminated such reporters as a cost-saving measure and
instead rely upon the National Reporter System, published by West
Group of Minneapolis, Minnesota.

JURISDICTION & COURT	REPORTER(S) AND SAMPLE CITATION(S)	DIGESTS	SHEPARD'S	LEGISLATIVE MATERIALS	ADMINISTRATIVE MATERIAL
United States Supreme Court	United States Reports* (407 U.S. 389 (1980)) (including slip opinions) Supreme Court Reporter (99 S. Ct. 406 (1980)) Lawyers' Edition (66 L.Ed. 2d 147 (1980)) U.S. Law Week (49 U.S.L.W. 4063 (1980))	Supreme Court Digest Federal Practice Digest 2d Modern Federal Practice Digest	United States Citations	*Codes:* United States Code (28 U.S.C. 1332) United States Code Annotated (28 U.S.C.A. 1332) *Session Laws:* Statutes at Large (41 Stat. 712 (1980)) Slip Laws	*Codes:* Code of Federal Regulations (29 C.F.R. 17.01(c)) *Registers:* Federal Register (67 Fed. Reg. 34,249 (1980)) *Decisions:* Specialized Reporters, such as Federal Trade
United States Courts of Appeals	Federal Reporter (621 F.2d 149 (5th Cir. 1980)) (slip opinions for some circuits, including Fifth)	Federal Practice Digest 2d Modern Federal Practice Digest	Federal Citations Part I	*Legislative History:* Committee Hearings Committee Reports U.S. Code Congressional & Administrative News (1980 U.S. Code Cong. & Ad. News 3412) Congressional Record (37 Cong. Rec. 32,451 (1980))	Commission Decisions (56 F.T.C. 203 1980))
United States District Courts	Federal Supplement (574 F. Supp. 37 (E.D. Wisconsin 1983)) Federal Rules Decisions (104 F.R.D. 136 (D. Maine 1985)) Federal Reporter (very early cases only)	Same	Federal Citations Part II		
State High Courts	Sometimes an official reporter, such as Hawaii Reports* (241 Haw. 301 (1962)) National Reporter System, such as Pacific Reporter (675 P.2d 9 (Colo. 1984))	State Digests, such as Pennsylvania Digest Regional Digests, such as Atlantic Digest Barclays' California Law Monthly	State citators, such as Indiana Citations Regional citators, such as Southwestern Citations	*Codes:* General codes, such as Equity's New Hampshire Revised Statutes Annotated (N.H. Rev. Civ. Stat. Ann. 377 776) Subject-matter codes, such as West's California Legislative Service	*Codes:* Individual state codes *Registers:* Individual state registers, such as Florida Administrative Register *Decisions:* Occasionally a specialized reporter
Intermediate State Appellate Courts	National Reporter System, such as Pacific Reporter (675 P.2d 649 (Alaska App. 1983))	Same	Same	*Session Laws:* Individual state session laws, such as Nebraska Laws (1973 Neb. Laws 1547 (1973))	
State Trial Courts	Usually Unreported Occasionally an official reporter, such as Miscellaneous Reports* (N.Y.) (23 Misc. 2d 301 (Fam. Ct. 1980)) New York Supplement (222 N.Y.S. 2d 331 (Fam. Ct. 1980))	All decisions in General Digest System	Same	Usually no slip laws *Legislative History:* Usually none	

* Denotes official reporter

The National Reporter System consists of seven **regional reporters:**

1. Atlantic
2. North Eastern
3. North Western
4. Pacific
5. South Eastern
6. Southern
7. South Western

Two special reporters are available for heavily populated states

1. *California Reporter*
2. *New York Supplement*

Each regional reporter contains decisions from a given geographical area of the country. For example, the *North Western Reporter* includes decisions from Iowa, Michigan, Minnesota, Nebraska, North and South Dakota, and Wisconsin.

While at one time it was thought that courts would be likely to follow the decisions of other courts in neighboring states, the grouping of states is today more a matter of tradition and convenience.

There are also a number of **specialized reporters** that gather court decisions in a particular branch of the law for easy reference. Examples include the *Federal Securities Law Reports*, the *Trade Regulation Reporter*, and the *Fair Employment Practices Cases*, to name a few. Unlike other reporters, which limit themselves to the decisions of specific courts but which include cases in all areas of the law, these specialized reporters publish cases from federal and state courts anywhere in the country. They are restricted to specific legal topics. For a legal practitioner who specializes heavily, they can be an invaluable resource.

Case reports are customarily issued in consecutively numbered bound volumes. Thus, for example, a case may appear at 389 U.S. 407: page 407 of volume 389 of the *United States Reports*.

Many reporters have more than one series. When the volumes of the first series reached a high number, the publisher started the numbering system over and called the new volumes a "second series." Thus, for example, there are nearly 1,000 volumes of the *Federal Reporter, Second Series*, containing cases dating back to 1925. In order to locate a particular case, it is important to know the series as well as the volume and page number.

A substantial amount of time elapses between the issuance of an opinion and its publication in a bound reporter volume. This delay is occasioned by the need for enough opinions to fill a full volume, by the occasional need for correction of an opinion after it has been issued, and by the usual delays of publication. Where a rapidly changing area of the law is involved, this delay can often cause problems for the legal researcher.

To eliminate these problems, various methods of getting opinions into the hands of those who need them before the publication of bound reporter volumes have been developed. Most reporters issue **advance sheets**, which are paperback versions of smaller groups of opinions that will eventually appear in the bound volumes. Whereas a bound volume may be issued from one to twenty times per year, advance sheets are often issued weekly, thus minimizing delay.

A few courts, such as the United States Supreme Court and the United States Court of Appeals for the Fifth Circuit, go one step farther in streamlining the process. These courts issue **slip opinions**, individual decisions in booklet form, which are mailed directly to subscribers within days after the opinions are issued.

For the United States Supreme Court, decisions are likewise published rapidly in *United States Law Week*, a legal newsletter that also provides summaries of important decisions by other courts. A few state supreme courts have similar publications, such as the *Texas Supreme Court Journal*, which provides rapid publication of decisions of that court. Same-day opinions are now provided on the Internet by value-added subscription services.

Legislation

The primary source of legislative materials is the statutory code of the United States and of each state. These codes represent a collection of all general statutes, grouped by subject matter. Annual supplements, called **pocket parts** because they are fitted into a pocket in the back of each volume, keep the volumes up-to-date as the statutes are amended.

Many code volumes also contain **annotations** to court decisions interpreting the sections of the code that are contained in the volumes. Sometimes it is necessary to refer to a statute as it was when originally enacted or as of a specific time in the past. The session laws contain the text of statutes and statutory amendments precisely as they were enacted at a given session of the legislature. **Slip laws**, similar to slip opinions, are sometimes issued.

Federal legislative history is contained in the published committee hearings and reports of the Senate and the House of Representatives, together with the *Congressional Record*, which is a verbatim transcript of all proceedings on the floor of the Senate and House. Important committee reports are reprinted in *U.S. Code Congressional and Administrative News* published by West Group.

With occasional exceptions, usually for important statutes, no published materials are available on the legislative history of state statutes.

Regulation and Administrative Decisions

Administrative regulations are published in the *Code of Federal Regulations* and in similar volumes on the state level. Just as the session laws give the text of a statute as enacted, the *Federal Register* may be consulted to determine the text of a regulation at the time it was enacted. A few states have similar volumes.

Administrative rulings and decisions are published much as are judicial opinions. Some agencies have official reporters, such as the *Federal Trade Commission Decisions* and *National Transportation Safety Board Decisions*. These and other administrative decisions are also published in unofficial specialized reporters such as those described above.

Secondary Sources

Secondary sources abound, and the most that can be done here is to list the most commonly used materials. There are two principal legal encyclopedias in general use, entitled *American Jurisprudence (2d edition)*, nicknamed "AmJur 2d," and *Corpus Juris Secundum*. Encyclopedias of state law are sometimes available.

Virtually every law school publishes at least one legal periodical (usually called a **law review** or **law journal**). Some major law schools publish several. A few legal periodicals, such as the *ABA Research Journal*, are not published by a law school.

Law reviews and journals feature articles on legal topics by noted legal scholars, including law professors and judges, together with material written by law students. While most law reviews are general in scope, a few are devoted to specific branches of the law (*e.g.*, the *Harvard Civil Rights – Civil Liberties Law Review*). Many law reviews place emphasis on the law of the state in which their sponsoring law schools are located.

Legal reference books, known as **treatises**, are often written by law professors and other legal scholars. These reference works, which may range from one thin volume to a twenty-volume set with periodic supplements, cover almost every conceivable legal topic. Their value, of course, depends upon the prestige and scholarly ability of the author.

An important set of legal reference works is the *Restatements of the Law*, published by the American Law Institute, which summarize the state of the law in a given area and indicate the trend of recent decisions.

Finally, **form books**, often written by practicing attorneys, provide sample forms of legal documents, such as wills, real estate documents, and court pleadings, that may be copied and adapted to fit a particular need.

Research Aids

As previously mentioned, some legal materials do not directly present the law but instead operate as aids to locating the law in other legal materials. First among these case-finding aids are **digests**. Each reported decision in the West Group reporter system is summarized in a series of **headnotes**, which are paragraphs written by the West editorial staff summarizing the important legal points contained in the decision. Each headnote is assigned to one or more topic designations that consist of the name of a legal topic (such as Negligence, Constitutional Law, and Federal Civil Procedure) and a number that represents a subtopic within the general topic.

For each state, region, or other grouping, a **digest** is published that reprints these headnotes, grouping them in systematic fashion by topic and subtopic. As new cases dealing with a given topic and subtopic are decided, their headnotes appear, appropriately classified, in the pocket part of the appropriate digest volume. Thus, to find additional cases dealing with a particular topic and subtopic, one need only consult the section of the appropriate digest dealing with that topic and subtopic and then look up the cases that correspond to the headnotes listed under that topic and subtopic.

Another important case-finding tool is *Shepard's Citations*. These volumes list, for each reported case, the later cases that have cited, or referred to, the case. They will also indicate whether the case, or any portion of it, has been overturned by a later decision. Citing also includes noting information in a form that will permit the reader to locate the information and will give the important characteristics in a compact form.

Headnote numbers are also given. Thus, once a case has been found that is relevant to a particular topic, other cases on that point can be located by using *Shepard's* to determine what cases have cited the original case for the proposition being researched. When a researcher consults *Shephard's Citations*, he or she is said to **Shepardize** the case.

Computer-assisted legal research systems are an important case finding tool. Two such systems, LEXIS and WESTLAW, are now in widespread use. These databases contain the full text of both federal and state cases reported in the official reporters over the past several decades. In addition, direct case histories (whether a case has been affirmed, reversed, granted certiorari, etc.) are available at the federal level as far back as prerevolutionary days, and at the state level back to the late nineteenth century.

Cases available in full text may be searched for a given word or combination of words relevant to the research topic, such as a subject, issue, name (i.e., party, judge, witness, etc.), or any other important reference. Once cases have been located, the researcher can examine the case synopsis, headnotes or the entire text, either on screen or by printing a case for future reference. In addition, sophisticated citation capabilities allow a researcher to Shepardize, as well as locate and verify citations to other cases. Cases available in full text can be accessed online, using a modem, and for many jurisdictions case databases are also available on CD-ROM diskettes, which can significantly reduce the cost of computer-assisted research.

Techniques of Legal Research

There is no one correct way to locate materials on a legal topic. For example, where the research question involves federal taxation, an appropriate starting point might be the Internal Revenue Code. With a question on the law of negligence, the researcher might turn to the *Restatement (Second) of Torts*, a treatise or law review article on torts, a legal encyclopedia, or a digest topic under the heading of "Torts" or "Negligence."

While the starting point depends on the nature of the problem, common starting places include digest topics, annotations to statutes, legal encyclopedias, the *Index to Legal Periodicals*, the index to *American Law Reports* (a collection of selected cases and articles relating to the cases), and treatises.

Another approach is to use a computerized research system. LEXIS and WESTLAW provide the legal researcher with literally thousands of databases containing not only cases, but federal annotated statutes, state annotated statutes, restatements, administrative law, regulations, federal tax abstracts, law review articles, law dictionary and encyclopedia entries and much more. Many of these sources are also available on CD-ROM diskettes. In addition, through NEXIS and DIALOG, these services give the researcher access to the text of newspapers, magazines, journals, abstracts, lists, and other data often critical to the outcome of a legal matter. For example, similar matters that are settled out of court or that have not yet reached the appellate level are often reported in newspapers and professional journals.

Another common use of these ancillary databases is the location and verification of expert witnesses, including educational credentials, professional writings, and even challenges from other professionals to an expert's opinions and points of view. With certain exceptions, NEXIS is available to subscribers of LEXIS, while DIALOG is included in WESTLAW subscriptions.

The newest source of online research is the Internet, a worldwide network of people and information available to subscribers of an Internet service provider. The Internet offers two services, access to information and communication. Through the Internet, information stored on computers around the world is available to users. Every day, literally millions of lines of new information are made available on the Internet, including vast amounts of legal data. For example, the U.S. Code of Federal Regulations is accessible through the Internet, as are the statutes of many states including California. Case law for several federal circuits and the U.S. Supreme Court since the 1970s is also online.

Dozens of law libraries maintain a presence on the Internet, each offering specialized information, such as summaries of U.S. Supreme Court decisions the day after they are released, and the text of bills currently in various state legislatures. Increasingly, international law is finding its way onto the Internet. This access is especially valuable because most law libraries in the United States maintain only limited international law collections.

Subscribers can even "attend" legal seminars on the Internet, or visit the home pages of law firms and peruse substantive legal information posted by the host firms. The Internet also provides a means to consult online with lawyer-subscribers and to discuss the law. For example, a lawyer working on a tough case can post questions to one or many other lawyers on the Internet and receive replies. Groups of lawyers can come together on the Internet to discuss legal topics of interest. For example, several criminal defense attorneys may analyze a televised trial as it progresses.

With many research problems, the starting point may be the ending point as well. Where only a quick answer to a simple problem is sought, it may not be necessary to refer to a wide variety of materials to research every aspect of a particular branch of law. For example, if what is needed is the statute of limitations for burglary, it will seldom be useful to locate the appropriate statute in the appropriate jurisdiction and then look up all cases decided under that statute, read all the law review articles ever written about burglary, compare the statutes of the other 49 states, and write a 20-page memorandum on the subject. In such a situation, an answer such as "four years" may be all that is necessary.

In more complicated research projects, the first materials that the researcher consults seldom provide all the information that is needed. The materials may not answer the precise question under investigation but instead answer a different, although related, question.

Alternatively, the legal question may be the same but the facts of the case that has been found may differ somewhat from the facts of the case under investigation. Even if the facts and the law are the same, the researcher may want to investigate further to be sure that the legal principle has not been changed or that exceptions to it have not been created.

Finally, even where the material answers the question (i.e., is "**on point**," in legal research parlance), it may be helpful to have more cases or other materials that state the same legal principle, for added persuasive value in convincing a court to adopt a particular position. This is especially true where the case on which the legal researcher is most relying is from a different jurisdiction or from a lower court, and a similar case from the jurisdiction in which the case is being heard or from a higher court is unavailable.

Obtaining further materials once the first materials have been located is usually not difficult, since each set of materials contains clues suggesting the avenues that the researcher should explore next. Statute books usually contain case annotations, and cases and other materials contain citations to relevant legal materials. "Bridges," such as the digest system and *Shepard's Citations*, can be used to find further materials.

Where the researcher is dealing primarily with judicial opinions, all relevant cases can be located in a systematic way once the first case has been found. Cases decided before the first case may be found by checking the digest topics under which the headnotes of the original case are classified or by looking up the cases that the original case cites in support of the relevant proposition.

Cases decided after this first case may be found by using the digest or by Shepardizing the original case to locate later cases that have cited it.

Finally, the later history of the first case itself may be determined from *Shepard's Citations*. If the case has been affirmed or reversed on appeal, this will materially affect the answer to the question being researched. Both LEXIS and WESTLAW provide researchers with the ability to Shepardize and track headnotes via computer, saving time and increasing accuracy.

Where does it all stop? Cases lead to more cases, which lead to more cases, and so on—if the researcher is lucky. In such a situation, research should continue until the precise question is answered by the highest authority in the controlling jurisdiction, or until the researcher determines that he or she has come as close to the exact answer as is reasonably possible.

The approach depends on the circumstances. It may be that only a quick look for an approximate and probably correct answer is all that is needed. Or, the researcher may be preparing a Supreme Court brief or law review article in which every fine point must be meticulously tracked down.

A frequent occurrence, especially where the question is detailed or abstract or where the branch of law being researched is new, is that too

few materials are located. Either no "first case" or other material can
be found, or the line of cases is too short or never answers the precise
question. In such a situation, a new approach, trying legal materials not
consulted on the first attempt, may open up a promising line of cases.
Alternatively, the question itself must be reformulated, and materials on
analogous points must be sought. In such a situation, it will often be
necessary to consult with the person requesting the research.

Finally, the inability to find relevant materials does not necessarily
signify failure. There are many legal questions that have never been
addressed by the law. Knowing that this is the case may be as valuable
as finding the exact answer would have been.

For an excellent and more detailed discussion of the basics of legal
research, see M. Cohen, *Legal Research in a Nutshell*. Detailed rules
for citing legal materials may be found in *A Uniform System of
Citations*, often known as the "Bluebook," published by the Harvard
Law Review, Gannett House, Cambridge, MA 02138.

TERMS TO KNOW

legal research
citation
stare decisis
precedent
statutes
common law
legislative history
secondary sources
reporters
official reports
unofficial reporters
specialized reporters
advance sheets
slip opinions
pocket parts
annotation
slip laws
Congressional Record

law review
law journal
treatises
form books
digest
headnotes
computer-assisted legal
 research
Shepardizing

Chapter Six

FEDERAL COURTS

In recent years, the federal courts have exerted an ever-increasing influence over virtually every aspect of American life. In addition to adjudicating ordinary damage disputes between private litigants, federal courts have become involved in social issues ranging from school desegregation and prison reform to abortion and the death penalty. Yet few Americans have a good understanding of the inner workings of the federal courts or the sources of and limitations on their authority. Since virtually every legal professional inevitably comes into contact with the federal courts at some time or other, a working understanding of their powers and procedures is essential.

Jurisdiction

As discussed earlier in Chapter Two, jurisdiction means the power and authority of a court to hear and determine cases. The rules involving jurisdiction are highly complex, and for each rule there are often several exceptions. Nevertheless, an understanding of the basic principles and sources of jurisdictional power is critical to an understanding of the American legal system.

Federal Court Jurisdiction

The federal Constitution created three equal branches of government:

1. Congress, which makes law
2. The Executive branch, which enforces the law
3. The Judiciary, which hears and decides cases and controversies arising under the laws of the United States.

Article III of the Constitution vests the judicial power of the United States in the Supreme Court and in such lower courts as Congress may, from time to time, establish.

According to Article III of the Constitution, federal judicial power extends to

- all cases in law and equity arising under this Constitution, the laws of the United States, and treaties made, or which shall be made, under their authority

- all cases affecting Ambassadors, other public ministers and counsel

- all cases of **admiralty** and **maritime jurisdiction**

- controversies to which the United States shall be a party

- controversies between two or more states

- controversies between a state and citizens of another state

- controversies between citizens of different states

- controversies between citizens of the same state claiming lands under grants of different states

- controversies between a state or its citizens, and foreign states, citizens or subjects.

Types of Federal Jurisdiction

Two types of federal jurisdiction are embodied in the above list. **Federal question jurisdiction** involves claims based on the Constitution, the laws of the United States, and treaties made under U.S. authority. **Diversity jurisdiction** involves controversies between different states or citizens of different states. In addition, the Constitution proclaims that the Supreme Court shall have **original jurisdiction** over cases affecting ambassadors, other public ministers and counsel, and also cases in which a state is a party, which means that the original trial of cases involving these types of parties shall be held in the Supreme Court.

Based on a reading of Article III, it would be logical to assume that federal courts have exclusive jurisdiction over claims arising under federal law, while states have exclusive jurisdiction over claims arising under state law. This is not the case. In fact state courts have **concurrent jurisdiction** with the federal district courts over many federal claims. Likewise, federal courts routinely hear claims based on state laws. In these situations, plaintiffs can choose to file suit either in federal or state court.

Federal law is enforceable in state courts because Article VI of the Constitution (called the "Supremacy Clause") charges state courts with this responsibility. When Congress passes a law, any claims that could arise under that law can be brought in either state or federal court unless Congress, when it writes the law, affirmatively divests state courts of jurisdiction over the claim. Thus, lower federal courts have **exclusive jurisdiction** over only those federal causes of action that Congress has expressly stated belong to them. Examples of exclusive federal jurisdiction include claims arising under federal laws involving bankruptcy, taxes, securities, patents, and laws covering trade with foreign nations. In these types of cases, civil plaintiffs can file suit only in federal court. Conversely, in those federal matters where federal district courts and state courts would normally have concurrent jurisdiction, if the amount of damages requested by the plaintiff is less than a threshold amount set from time to time by Congress, the matter can be heard only in state court. In these situations, state courts serve more or less as small claims courts for federal matters.

Federal courts have the power to decide matters arising under state laws. This usually occurs in one of two situations:

1. when the plaintiff has different claims based on both federal and state laws, and

2. when the plaintiff and defendant are from different states.

In the first situation, the federal court has federal question jurisdiction over the federal claim and **pendent jurisdiction** over the state claim. Pendant jurisdiction over state claims is based on the notion that a plaintiff should not have to sue twice, once in state court and once in federal court, to get all the relief to which he or she is entitled. When the plaintiff and defendant are from different states, the federal district court will hear the case even if the plaintiff's claims arise solely under state law. Diversity jurisdiction is based on the historical assumption that a state court will tend to be biased toward its own citizens and against parties from other states, whereas the federal court will treat the parties equally.

Federal court rulings on matters of state law, whether at the trial court or appellate level, are binding on the parties. But they do not create binding precedence on the courts of the state in future cases. For example, if the Fifth Circuit Court of Appeals hears an appeal from the federal district court for the Eastern District of Texas on a matter of Texas state law, Texas courts are not bound by that decision in future cases involving similar matters of law and fact. Nevertheless, the Fifth Circuit decision will be considered "persuasive authority."

Civil Removal to Federal Court

When a plaintiff has the choice of suing either in state or federal court, and chooses to sue in state court, the defendant usually has the option to ask the nearest federal district court to take the case, an action known as **removal**. If the federal court chooses to take the case, all state court jurisdiction to hear and determine the case immediately ceases. In deciding whether to take the case, the federal district court will consider whether or not the state court has the power to fully satisfy the parties. For example, if the case involves one claim that arises under nearly identical state and federal laws, and both courts can award the same range of damages, removal will generally be denied. Conversely, if the plaintiff has a uniquely federal claim, or damages available at the federal level are more extensive, the federal district court will usually take the case.

Deciding whether or not to pursue removal is a question of strategy. Some attorneys, for example, dislike trying cases in federal court; thus, merely threatening removal will induce a plaintiff to settle a case. In certain types of claims, state court juries have a reputation for awarding higher (or lower) damages as compared with federal juries. In these instances, defendants will want to seek a jurisdiction where damages are more likely to be lower. Claims involving political figures from one party may do better in the jurisdiction where the judge is more likely to be from the politician's political party.

Criminal Jurisdiction

As a part of their "federal question" jurisdiction, the United States District courts have a broad jurisdiction over all offenses that are against the laws of the United States. This jurisdiction, as defined by statute, is exclusive.[1]

The Supreme Court has ruled that there are no federal "common law crimes."[2] In other words, a federal crime must be clearly defined by an act of Congress. The United States Code, the body of law in which most federal statutes are recorded, enumerates a broad variety of federal crimes.[3]

It is possible that an act might violate both a federal and state law and thus constitute both a federal and a state crime. The offender may then be prosecuted by either the federal or the state court or both without violating the rule against placing a person in **double jeopardy**.

Judicial Restraint

The courts within the federal system are constantly struggling with the problem of how to sift through the thousands of cases filed each year and determine which ones present the type of controversy that they should hear. Both the trial courts and the appellate courts in the federal system have adopted certain criteria to resolve this problem. Collectively this set of criteria is known as the **doctrine of judicial self-restraint**.

Judicial self-restraint is the practice of using these criteria to refuse to accept jurisdiction in certain cases. If the federal courts did not exercise some sort of restraint, they would quickly be submerged under a

---

1. C. Wright, *The Law of Federal Courts* 124 (5th ed. 1994).

2. *United States v. Hudson and Goodwin*, 11 U.S. (7 Cranch) 32 (1812).

3. 18 U.S.C.

steadily increasing tide of incoming cases. Some of the more important principles of judicial restraint[4] are:

Justiciable Controversy

The Constitution requires that before the federal courts accept jurisdiction over a matter, a "case or controversy" must exist. Courts have interpreted this constitutional directive to mean that a case

- must be between *bona fide* adversaries *and*
- must involve
    - the protection or enforcement of valuable legal rights, *or*
    - the punishment, prevention, or redress of wrongs that directly concern the party or parties bringing suit.

The matter must be definite, and the remedy requested must be capable of being granted through specific relief, such as a specific amount of damages or an injunction. Should two friends try to use the courts to decide whose home is more aesthetically appealing, to decide whose child is a better baseball player, or simply to settle a friendly wager, no **justiciable controversy** would be presented. The parties would not actually be adversaries. They would not be asking the court to grant any specific relief but would instead be asking it to make a value judgment.

Standing

A person bringing suit must have a personal stake in the litigation of a sufficient nature to justify the federal court in accepting jurisdiction. **Standing,** as this personal stake is usually called, is measured by determining whether the litigant can establish a sufficient personal economic interest in the controversy or whether the litigant claims that his or her own basic rights are being violated.

A person residing in Palo Alto, California, who owns no real property within the limits of the City of San Francisco, would not have standing to sue the Corps of Engineers, a federal agency, in federal court to

---

4. J. Ferguson and D. McHenry, *The American System of Government* 434 (12th ed. 1973).

obtain an injunction to prevent the Corps from building a dam that would flood residential property in San Francisco. Not being a resident or property owner, the Palo Alto resident would have no economic interest at stake. Actual property owners whose property would be affected, however, would have standing to sue in federal court.

Advisory Opinions

The federal courts will not issue "advisory opinions." **Advisory opinions** are judicial rulings upon the legality of governmental actions, whether already accomplished or contemplated, when there is no *bona fide* case or controversy to decide. The rule against advisory opinions was first established when the Supreme Court refused to answer 29 questions proposed by Secretary of State Thomas Jefferson in 1793.[5]

Because of the rule against advisory opinions, the Congress, in deciding whether to enact a particular law, cannot ask the Supreme Court for its opinion as to whether, if passed, the law would be unconstitutional. Instead, the Supreme Court can only address the question of the law's constitutionality after Congress has enacted the law and a person who claims that the law violates his or her constitutional rights has brought suit in federal court.

Similarly, a federal court will not decide a case brought by an individual party who merely anticipates a dispute in the future. Called the **ripeness doctrine**, this doctrine provides that a party who believes that some future action or event will pose a threat or cause damage may not bring suit until the threat or damage materializes. Thus, a property owner is not allowed to challenge a local government for taking his or her property for public use merely because the city counsel is debating the possibility.

Political Questions

Federal courts have also refused to decide political questions in cases involving certain legislative or executive actions. In declining

---

5. C. Wright, *supra*, at 65.

jurisdiction over such matters, courts have relied on the policies of separation of powers and judicial self-restraint.[6]

The principal application of this doctrine is to questions of international and domestic law that immediately concern the country's political or military interaction with foreign nations.[7]

Other examples of political questions are cases involving the processes by which statutes or constitutional amendments are adopted[8] and questions about which group is the legitimate government of a particular state.[9]

Hypothetical Questions

A hypothetical question involving an intellectual difference of opinion, as opposed to a real dispute, will not be entertained by the federal courts.[10] In legal parlance there is no **justiciable controversy**. Such great philosophical debates as the existence of God or the presence of life on other planets are too vague and imprecise to present the concrete issues necessary to litigate in court. One federal district judge, for instance, refused to accept jurisdiction in a case where a man sued God because the United States Marshals were unable to locate and serve a summons on the defendant.[11]

Mootness

A moot case is one that does not present a case or controversy because the matter has already been resolved. Something has happened to the case before the court has decided it, rendering any action by the court unnecessary. Suppose, for instance, that a city passes an ordinance making it illegal for a woman to be a firefighter. A woman who wants

6. *Id.* at 84.

7. *Id.* At 88-91.

8. *Coleman v. Miller*, 307 U.S. 432 (1939).

9. *Luther v. Borden,* 48 U.S. (7 How.) 1 (1849).

10. C. Wright, *supra*, at 60-61.

11. *Dallas Times Herald*, Sunday Magazine, Nov. 2, 1975.

to become a firefighter files a lawsuit in federal district court seeking to have the ordinance declared unconstitutional and to have the city enjoined from enforcing it. Before the case is filed or before it comes to trial, the city repeals the ordinance, passes a resolution pledging that it will never enact a similar ordinance and hires the plaintiff as a firefighter with back pay. Here the matter has been resolved. It is moot, and nothing remains for the court to decide. The principles of judicial restraint discussed above are applicable to state as well as federal courts.

Structure of the Federal Courts

Article III of the Constitution creates the Supreme Court and empowers the Congress to create such other lower federal courts as it deems necessary. Congress has used this constitutional grant of power to establish two levels of courts below the Supreme Court. At the lowest level are the United States district courts, which are the trial courts of the federal system. The middle level is the United States courts of appeals.

Following is an examination of the complementary roles of these three tiers: the district courts, the courts of appeals and the Supreme Court.

Federal District Courts

More than 646 active judges preside over the 94 judicial districts that cover the United States and its territories. Naturally, the more sparsely populated judicial districts have fewer judges than the heavily populated districts. In fact, in the least populated areas some federal district judges may serve several districts. Some heavily populated judicial districts, on the other hand, may contain as many as 28 judges. Congress establishes the district configuration, basing it on such factors as population, distance, and caseload.[12]

Federal district court judges are required to reside in the district in which they sit. Their offices are maintained in a principal city in the district, usually at the nearest federal office building.

---

12. J. Ferguson and D. McHenry, *supra*, at 431.

Each district has a number of federal officers and agencies that assist the federal district courts in the administration of justice, including a United States District Clerk's Office, a United States Marshal's Office and a United States Attorney's Office. These supporting officers and agencies are discussed in detail later in this chapter.

With limited exceptions discussed in the section on the Supreme Court, these district courts conduct the trials of all cases in the federal judicial system. In these cases, the district court judge supervises pretrial matters, conducts the trial, and enters the judgment.

The district judge may decide to write an opinion on the issues of law or fact in a particular case. Such opinions often are published to provide guidance for other courts faced with similar issues. They appear in the *Federal Supplement*.

As a court of record, the district court has a court reporter or an electronic recording device present at all times to transcribe proceedings. If one of the litigants later decides to appeal the decision of the district judge, the appellate court refers to this complete record of the district court proceedings.

United States Courts of Appeals

The United States courts of appeals are the intermediate appellate courts in the federal judicial system. The main purpose of these courts is to hear appeals from district court decisions, thereby facilitating the prompt disposition of cases and easing the caseload of the Supreme Court.

There are 13 United States courts of appeals, one in each of 12 geographic regions known as circuits, plus a thirteenth court – the United States Court of Appeals for the Federal Circuit – that hears appeals in certain patent, copyright, and other special cases.

Each circuit, with the exception of the District of Columbia Circuit, encompasses three or more states or territories. The Ninth Circuit is the largest in area, embracing nine states and the territory of Guam. A Court of Appeals has a primary city in which it usually sits, but it may also sit in other cities in the states it serves. Each Court of Appeals has jurisdiction to hear appeals from federal courts and administrative agencies operating within its circuit.

Currently some 179 active and 80 senior judges serve on these courts in the 13 circuits. Each court is composed of at least four judges with the largest court, the Ninth Circuit, now having 28 judges plus 18 senior judges. The chief judge of a particular circuit is the judge with the longest active service who has not yet reached the age of 70.

Most cases appealed to the courts of appeals are heard by panels three judges.[13] However, when a case is heard by a panel, there must be at least two judges present, and at least two must agree before there is a valid decision.[14]

Sometimes, however, all the judges in a particular circuit sit *en banc* to hear a case. When a hearing *en banc* is ordered by a majority of the judges in regular active service on a United States court of appeals, then all the active judges on the court sit to determine the result in the case.[15] A majority of the active judges in the circuit sitting *en banc* constitutes a quorum, and a majority has the authority to render a decision.

En banc courts are the exception rather than the rule. Only in cases of great importance to the circuit as a whole, and possibly to the nation, do all the judges of a federal court of appeals sit *en banc* to determine major developments in the law.[16]

The primary advantages of *en banc* decisions are avoiding conflicts of views and promoting finality among the judges within a particular circuit.[17] Their major disadvantages, especially since the number of judgeships in each circuit has been expanded, are the difficulties in

---

13. 28 U.S.C. §46.

14. *United States v. Allied Stevedoring Corp..* 241 F.2d 925, 927 (2d Cir.), *cert. denied*, 353 U.S. 984 (1957).

15. 28 U.S.C. §46.

16. 363 U.S. 685 (1960).

17. C. Wright, *supra*, at 11.

convening all the judges in the circuit and the enormous length of time
it sometimes takes to render a decision.

The United States courts of appeals are primarily appellate courts that
hear appeals from final decisions of United States district courts.[18] A
final decision has been defined as one that ends the litigation on the
merits and leaves nothing for the court to do but to execute the
judgment.[19]

In certain cases, however, an appeal may be pursued even though the
judgment of the district court is **interlocutory**, i.e., not final.
Interlocutory orders are rulings of the court that do not finally dispose
of the case but require some further action of the court before a final
decision can be rendered. Appeal may be had from an interlocutory
order by a federal district judge to the United States courts of appeals in
the following circumstances:[20]

- Interlocutory orders dealing with injunctions, except where
  direct review may be had in the Supreme Court

- Interlocutory orders appointing receivers or affecting receivers.
  (A **receiver** is a neutral party who is appointed by a court to
  preserve property during the course of the litigation.)

- Interlocutory decrees determining the rights and liabilities of
  parties to admiralty cases

- Certain bankruptcy decisions.[21]

In addition to hearing the appeals of criminal and civil cases decided by
the federal district courts, the United States courts of appeals hear most
appeals from orders of federal administrative agencies.[22] The tax court

---

18. 28 U.S.C. §1291.

19. *Catlin v. United States*, 324 U.S. 229 (1945).

20. 28 U.S.C. §1292.

21. 28 U.S.C. §1293.

22. C. Wright, *supra*, at 758-60.

is considered an administrative agency for appellate purposes, and the court of appeals is the proper forum to review its decisions.[23]

Under the Federal Rules of Civil Procedure, the procedure for filing an appeal to the court of appeals is simple. First, a litigant, known as the **appellant**. must file a notice of appeal, which is an uncomplicated document. Defects in the notice of appeal that are not material can be waived so long as the **appellee** is not misled by the defect and the intention to appeal clearly appears. In civil cases, notice of appeal must be filed within 30 days after the entry of the judgment except when the United States is appealing, in which case 60 days are allowed. Notice of appeal must be filed within 10 days in criminal cases.

An appellant must also file the record on appeal, must docket the appeal, and must file both its brief and an appendix. Each court of appeals appoints a clerk who makes sure that all these documents are properly and timely filed.

Decisions of the United States courts of appeals are required to be in writing, stating facts and making conclusions of law. The courts of appeals have a duty to follow majority opinions of the Supreme Court,[24] just as United States district courts are bound by the law established by the appeals court in the circuit in which they are located.[25] All decisions of the courts of appeals are reported in the *Federal Reporter* series published by West Group.

United States Supreme Court

The Supreme Court of the United States sits at the pinnacle of the federal judicial system. The first legislative act to define its jurisdiction was the Judiciary Act of 1789, which made it clear that the individual states, Congress, and the president were subject to the Court's judicial authority.[26] The Judiciary Act required members of the Court to travel

---

23. United States Government Printing Office, *The United States Courts* 5 (1975).

24. *United States v. Vida*, 370 F.2d 759 (6th Cir. 1966).

25. *Bauer v. Orser*, 258 F.Supp. 338 (D.N.D. 1966).

26. R. McCloskey, *The American Supreme Court* 4 (1960 ed.)

twice a year to distant parts of the nation and preside over courts of appeals sitting in various circuits, a practice that soon fell into disfavor with the justices.[27]

The Supreme Court was treated like a poor relation during its first 150 years, shuffled from New York to Philadelphia to a vacant part of the U.S. Senate in Washington. It was not until 1935 that the Supreme Court obtained a home of its own—the present extraordinary and overwhelming Supreme Court Building designed by architect Cass Gilbert.[28]

Like other federal judges, the chief justice and the eight associate justices are appointed by the president with the advice and consent of the Senate and serve for life. The presence of six justices constitutes a quorum, and five justices must agree before a decision of the Supreme Court becomes official and binding.[29] The regular term of the Supreme Court always commences on the first Monday in October of each year and continues until the latter part of June.[30] On rare occasions, the court will convene in special session during the summer to hear important cases, such as the Nixon tapes case and President Truman's seizure of the steel mills.

The Chief Justice of the United States, in addition to the primary function of presiding over the sessions and deliberations of the court, has many important administrative functions that often take that official far from the chambers of the court. The Constitution requires the chief justice to preside over impeachment trials of the president in the Senate, a duty that the Chief Justice has exercised only twice during the history of our nation.

By statute, the Chief Justice is chair of both the Federal Judicial Center and the Judicial Conference of the United States. The Federal Judicial

---

27. *Id.*

28. R.L. Williams, *The Supreme Court of the United States: the Staff That Keeps It Operating. Smithsonian*, Jan. 1977, at 41.

29. 28 U.S.C. §1.

30. 28 U.S.C. §2.

Center is the research and development arm of the federal judiciary and plays an important role in the training of new federal judges. Acting as a kind of board of directors for the approximately 1600 federal judges, the Judicial Conference of the United States considers such problems as proposed legislation in new areas of law, the need for increased efficiency of court calendars, and more efficient use of jurors' time. Former Chief Justice Warren Burger estimated that nearly a third of his time was spent on administrative and cultural duties that had little to do with the judicial functions of the Court.

The Supreme Court exercises both a limited original jurisdiction and an extensive appellate jurisdiction. Jurisdiction of the Supreme Court extends to criminal and to civil matters.

The Court's jurisdiction is complex and often confusing.

Direct Review of the Decisions of Federal District Courts

There are three circumstances when an appeal may be made from a federal district court directly to the Supreme Court without first going through the United States court of appeals.

- Any civil action brought by the United States seeking to

  ♦ obtain equitable relief such as an injunction or violation of the antitrust laws

  ♦ enforce provisions of the Interstate Commerce Act, or

  ♦ recover under the common carriers section of the Communications Act where the district court judge makes an order stating that immediate consideration of the appeal by the Supreme Court is of such general public importance that it requires the Court's attention due to its significance in the administration of justice.[31]

---

31. C. Wright, *supra*, at 770-71.

- Appeals from an order granting or denying an interlocutory or permanent injunction in any civil action that is required to be heard by a three-judge federal district court.[32] (In 1976, Congress drastically limited the circumstances under which a three-judge federal district court may be convened.)

- Appeals from an interlocutory or final judgment of any federal court holding an Act of Congress unconstitutional in any civil action, suit or proceeding to which the United States, or any of its agencies, officers or employees are a party.[33]

Review of Decisions of the Courts of Appeals

Under two basic circumstances cases are appealed from the United States courts of appeals to the Supreme Court:

- Review by **writ of certiorari** upon the petition of any party to the suit in the court of appeals.[34] This is the most commonly used means of appeal from circuit court decisions. The Supreme Court has the discretion to decide which applications for writ of certiorari it will grant. The court frequently "grants cert" to resolve conflicts between circuit court decisions or to decide new and significant issues of law.

- Review by appeal from a court of appeals where:

  - The appellate court has held an Act of Congress unconstitutional in a case to which the United States is a party.[35]

  - A court of appeals has held a state statute unconstitutional or in conflict with the laws and treaties of the United States.[36]

---

32. 28 U.S.C. §1253.

33. 28 U.S.C. §1252.

34. C. Wright, *supra*, at 774-75.

35. 28 U.S.C. §1252.

There is a third, rarely used method of taking appeals from the United States courts of appeals to the Supreme Court. This method is by **certificate**. A federal court of appeals may issue a certification to the Supreme Court asking for instructions in either a criminal or civil case.[37] Certificates are issued only for questions of law, and these questions must be distinct and definite.[38]

Review of State Court Decisions - Direct Review

The Supreme Court may also review a decision from the highest court of a state when[39]

- the highest court in the state has rendered a final judgment and when

- the validity of a treaty or statute of the United States is drawn into question, or

- the validity of a state statute is drawn into question on the basis of its conflicting with the Constitution, treaties or laws of the United States, or

- any title, right, privilege, or immunity is specifically claimed under the Constitution, under treaties or statutes of the United States, or under a commission held or authorized or exercised by or under the authority of the United States.

The Supreme Court's power to review cases under this provision does not depend on the amount in controversy or on diversity of citizenship, but upon the existence of a genuine federal question.[40]

---

36. 28 U.S.C. §1254(2).

37. 28 U.S.C. §1254(3).

38. *United States v. Mayer*, 235 U.S. 55 (1914).

39. 28 U.S.C. §1257(3).

40. C. Wright, *supra*, at 786.

Original Jurisdiction

As discussed earlier, the Constitution states that "in all Cases affecting ambassadors, other public ministers and consuls, and those in which a State shall be a party, the Supreme Court shall have original jurisdiction."[41]

Despite this grant of original jurisdiction, full-blown trials with the parade of witnesses, objections, and arguments of attorneys and the presentation of evidence that we would normally associate with a trial on the merits in federal district court rarely occur in the Supreme Court.

Although a federal statute grants parties the right of a trial by jury in original actions in the Supreme Court against citizens of the United States,[42] no jury trial has been held in the Court since the 18th century.[43] Instead, the Supreme Court typically appoints a distinguished lawyer or retired judge to serve as master and to hear the evidence and make recommendations to the Court.

Procedure

Procedure in the federal district courts in civil cases is governed by the Federal Rules of Civil Procedure. These rules tell the parties how to

- file a lawsuit
- pursue pretrial preparation and discovery
- conduct themselves during a trial
- obtain a final binding judgment.

Although these rules and the underlying federal procedural system vary from those in the different state courts, they are remarkably similar to state systems in many ways. This similarity results in part from the fact that many state systems have modified their rules to be more in line with the federal system. Thus, a student who studies federal procedure

41. U.S. Const. Art. III, §2.

42. 28 U.S.C. §1872.

43. C. Wright, *supra*, at 813-14.

also inevitably learns principles that are applicable to the various state systems. Following is a description of **litigation** and trial in civil cases under the Federal Rules of Civil Procedure. Criminal cases are governed by the Federal Rules of Criminal Procedure, which are both similar to and different from their civil counterpart.

The Complaint

An action commences in federal court with the filing of a **complaint** with the court pursuant to Rule 3. Pursuant to Rule 8, this complaint must contain three essential elements:

- A "short and plain statement of the claim showing that the pleader is entitled to relief"

- A statement of the ground on which the court's jurisdiction is based

- A demand for judgment for the relief that the plaintiff seeks.

"A short and plain statement of the claim" has generally been construed to require a simple statement of circumstances demonstrating that the plaintiff has been wronged.

A complaint's purpose is to inform the defendant and the court of the basis of the plaintiff's claim – nothing more. The defendant is entitled to find out all the details in the process described below known as **discovery**.

The Defendant's Response to the Complaint

When a defendant has been served with a complaint, the Federal Rules require that the defendant make a response. Just as the plaintiff must let the defendant know the grounds of the plaintiff's claim, the defendant must reveal his or her defenses. The defendant may assert numerous defenses, such as:

- that the claim cannot be brought in any federal court because those courts lack jurisdiction

- that the claim cannot be brought in that particular federal court, either because that court does not have jurisdiction over the defendant or because the federal venue rules require that under the circumstances the case should be brought in a different federal court

- that a necessary party to the lawsuit has not been joined.

These defenses have nothing to do with the merits of the plaintiff's claim. There are, however, other defenses that do address the merits:

- that the plaintiff's claim is untrue – this is a **denial**

- that the law does not entitle the plaintiff to relief based on the facts alleged

- that even if what the plaintiff claims is true, the defendant has an **affirmative defense**; that is, that other pertinent facts relieve the defendant of liability. *Example*: Whether or not the defendant may have been responsible for the plaintiff's injuries, the plaintiff has waited too long to sue and the **statute of limitations** has run out.

Finally, while it is true that the plaintiff's complaint need only contain a "short and plain statement," Federal Rule 12(e) states that it cannot be "so vague and ambiguous that a party cannot reasonably be expected to interpose his responsive pleadings." The defendant may object to the complaint on such grounds and request that the plaintiff be required to file a more definite statement.

The next question is: How may the defendant present these various defenses and obligations? The Federal Rules provide two means.

First, all matters may be raised in an **answer**. Second, certain enumerated defenses set forth in Rule 12(b) may, at the option of the defendant, be raised by **motion**. These defenses are:

- lack of jurisdiction over the person
- lack of jurisdiction over the subject matter
- improper venue

- insufficiency of process
- insufficiency of service of process
- failure to state a claim on which relief can be granted
- failure to join a necessary party.

In Rule 7(b)(1) a **motion** is defined as "an application to the court for an order." In other words, it is a document in which a party requests the court to take certain action.

The various motions that defendants may file to assert any of the seven defenses set forth above are collectively known as **motions to dismiss**. If the court denies the defendant's motion to dismiss, or if the defendant chooses not to file such a motion, then the defendant must file an answer.

Counterclaims

Often controversies arise in which each party claims to have been wronged by the other. After one party sues the other, the defendant wants to assert his or her own claim against the plaintiff. This may be a claim growing out of the same set of facts on which the plaintiff's claim is based, or it might be based on an entirely different incident. Rather than requiring the defendant to file a separate lawsuit, the Federal Rules permit the defendant to file a **counterclaim** against the plaintiff in the same action.

There are two types of counterclaims: **compulsory** and **permissive**. A compulsory counterclaim is one arising out of the same transaction or occurrence that is the subject matter of the plaintiff's action. Failure to assert a compulsory counterclaim in the defendant's answer bars the defendant from raising that claim in the future, either in the pending action or in the defendant's own separate lawsuit against the plaintiff.

A permissive counterclaim is a claim that the defendant has against the plaintiff that arises out of a separate incident. For example, the plaintiff claims that the defendant negligently drove into the plaintiff's car; the defendant claims that the plaintiff breached a contract with the defendant.

Under Rule 13(b), the defendant may assert his or her permissive counterclaim against the plaintiff, but the defendant is not required to do so. If the defendant chooses not to raise it, he or she may later bring an action against the plaintiff.

Discovery

After the parties have completed the pleading process described above, each side may only have a very sketchy view of its adversary's position. If the parties had no other means of finding out what their opponents could prove, they would be faced with countless surprises at trial against which they might be ill-equipped to defend. For example, one side might introduce unexpected testimony that the opposing side could have effectively rebutted had it only known in advance.

To avoid these problems, the Federal Rules provide for discovery. Through use of the discovery tools created by the Rules, a party can become thoroughly acquainted with an adversary's position and with the testimony of the opponent's witnesses. A party has the opportunity to prepare his or her best possible case and to dispose of nonexistent issues.

Often, discovery encourages **settlement**. Each party learns the strengths and weaknesses of his or her own, as well as the opponent's, position and is better able to assess the likelihood of success and, hence, the monetary value of the case.

Rule 26 prescribes the scope of discovery. The rule states that the parties "may obtain discovery regarding any matter, not privileged, which is relevant to the subject matter involved in the pending action." This includes, among other things:

- the identity and location of persons
- their knowledge of the subject matter
- the existence, location, and content of relevant documents.

Rule 26 adds that discovery may be had even if "the information sought will be inadmissible at trial, if the information sought appears to be reasonably calculated to lead to the discovery of admissible evidence."

The following are the various means of discovery:

Deposition upon oral examination

A **deposition** is the oral examination by any party of any person who the party believes has relevant information. The taking of deposition testimony is like the taking of trial testimony in that the entire process is recorded by a court reporter.

First, the deponent is sworn by the court reporter, who is a notary public. Then the party taking the deposition questions the deponent in the same format that is used at trial. The opposing party may make objections to the questions or answers.

When a party objects to a question, one of several things may happen. If the party objects on the ground that the question inquires into matters that are within the scope of discovery but inadmissible at trial, the court reporter merely records the objection and the deposition proceeds. Then, if the deposing party later wants to introduce the deposition at trial, the judge will rule on the validity of the objection, and, depending on the judge's ruling, either admit or exclude the testimony. In order to speed up the deposition, attorneys taking depositions often agree (**stipulate**) that this type of objection may be made at the time of trial.

If the party objects to the question because it is not within the scope of discovery, his or her opponent may simply withdraw the question. Sometimes, the objecting party instead may decide to let the inquiry proceed. Occasionally, however, the objecting party will instruct the witness not to answer the question. In that case, the party taking the deposition may decide to file a **motion to compel** with the court. This type of motion asks the judge to rule that the witness must answer.

Interrogatories

Another commonly used method of discovery is the use of **interrogatories**. Interrogatories are a series of written questions that one party submits to another that must be answered in writing and under oath. Interrogatories, like questions in a deposition, may relate to any matter not privileged that is relevant to the subject matter of the pending action.

The party on whom the interrogatories are served may object to any or all interrogatories on various grounds. Some examples of common objections are that an interrogatory inquires into matters that are privileged or beyond the scope of discovery or that it is overly burdensome.

Interrogatories are frequently used to gather preliminary information about the opponent's position and about any expert witnesses that a party intends to call at trial. An interrogatory may inquire about the subject matter of the expert's planned testimony and the grounds of the expert's opinions.

Interrogatories have the advantage of being comparatively simple and inexpensive. They do not provide the examining party with the flexibility of a deposition, however, in which the questioner may ask follow-up questions and probe the witness responses in depth. Moreover, interrogatories, unlike depositions, may only be directed to parties in the case and not to third persons.

Requests for Admissions

Another useful discovery device is the **request for admissions**. One party may send to the other written requests that the recipient admit or deny the truth of any matter within the scope of discovery that relates to statements or opinions of fact or to the application of law to fact, including the genuineness of any document described in the request.

The Federal Rules state that if the opponent fails to answer any request for admission within 30 days, the unanswered request is deemed admitted. The opponent, instead of answering a request, may object to it on various grounds including, but not limited to,

- that the request requires the revelation of privileged material
- that the request inquires into matters that are beyond the scope of discovery
- that the request is argumentative, ambiguous and unclear.

If the opponent does not object to the request, he or she must either admit or deny, or state in detail why he or she cannot admit or deny the matter.

Often a party will be unable to respond to a request for admission because he or she lacks the requisite information or knowledge. The Federal Rules specifically state that lack of information or knowledge is a permissible reason not to admit or deny the truth of the request. Requests for admissions are useful devices for discovering the areas of agreement between the parties and sharpening the focus of disputed matters.

Production of Documents

Federal Rule 34 provides that a party may serve on any other party a **request to produce,** and to permit the party making the request to inspect and copy any designated documents. A party may also request the opportunity to inspect and copy, test, or sample any tangible things that constitute matters within the scope of discovery.

The rules further provide that a party may request that any other party permit the requesting party's entry on designated land or other property for the purpose of inspecting, measuring, surveying, photographing, testing, or sampling the property or a designated object on the property. These requests must be served in writing. The other party must respond in writing and either agree to the request or object to it.

Physical and Mental Examinations

If the physical or mental condition of a party is in controversy, any other party may request that the court order him or her to submit to a mental or physical examination. The moving party is required to show "good cause" why this examination should be required. Often good cause is apparent from the face of the pleadings, as where the extent of the plaintiff's injuries forms an important area of dispute. If the court orders the physical examination, the party examined is entitled to receive from the discovering party a copy of the written report of the examination.

Failure to Make Discovery

Rule 37 provides that if one party refuses to give the other the discovery that the other requests, the discovering party may ask the court to enter an order compelling discovery. This request is called a motion to compel. The court reviews the request and the other party's objections, then either enters the desired order or denies it.

If the judge grants the motion in whole or in part, he or she may also enter a protective order. Rule 26(c) states that a protective order should be used to shield a party or person from annoyance, embarrassment, oppression, or undue burden or expense. A protective order may require, among other things, that

- certain matters not be inquired into
- discovery should be had only on specified terms and conditions, including a designation of the time or place
- discovery should not be had at all
- only a particular method of discovery may be used
- a deposition should be sealed and opened only by order of the court.

Often a party who files a motion to compel will request the court to order that it should be reimbursed for the expense of preparing and pursuing the motion, which the court will often do if it grants the motion. If the court denies the motion to compel, it may instead order the moving party to pay his or her opponent the reasonable expenses that the opponent incurred in opposing the motion. Whatever the decision on the motion, the court should not order either party to pay the expenses of the other if it finds, under the law and the facts and circumstances, that the opponent's failure to give discovery or the discovering party's motion to compel was substantially justified.

Motion Practice – Termination of the Litigation Without Trial

As discussed in the section on responsive pleadings, a party can obtain dismissal of the case in a number of ways before it has progressed past the filing of a complaint. Two other motions, not previously discussed, that are usually not filed until all pretrial proceedings are complete, also may terminate the case.

The first is a Rule 12(c) **motion for judgment on the pleadings**. This motion, which is not appropriate until all pleadings have been filed, is relatively rare. The most common circumstance in which it arises is one in which the defenses raised by the defendant's answer, even if proven, do not relieve the defendant of liability. For example, if a defendant admits the truth of the matters alleged in the complaint but asserts an affirmative defense, the plaintiff may file a motion for judgment on the pleadings in which the plaintiff claims that the affirmative defense is legally insufficient.

A **motion for summary judgment** under Rule 56 is perhaps the most commonly used method of disposing of litigation before trial. Parties use this device when the court records, on their face, show no disputed issue of fact. A motion of summary judgment permits a court to look to evidence beyond the pleadings to determine whether there is any genuine issue of material fact. If there is no such issue, then a trial is unnecessary because the court may simply decide the issues of law and rule in favor of one party or the other.

A party filing a motion for summary judgment submits with the motion any additional evidence that the party wants the court to consider. The evidence might be in the form of deposition excerpts, affidavits in which a witness swears in writing to the truth of a particular fact, or other documentary evidence. The opposing party may then file whatever controverting evidence it wants the court to consider.

Suppose, for example, that a plaintiff sued a defendant for breach of contract, claiming that a contract between the plaintiff and the defendant required the defendant to deliver to the plaintiff 1000 bushels of corn on or before July 1, that the defendant had delivered only 100 bushels of corn on July 1, and that the plaintiff had suffered damages in the amount of $1.00 per undelivered bushel.

The defendant filed an answer admitting that he had delivered 100 bushels of corn on July 1 but denying that the terms of the contract were as the plaintiff claimed.

The plaintiff then filed a motion for summary judgment, attaching to the motion a contract signed by the plaintiff and the defendant that required the defendant to deliver 1000 bushels of corn on July 1, which set the price of the corn at $2 per bushel. The plaintiff also filed an affidavit in which she swore that, because the defendant failed to deliver the 900 additional bushels of corn, the plaintiff had been forced to buy 900 bushels of corn elsewhere and had paid $3 a bushel for it.

The defendant filed a response in which he merely stated that he did not recall that the contract required him to deliver 1000 bushels.

On the basis of these documents, the court should grant summary judgment in favor of the plaintiff. The plaintiff proved both the contract term that defendant's answer had denied and, through her sworn and uncontested affidavit, the amount of her damages.

It should be remembered that, if there are any contested issues of material fact, a summary judgment motion cannot be granted. Suppose in the preceding example that the defendant's answer had stated that, contrary to the plaintiff's charges, he had in fact delivered 1000 bushels of corn. The plaintiff then filed a motion for summary judgment, attaching an affidavit in which she swore that she had received only 100 bushels. In his response, the defendant filed his own affidavit in which he swore that he had delivered the full 1000 bushels. These conflicting affidavits present a **contested issue of material fact**. The court must deny the motion for summary judgment and have the factual dispute resolved at trial.

A court may grant summary judgment on the entire case or only on certain issues. If the action is an automobile collision case, for example, the court may grant the plaintiff's motion for summary judgment on the issue of negligence and deny it on the issue of damages. The trial will then focus only on the remaining factual question—the amount of damages.

Any party to a proceeding may move for summary judgment at any stage in the proceeding after 20 days have elapsed from the filing of the complaint and before trial. In a complex case in which there are numerous allegations, summary judgment is often a useful means of narrowing the issues. In all cases in which there is no genuine dispute as to the facts, such a motion averts an unnecessary trial and saves the court valuable time.

The Trial

In a trial, either a jury or the judge may decide the disputed issues of fact. Rules 38 and 39 provide that any party may request a jury, but if neither party makes such a request, the case is tried to the court. The court, however, in its discretion, may order that the case be tried in whole or in part by a jury.

If the case is to be tried by a jury, after the parties have selected a jury, the attorney for each side makes an **opening statement**. This statement is a brief explanation of that party's position and what that party intends to prove.

The parties then proceed with the presentation of the **evidence**, with the plaintiff going first. The plaintiff calls the plaintiff's first witness, who is sworn and then questioned by the plaintiff's attorney. Following this **direct examination**, the defendant's attorney has the opportunity to **cross examine** the witness. Cross examination may be followed by **redirect examination** and **recross examination** until each side has exhausted its questions.

The plaintiff then calls the plaintiff's second witness, and so on, until the plaintiff's attorney decides that he or she has proven a *prima facie* **case**, that is, the essential elements of the party's claim. The plaintiff's attorney then states that the plaintiff **rests** his or her case.

At this time, the defendant's attorney may move for a **directed verdict** under Rule 50(a). In this motion the defendant's attorney states that the plaintiff did not prove the essential elements of the plaintiff's claim and that the defendant is entitled to judgment.

A directed verdict may be proper in two circumstances. If, for example, the plaintiff had the burden of proving the defendant's negligence but presented no evidence that the defendant was negligent, then the court should grant a directed verdict.

The second circumstance in which a judge may grant a directed verdict is one in which the plaintiff presented on the issue of the defendant's negligence some evidence, but so little that reasonable people could not possibly believe that the defendant was negligent.

If the court grants the defendant's motion, the case is withdrawn from the jury, because there remains nothing for the jurors to decide. If the motion is denied, the defendant then presents the defendant's case.

In some federal courts, the defendant's attorney makes his or her opening statement after the plaintiff rests rather than at the beginning of the trial. The defendant's attorney then proceeds to call the defendant's witnesses, examines them, and offers them to the plaintiff's attorney for cross examination. As in the plaintiff's case, the attorneys have the opportunity for redirect and recross examination.

After the defense rests, the plaintiff's attorney may move for a directed verdict. If such motion is denied, the plaintiff may put on **rebuttal evidence** to contradict facts that the defendant introduced. The defendant may then put on his or her own rebuttal evidence, called **rejoinder**. At the end of the evidence, both parties rest.

During the trial, each party's attorney may object to the evidence that the other is about to introduce. When an attorney objects, he or she must state the grounds of the objection. The party who is trying to introduce the evidence will then explain why he or she believes that it is admissible. The judge then applies the Federal Rules of Evidence to determine whether admission of the evidence is proper.

An attorney who makes an objection does so with a dual purpose. First, the attorney wants to keep the evidence out. Second, if the judge admits the evidence, the attorney wants to preserve the right to complain about the erroneous admission of the evidence. The failure of an attorney to object generally waives that party's right to complain on appeal that the evidence should not have been admitted.

At the close of all the evidence, each party again has the opportunity to move for a directed verdict. If the judge does not grant any such motions, the parties then proceed with their **closing arguments**.

Following closing arguments, the judge **charges** the jury. In the charge, the judge explains the applicable law and the standards of proof that the jurors must use. The judge has the option to summarize or even comment on the evidence. A judge who comments on the evidence, however, must make clear that the jurors alone are the finders of fact.

Because of the danger of prejudicing the jury and thereby forcing a new trial, most federal judges use their power to comment on the evidence only sparingly.

After the jury has been charged, it retires to deliberate. Rule 49 states that a court may require the jury to return with either a **general verdict** or a **special verdict**. If a special verdict is required, the judge submits specific written questions to the jury on each factual issue and asks them to respond in writing.

If the judge instead requests a general verdict, the jury returns with a simple statement either that the jurors find for the defendant or that the jurors find for the plaintiff and award damages in the amount of a certain number of dollars.

If there is no jury, the judge must specify in writing his or her findings of facts and conclusions of law.

Motion for Judgment Notwithstanding the Verdict

Rule 50(b) provides that after the jury has rendered its verdict, the unsuccessful party may request the court to enter **judgment notwithstanding the verdict**, technically known in Rule 50(b) as "judgment as a matter of law." Essentially, the moving party requests the court to set aside the jury verdict and enter judgment in its favor. In order to make this motion, the moving party must have made a motion for directed verdict at the close of the evidence. Such a motion "**j.n.o.v.**" must be made no later than 10 days after the court has entered a judgment on the verdict. Rule 50(b) implies that the court should apply the same standard in evaluating a motion for judgment notwithstanding the verdict as it does in reviewing a motion for directed verdict. The rule gives a judge the power to determine that the jury rendered a verdict that was clearly contrary to the facts proven during the trial.

Motion for a New Trial

Federal Rule 59(b) permits a dissatisfied party to file with the court a motion for a new trial not later than 10 days after the entry of judgment. A judge will grant such a motion if the judge believes that during the course of the trial he or she made a decision that constitutes reversible error or if the judge believes that the jury acted unreasonably or improperly or misunderstood the judge's charge.

Judgment

Rule 58 provides that after the jury has rendered its verdict or the court has decided the case in favor of one party or the other, the court shall enter **judgment,** either awarding relief, including the specific amount of damages, or denying relief. The various types of relief that a judgment may grant are discussed in Chapter Three.

A judgment has the power of the government behind it. If it awards money damages to the plaintiff and the defendant fails to pay, a sheriff or, upon order of the court, a United States Marshal, may execute on (**seize**) the defendant's property to satisfy the judgment. If relief granted is **injunctive** (that is, ordering the defendant not to perform a certain act or, less frequently, requiring that he or she perform a particular act), then the defendant can be jailed for failing to obey. The entry of final judgment is the last step in a federal district court proceeding.

Personnel of the Federal Courts

The Federal Judge

The Constitution, which sets forth the method for selecting federal judges, provides that the president nominates a person to the position and the Senate confirms the person. In practice, the senior U.S. senator of the president's political party from the state where the judge will sit has a powerful voice as to who will be nominated or confirmed. The Senate Judiciary Committee will authorize a background check on each nominee, hold public hearings on his or her fitness to serve and recommend that a nominee be confirmed by the Senate or decline to recommend. The Senate's power to approve presidential nominees for federal judge is one means by which Congress can check the power of the executive branch.

This system of political patronage and expediency has resulted in the selection of some outstanding jurists and "many complacent mediocrities."[44] Few qualifications have been established for federal judges. The primary requirement is that they be competent to sit.

Although the law does not require that federal judges must be lawyers, pursuant to 28 U.S.C. §132 this requirement of competency by implication excludes nonlawyers. To help ensure that only qualified persons become federal judges, a screening process involving several prominent legal organizations was established to pass on the qualifications of candidates for federal judgeships. This screening process involves both the American Bar Association and the United States Department of Justice.

Once selected, all new federal judges go through a training program, regardless of their legal background. Educational programs, which include orientation seminars for the newly appointed judges, are provided at the Federal Judicial Center. The Federal Judicial Center carries on research activities and conducts training programs not only for federal judges but also for other court personnel.[45] The orientation seminars for the new judges cover federal laws, civil and criminal procedure, sentencing, and court management.[46]

Compensation for federal judges is established by statute. The Constitution provides, however, that federal judges ". . . shall receive for their Services, a Compensation, which shall not be diminished during their Continuance in Office."[47]

The constitutional provision serves a very important purpose: it ensures that if a judge makes a politically unpopular decision, Congress cannot punish the judge by lowering his or her salary. Thus, a judge who is asked to protect the rights of a disliked minority or individual can make a decision strictly on the merits of the case, without fearing that, in reprisal, his or her salary will be reduced.

---

44. *Dallas Times Herald*, Nov. 15, 1977.

45. *The United States Courts, supra*, at 11.

46. E. Pearson, *Federal Judicial Personnel* 1 (1978).

47. U.S. Const. Art. III, §1.

Once nominated and confirmed, federal judges serve for life.[48] They can be removed only through the process of **impeachment** for official misconduct, *i.e.*, on conviction of treason, bribery, or other high crimes or misdemeanors. Because federal judges are appointed by the President and serve for life, they become a means for the President and the political party he or she represents, to wield power long after the appointing President has left office.

This tenure provision of the Constitution does not protect a federal judge from prosecution for a crime that the judge committed during his or her term of office or before taking judicial office.[49] Although conviction of a serious crime or high misdemeanor might not automatically result in the removal of a federal judge from office, such a conviction would probably trigger the impeachment process. For example, any justice or judge appointed under the authority of the United States who practices law by representing private clients while in office is deemed guilty of a high misdemeanor that would constitute grounds for impeachment.[50]

Impeachment of a federal judge involves the same process used to impeach a president. The House of Representatives would first adopt Articles of Impeachment that serve the same purpose as an indictment in ordinary criminal proceedings. Trial on these Articles of Impeachment would then be held in the Senate, with the accused judge having the right to appear on his or her own behalf. A two-thirds vote in favor of impeachment is necessary for a conviction.[51]

As might be expected, the impeachment of a federal judge rarely occurs. Only about a dozen federal judges have had Articles of Impeachment voted against them by the House of Representatives

---

48. *Id.*

49. *United States v. Isaacs*, 493 F.2d 1124 (7th Cir. 1974).

50. 28 U.S.C. §454.

51. J. Ferguson and D. McHenry, *supra*, at 348.

during the entire history of the federal judiciary, and only about half of those were ultimately convicted by the Senate.[52]

The relative security of federal judges, when compared to the political vulnerability of elected state court judges, has often been the subject of heated debate. Opponents of the federal method of appointment have criticized the federal judiciary as being too isolated from the political process, accusing federal judges of living in "ivory towers" with the thick walls provided by life tenure forming effective barriers to public opinion. Critics have suggested election or shorter terms as methods of making federal judges more sensitive to public opinion. As discussed in Chapter One, however, federal judges need to be autonomous and removed from political pressures in order to make hard but just decisions in difficult situations.

A federal judge is not subject to a mandatory retirement age. When a judge reaches 65, with 15 years of active service on the bench, or when he or she reaches the age of 70, with at least 10 years of active service, the judge may retire.[53] A retired judge often remains very active, however, continuing to discharge the same judicial duties as other judges, although often with a substantially reduced caseload.[54]

The United States District Judge and the Judge's Staff

The first major function of a federal district judge is that of presiding over and ruling on trials. During the progress of a trial, a judge makes numerous decisions (**rulings**) on what evidence should be allowed and what law applies. Not infrequently, a judge may preside over a case that presents new and previously unresolved issues of law. In such a case, the judge has the challenging responsibility of determining what the law ought to be.

---

52. *Id.*

53. 28 U.S.C. §371.

54. *In re National Recreation Products, Inc.*, 403 F.Supp. 1399 (C.D. Cal. 1975).

As discussed in Chapter One, a judge who is presiding over a non-jury trial must perform an additional, often difficult task. He or she must take on the role of a jury and decide the facts.

While a judge is hearing one case, as many as three or four hundred cases may be pending that require hearings and rulings. A **docket** is a record of the cases waiting to be tried. Because of the great number of cases on a judge's docket and because new cases are filed daily, a judge must keep all cases moving toward trial or other resolution.

Many judges find that the best way to move their cases is to set deadlines for the lawyers, including deadlines for completing discovery, conducting settlement conferences, and commencing the trial. Without such deadlines, some cases might not progress at all. A plaintiff's attorney who has a weak case may prefer to keep the case pending indefinitely. Defendants' attorneys normally prefer to delay the trial. Most judges find that if they were to allow cases to remain inactive for long periods of time, their docket would soon become so bloated that it would be totally unmanageable.

At a 1971 seminar for federal judges, Judge Carter of the U.S. District Court for the Southern District of California[55] discussed the problems inherent in lack of control of the docket. He stated the inevitable results:

> Cases that should be settled or disposed of clog the docke; . . . congestion breeds congestion, and the more the trial calendar becomes crowded or delayed, the less activity there is by lawyers on pending cases, and this congestion leads to further congestion . . . We therefore recommend as a matter of principle that calendar control by a court is far superior in the administration of justice, to a system which for all practical purposes, surrenders the control of the calendar to the attorneys who practice in the court.

---

55. Federal Judicial Center, *Seminars for Newly Appointed United States District Judges* (1971).

Feeling the pressure of a trial date, lawyers have an incentive to work out an amicable settlement. Pretrial and scheduling conferences are set to encourage the parties to meet and discuss the issues and to offer opportunities for settlement. In many courts, parties are strongly encouraged to make a good faith effort to settle their dispute, and settlement discussions are promoted well in advance of any pretrial conference.

In 1990, Congress passed the Civil Justice Reform Act[56] that requires every federal district court to develop a plan to curtail the costs and shorten the time involved in most litigation. Every district court plan requires the parties to a lawsuit to attend a nonbinding "neutral evaluation conference" to present the legal and factual basis of their case before a court representative. This process enables each side to evaluate the strength of their case by hearing what the other side has to say, and thus encourages settlement. In addition, every federal court provides some means by which cases are evaluated for their suitability to mediation, arbitration, or some other alternative to actually bringing the case to trial. If these methods of early resolution fail, the case goes to trial.

Members of the judge's staff play a major role in helping the judge decide his or her cases and move the docket. These include the **law clerks**, the judge's secretary, the court reporter, and the courtroom deputy. Technically, the latter two are under the supervision of the office of the U.S. District Clerk.

Law Clerks

Law clerks are usually lawyers who have recently graduated from law school at the top of their class. Usually they are employed by the judges for a one- or two-year term as assistants to the judges, although it is possible to become a career law clerk.

Law clerks serve at the direction of the judge and perform a broad range of functions that vary from court to court. Frequently, the law clerk's activities center around legal research and writing. The clerk

---

56. 1 U.S.C. §101.

engages in discussions with the judge on pending matters. He or she prepares the judge for and attends conferences in chambers with attorneys.

Such law clerks generally perform three other functions: researching motions, drafting memorandum opinions, and preparing jury charges.

As discussed in the previous section, motions are requests of various types submitted to the court for rulings on particular issues. After studying the motion, the response to the motion, and the applicable law, the law clerk may prepare a memorandum for the judge. The judge, based on the law clerk's memorandum, may make a ruling on the motion or request oral argument. If the ruling is complex and involves important legal question, the judge may want to file a **memorandum opinion** that law clerks help the judge prepare. In a memorandum opinion, the judge not only rules for one side or the other but also sets forth in detail the law on which he or she relied in making the decision. The memorandum opinion is one way for a judge to avoid having a verdict overturned on appeal because it explains to the appeals court the trial judge's reasoning behind his or her decision.

Jury charges, which law clerks may also help prepare, are the written instructions for the jury. They may include one or more specific questions that the jury must answer. These questions are ones of fact around which the resolution of the case revolves.

In a lawsuit over an automobile accident, for example, the jury might be asked: "Do you find that the defendant John Smith drove through the red light at the intersection of 34th and Main Streets?" In answering yes or no to this question, the jury effectively decides the case.

In order to draft a jury charge, a law clerk not only must be completely familiar with the important facts of that particular case but also must understand the applicable law. Only if the clerk understands the law will he or she be able to ask the relevant questions. For example, the question about running a red light is only pertinent if the law requires a person to stop at a red light.

Some judges do not permit their clerks to draft jury charges. Instead, they prepare the charge themselves, leaving their clerks to perform other tasks. Lawyers for the parties will typically submit proposed jury charges to be considered by the judge.

In addition to legal research, law clerks also perform administrative functions that help the judge keep the docket moving. These clerks serve as the court's contact with the lawyers, working with them to resolve disputes that arise in connection with trial preparation and arranging conferences between the lawyers and the judge. The clerk performing such administrative tasks serves many of the functions of a courtroom deputy, discussed below.

Some judges may prefer their law clerks to perform these jobs, in which case a courtroom deputy performs purely clerical tasks. Other judges choose to allocate all such administrative jobs to their deputy and ask their clerks to work on entirely legal matters.

Most district courts have two law clerks. Case assignments to the law clerks are made in a variety of ways, but most judges assign all even-numbered cases to one clerk and all odd-numbered cases to the other. If a clerk has a preference for a particular subject matter, many judges try to accommodate that preference.

Law clerks must operate under the same high code of conduct as the judge and other members of the judge's staff. Law clerks who have regular contact with attorneys must be impartial and walk a delicate line between being helpful, courteous, and friendly and resisting efforts by lawyers to gain improper advantage or win favors. This balance is sometimes difficult to maintain. For this reason, many courts have delegated the responsibility of dealing with lawyers to the courtroom deputy.

State court trial judges generally do not employ law clerks. Most rulings on motions at the state court level are more routine as compared to federal trial courts. Thus, state judges can rely on their experience with similar matters to make decisions. If legal research is needed or a document must be drafted, the judge will do it himself or herself.

Secretary

In addition to traditional secretarial duties, the judge's secretary handles a wide range of responsibilities to help the judge with public and private matters. The secretary generally types opinions for the judge and the law clerks. If the judge does not use a courtroom deputy for administrative functions, the secretary often shares in the administrative duties by keeping track of the docket and scheduling trials and conferences. In courts where there are as many as 500 cases pending, such a job is extremely demanding.

Court Reporter

The court reporter's responsibility consists of recording all proceedings verbatim by shorthand or by mechanical means and transcribing any proceedings upon the request of a judge or any party to the proceeding. He or she receives a salary from the court and fees from **litigants** for transcripts requested by them and prepared by the reporter. In many courts, the court reporter also takes responsibility for keeping exhibits introduced during trials.

Court reporters are primarily assigned to a particular judge, although they serve the district court *en banc*. Court reporting services must be available to each judge in all divisional offices.

Under the direction of the district judges, the overall management of court reporters is delegated to the clerk of court. The clerk must:

- equitably apportion the court reporting tasks, known as "pooling"

- ensure that the fee charged and format used for all transcripts are in compliance with regulations of the Judicial Conference

- ensure that all transcript preparation is done in a prompt and timely manner and that the quality of transcripts is maintained

- ensure that appeals delivery deadlines are met.

While certification by the state is a requirement for court reporters in most state courts, it is not mandatory for federal court reporters. Unless one is certified, however, one stands little chance of obtaining a position as a federal court reporter. In the past, court reporters experienced a great deal of independence. The Judicial Conference now requires each court to have in place a court reporter management plan that increases supervision and ensures the timeliness and quality of transcripts. As a result of this directive, sanctions can be imposed for a case on appeal in which the transcripts have not been delivered within 30 days of the date ordered.

Courtroom Deputy

Formerly, the courtroom deputy's primary function was that of a minute clerk who recorded minutes of courtroom proceedings and had responsibility for marking and keeping exhibits. With the increase in litigation, some judges have found it necessary to delegate administrative and management matters to para-judicial personnel.

Many judges have taken the courtroom deputy out of the courtroom and made this individual responsible for managing the court's docket and the court calendar. In fact, the Federal Judicial Center recommends that courtroom deputies be used in this manner.

The courtroom deputy who has calendar responsibility may regulate the movement of cases by fixing dates and times for status conferences and motion hearings. During these conferences the judge may discuss a discovery schedule in the case and a date for trial.

Some cases are not set for trial. For example, social security and bankruptcy reviews are typically decided on the basis of motions. The courtroom deputy may set schedules and follow up on such motions.

Since managing the docket entails a great deal of contact with the attorneys, either by phone or in person, many judges have designated the courtroom deputy as the liaison or contact person for the court in all matters.

In addition to the responsibilities outlined above, the courtroom deputy performs traditional courtroom responsibilities such as administering oaths to jurors, receiving verdicts, and recording minutes of proceedings. In criminal cases, the courtroom deputy may record actions taken during arraignments and sentencing and may prepare appropriate judgments.

The United States District Clerk

The United States district clerk is appointed by and serves at the pleasure of the district judges within a particular judicial district. The clerk's office is the nucleus of the recordkeeping and service function of the courts. All pleadings are filed with, and official records are maintained in, the clerk's office. The size of the clerk's staff varies with the size of the district and the volume of litigation. In metropolitan area courts, the clerk may have as many as 150 deputy clerks. Small division offices may have only one deputy clerk.

The responsibilities of deputy clerks may include:

- receiving and filing new cases and pleadings
- setting up new files
- recording (**docketing**) pleadings on central docket sheets, both paper and automated
- mailing out orders
- assisting the public with locating files
- copying records
- preparing statistical data reflecting the performance of the courts
- receiving, administering, and disbursing court funds
- purchasing supplies
- handling personnel functions.

The summoning of jurors is also handled by the clerk's office. One or more jury clerks are usually assigned the responsibility of administering the jury program. The objective of the program is to make the best use of the jurors' time, while at the same time ensuring that the judges have jurors available whenever they are needed. Cases frequently settle at the last minute, sometimes after a jury panel is already in the courtroom. Often it is difficult to predict exactly when jurors may be needed if a judge plans to start a new case immediately after concluding the current one. The jury clerk must thus develop frequent and open communication with the judge's staff.

When a new case is filed in the clerk's office, it is usually randomly assigned to a judge. This method is called the **individual calendar system**. In such a system each judge must become thoroughly familiar with his or her cases and maintain responsibility for the handling of each case from the time that it is filed until the dispute is resolved.

An alternate way of handling cases is the **master or central calendar system**, where several judges may conduct different hearings in one case and no one judge has responsibility for the case.

The United States Magistrate Judges

To help with administrative and judicial functions, judges often look to magistrate judges. The authority of magistrate judges derives primarily from the Federal Magistrates Act of 1968, 28 U.S.C. §636, as interpreted by *Mathews v. Weber*, 423 U.S. 261 (1976).

Magistrate judges are appointed by a majority of the judges of the district court for a term of eight years. They may be removed from office by a majority of the judges for incompetency, misconduct, neglect of duty or mental disability.[57]

To qualify for appointment as a magistrate judge, a person must be under 70 years of age, a member of the bar in good standing, competent to perform the duties of the office, and unrelated by blood or marriage to a judge of the appointing court. Additional requirements may be imposed by district courts.[58]

Generally, each judge determines which duties a magistrate judge will perform for the judge. Ideally, magistrate judges are given the broadest possible powers within a framework established by judges and within the confines of the law. The Federal Rules for United States Magistrate

---

57. 28 U.S.C. §631.

58. Federal Judicial Center, *Law Clerk Handbook* (1977).

Judges became effective in May 1969 and prescribe procedures for magistrates judge.[59]

A typical magistrate judge might:

- issue arrest warrants or summonses upon a finding of probable cause in a criminal complaint

- issue search warrants upon a finding of probable cause from the affidavit in support of the application

- conduct preliminary hearings in criminal cases to determine whether there is probable cause to believe that an offense has been committed and that the defendant has committed it

- appoint counsel and set bail and conditions of release under 18 U.S.C. §3146

- serve as special master in civil actions and in habeas corpus proceedings

- assist a district judge in the conduct of civil and criminal pretrial and discovery proceedings

- where all parties consent, sit as a judge for the trial of cases.[60]

The United States Probation Office

The United States Probation Office is probably best known for its responsibility in supervising persons on probation and parole.

Probation officers perform many other functions as well. They serve at the pleasure of the court and assist the court in criminal matters. Their duties involve preparing pre-sentence investigation reports for use by judges in making sentencing decisions. They also perform

---

59. F. Klein, *Federal and State Court Systems — A Guide* (1976).

60. Federal Judicial Center, *Law Clerk Handbook* (1977).

investigations and make recommendations to the judges about persons who have allegedly violated the terms of their probation.

The sentencing of a defendant is based upon formulas set forth in the *Federal Sentencing Guidelines*. These guidelines take into consideration the type and seriousness of the offense, contributing circumstances, and the criminal history of the defendant. The guidelines set forth a range within which a judge must sentence the offender. While a judge may depart from the sentencing guidelines when there are aggravating or mitigating circumstances in a particular case, these departures are rare. Reasons for such departures must be specified.

Probation officers also make recommendations to the United States Parole Commission. In this connection, they conduct investigations, make evaluations, and prepare reports concerning parole considerations and recommendations concerning alleged parole violators.

When a defendant requests modification of his or her sentence, the probation officer may assist the court by providing background information and recommendations. Probation officers are often helpful to the judge in preparing responses to the many letters and pleas that judges receive from prisoners.

The United States Marshal

Deputy United States marshals are sometimes referred to as the police officers of the courts. Although the marshal's office works very closely with the courts, organizationally the marshal's office is part of the executive branch of government rather than the judicial branch. The marshal's office reports to the Attorney General of the United States.

The United States marshal for each district is appointed in a manner similar to that of a federal judge. A candidate is recommended by the senior U.S. senator of the president's political party from the state where the marshal will serve. After a full Senate confirmation, the marshal is appointed to a term of four years, although he or she serves at the pleasure of the president.

In addition to providing security in the courtroom during court proceedings, the marshal is responsible for serving subpoenas, summonses, court orders, writs and, at times, the original complaint. Service of the original complaint is, however, usually made by certified mail or through a private process server. Anyone over 18 who is not a party to the suit may be a process server.

The marshal's office also has responsibility for transporting and retaining custody of defendants who are appearing in court for arraignment in criminal and, sometimes, in civil cases, for trial or sentencing. In many courts a deputy marshal formally opens and closes court and is present during trial.

In the case of jury trials, the marshal is in charge of the jury and is the only court officer communicating with the jurors outside the courtroom. During a criminal jury trial, several deputy marshals are usually in the courtroom, one in charge of the jury, one to watch the defendant, and one to maintain security in the courtroom in general.

The marshal's office is responsible for protecting the safety of the judge and the judge's staff. This task is an important one. Judges try controversial cases and have the difficult job of sentencing criminal defendants. They often receive threats and need constant, diligent protection.

The United States Attorney

The United States attorney is appointed for a term of four years by the President with the advice and consent of the Senate. The Attorney General of the United States may appoint assistant United States attorneys as needed. Assistant U.S. attorneys can do anything a U.S. attorney can do.[61]

The U.S. attorney's office is a part of the court system only in the sense that the U.S. attorney and assistant U.S. attorneys, like all lawyers, are considered to be officers of the court. Organizationally, the U.S. attorney reports to the Attorney General as head of the Department of Justice.

---

61. 28 U.S.C. §542.

The Department of Justice is sometimes referred to as the "largest law firm in the nation."[62] It represents the citizens of the United States

> "in enforcing the law in the public interest. The Department also plays a key role in protecting citizens against criminals and subversion, in ensuring healthy competition of business in our free enterprise system, in safeguarding the consumer, and in enforcing drug, immigration, and naturalization laws."[63]

The Justice Department is divided into several major divisions.

With a few exceptions, the Criminal Division is responsible for the enforcement of all federal criminal laws except those specifically assigned to the Antitrust, Civil Rights, and Tax Divisions. The division has special responsibility for enforcement against organized crime from the initial investigation through the handling of prosecution and appeal. In recent years the number of civil suits filed by inmates of prisons against federal officials has greatly increased. The Criminal Division defends the federal officials named in these actions. The general supervision of laws relating to subversive activities and certain other activities directed against internal security has been transferred to the Criminal Division.[64]

The Antitrust Division is responsible for enforcement of federal antitrust laws. This involves investigating possible antitrust violations, conducting grand jury proceedings, preparing and trying antitrust cases, prosecuting appeals, and negotiating and enforcing final judgments. Such criminal actions arise from alleged restraint on and monopolization of trade. The Consumer Affairs Section of the Antitrust Division is responsible for the institution of civil and criminal proceedings in cases referred to the department by other agencies such

---

62. United States Government Printing Office, *United States Government Manual* (1978).

63. *Id.*

64. *Id.*

as the Food and Drug Administration and the Federal Trade
Commission. ·

The Civil Rights Division was established in 1957 to secure effective
federal enforcement of civil rights laws that prohibit discrimination on
the basis of race, sex, color, religion, or national origin. Although
litigation in the Civil Rights Division is primarily civil, the division
also enforces specific criminal statutes, including those concerning
willful deprivation of constitutional rights while acting under **color of
law** or through conspiracy and violent interference with federally
protected activities.[65]

The Tax Division handles litigation arising under the Internal Revenue
Code. This litigation may be civil or criminal in nature.

The Civil Division is responsible for representing the United States in
civil litigation except certain specialized areas that are assigned to other
divisions of the Department. The Civil Division is responsible for
"suits and claims on behalf of the government and suits filed against the
United States, and actions for injunctive relief and judicial review
brought against Cabinet members, the heads of federal agencies, and
other government officials."[66]

TERMS TO KNOW

admiralty jurisdiction	double jeopardy
maritime jurisdiction	pendent jurisdiction
limited jurisdiction	doctrine of judicial self-
federal question jurisdiction	restraint
diversity jurisdiction	justiciable controversy

---

65. 18 U.S.C. §§241, 242, and 245.

66. United States Government Printing Office, *United States Government
    Manual* (1978).

standing
advisory opinions
receiver
final decision
interlocutory
appellant
appellee
writ of *certiorari*
"grants cert"
certificate
original jurisdiction
litigation
litigant
complaint
denial
discovery
affirmative defense
statute of limitations
answer
motion
motions to dismiss
compulsory counterclaim
permissive counterclaim
settlement
deposition
stipulate
removal
motion to compel
interrogatories
request for admissions
request to produce
motion for judgment on the
 pleadings
motion for summary
 judgment
ripeness doctrine
contested issue of material
 fact
opening statement

evidence
prima facie case
direct examination
cross examination
recross examination
directed verdict under Rule
 50(a)
rebuttal evidence
rejoinder
closing arguments
charges
general verdict
special verdict
judgment notwithstanding
 the verdict
judgment
injunctive
impeachment
rulings
docket
law clerks
memorandum opinion
docketing
individual calendar system
master
central calendar system
en banc
color of law

Chapter Seven

CONCLUSION

This book has given you a view of the American legal system much like
the view of America an airline passenger receives by traveling from
New York to Los Angeles: The great landmarks are clearly visible, but
the intricate byways of each little city or town are too small to be seen
with the naked eye.

Like an airplane flight, this condensed approach gives you "the lay of
the land." There remains much to be seen, and the authors can only
hope that you will explore the areas that have piqued your interest,
observing firsthand the intricate maze that the law can sometimes be.

Bon voyage!

ABA Code of Professional Responsibility – Ethical guide promulgated by the American Bar Association

ABA Model Rules of Professional Conduct – Ethical rules promulgated by the American Bar Association

Abstract of title – Summary of the transactions by which property has changed hands over the years

Abuse of process – Malicious prosecution in a civil case

Acceptance – Receiving a thing offered or tendered by another; consenting to the terms of a contract

Accord and satisfaction – Method of discharging a contract through compromise between parties disputing the contract

Actual damages – Damages awarded the victim of a tort, designed to place the tort victim in the place the victim would have occupied had the tort not occurred, to the extent that goal may be reached through a monetary payment

Adeemed legacy – Legacy destroyed because the specific property in question was destroyed or sold before the testator's death

Adhesion contract – A standard contract to which the weaker party must agree if the weaker party wishes to do business with the stronger party

Admiralty jurisdiction – Jurisdiction assigned to the federal courts by the United States Constitution over matters involving things done upon and relating to the sea, such as navigation, commerce and injuries. Also known as maritime jurisdiction

Advance sheets – Paperback versions of smaller groups of court opinions that will later appear in bound volumes

Advisory opinion – Judicial ruling upon the legality of a governmental action, whether already accomplished or contemplated, when there is no case or controversy for the court to decide

Adverse possession – Doctrine under which a party who remains in open, continuous, and adverse possession of a tract of land for a specified amount of time acquires title to the tract of land

Affirmative defense – Presentation of other pertinent facts that relieve a defendant of liability, even though the defendant may have committed the act with which he or she is charged

Annotation – A critical or explanatory note

Answer – Defendant's reply to a complaint

Antitrust Division – Division of the Justice Department responsible for enforcement of federal antitrust laws

Appeal – Request by an unsuccessful party that the decision of a lower court be reconsidered by a court of higher authority, such as an appeal from a trial court

Appearance bond – Bail bond for a minor offense

Appellant – Party who initiates or files an appeal seeking to set aside a lower court decision

Appellee – Party who argues against an appeal and for the decision of a lower court in its favor

Arraignment – Occasion at which the defendant is brought into court and the charge or charges against the defendant are read

Arrest – Taking an individual into custody

Assault – Intentional tort; placing another person in apprehension of battery

Assignment of the lease – Transfer of all of a tenant's interest in property under a lease to a third party

Assumpsit – Old English writ of an agreement between two citizens from which arose the modern law of contracts

Attractive nuisance – Condition constituting an unreasonably dangerous condition, which condition might result in injury to children who cannot learn or appreciate the danger

Award – Decision rendered by an arbitrator or panel of arbitrators in an arbitration hearing

Bail bond – Legal document containing the promise of a defendant to appear for trial or to forfeit a sum of money

Battery – Intentional tort; the harmful or offensive touching of another person, including that person's clothing or an object closely associated with that person

Beneficiary – Third party who benefits from a trust. Also, one who benefits under a will

Bilateral contract – Contract in which a promise is exchanged for a promise

***Bona fide* purchaser** – Purchaser who is unaware of any ownership interests not reflected in the deed records

Business tort – Civil wrong that interferes with the conduct of a person's business. May be created by statute, such as federal securities fraud rules and regulations

Cash bond – Bail bond for which guarantee is made by a deposit of cash

Causation in fact – Negligent conduct causing a resulting injury, which injury would not have occurred if the negligent conduct had not occurred

Central calendar system – System of assigning new court cases under which several judges may conduct different hearings in one case with no single judge completely responsible for that case

Certificate – Document issued by a governmental agency, such as the Secretary of State

Cestui que trust – French term for the beneficiary under a trust; see "beneficiary"

Challenge for cause – A request to remove a potential juror for a specific reason

Charges – See jury charge

Chattel – Physical object, as opposed to an abstract concept; personal property

Citation – Order to appear before a judge at a later date

Civil action – Action by one person against another seeking redress for injury that the first person claims to have suffered; as opposed to criminal action

Civil Division – Division of the Justice Department responsible for representing the United States in civil litigation, except in those certain specialized areas assigned to other divisions of the Justice Department

Civil Rights Division – Division of the Justice Department responsible for enforcement of civil rights laws that prohibit discrimination on the basis of race, sex, color, religion or national origin

Closing – Meeting of a buyer and seller during which a purchase and sale is consummated by such actions as the transfer of deeds, mortgages and money

Closing argument – Counsel's final address to the jury in which counsel summarizes the case, interprets the evidence, and attempts to persuade the jury to reach a desired verdict

Cloud on the title – Lien or an actual or potential ownership interest by a third party

Color of law – Action by someone or some entity, generally a government employee or agency, that purports to be authorized by law but which, in fact, is illegal (*e.g.*, police brutality)

Commercial paper – Specialized contract governed by Article 3 of the UCC: promissory notes and drafts

Common law – Law derived from cases decided by courts rather than from legislated statutes; ancient British tradition on which American jurisprudence system is based

Community property state – One of the fourteen states in which a husband and wife automatically own property jointly

Community service – Type of criminal sentence that requires the convicted defendant to perform a certain number of hours of work within a stated period of time that is of benefit to the community, and which may embody principles of restitution on the part of the defendant for the damage caused by his or her criminal acts, and of rehabilitation of the criminal

Comparative causation – Doctrine in strict tort liability under which a defendant's liability may be reduced by a percentage that represents the degree to which the plaintiff's misconduct participated in causing the injury

Comparative negligence – Theory under which a plaintiff is permitted to recover damages so long as the plaintiff's negligence is not greater than the negligence of the defendant

Compensatory damages – See "actual damages," above

Complaint – Charging document that initiates a litigation proceeding; document filed with the court outlining the wrong a plaintiff feels has been done

Compulsory counterclaim – Defendant's counterclaim arising out of the same transaction or occurrence that is the subject matter of the plaintiff's action

Computer-assisted legal research – Research conducted electronically through an online database rather than in printed volumes

Condemnation – Proceeding brought by a government agency asking that land be transferred to the government and the current owner paid a fair price therefor

Confidences – Information protected by attorney-client privilege

Congressional Record – A verbatim transcript of all proceedings on the floor of the Senate and House

Consideration – Act that a party performs, or promises to perform, even though he or she has no legal duty to do so, or forbearance, or promise of forbearance, from an act that he or she has a legal right to do.

Contested issue of material fact – Conflicting statements of fact that must be resolved through trial or settlement

Constructive eviction – Situation in which a landlord so interferes with a tenant's right to possession that the interference is equivalent to a forcible eviction and the tenant is relieved of any further obligations toward the landlord

Contract implied-in-fact – Contract under which parties have not formally agreed to be bound but have a mutual intent to create a contract, which intent may be inferred from their conduct

Contract implied-in-law – Contract created by the court when requirements are imposed on a party even though that party has not agreed to be bound by those requirements, so imposed because not to do so would be unfair

Contract of adhesion – Contract, usually preprinted and standard, to which the weaker party must agree if the weaker party wishes to do business with the stronger party

Contributory negligence – Theory under which a plaintiff whose own negligence was a contributing cause of his or her injuries can be barred from recovery

Conversion – Intentional tort consisting of the intentional exercise of dominion or control over a chattel that so seriously interferes with the right of another person to control the chattel that the person controlling may justly be required to pay the other person the full value of the chattel

Counterclaim – Claim filed by a defendant against a plaintiff

Court of limited jurisdiction – Federal court that may only hear those types of cases that the Constitution empowers it to hear

Court of record – Court in which the proceedings are recorded by an official or unofficial court reporter (meaning the series of books, not the individual who records the proceedings)

Crime – Action that offends the morality of society and that society will not tolerate

Criminal action – Litigation in which the state prosecutes a citizen for breaking criminal laws, as opposed to citizens opposing each other

Criminal Division – Division of the Justice Department responsible for enforcement of all federal criminal laws except those specifically assigned to the Antitrust, Civil Rights and Tax Divisions

Criminal justice system – System whereby the federal or a state government brings an action against an individual alleging that the individual has broken a law or laws, thereby committing a crime

Cross-examination – Questioning of a witness by counsel for the "other side" after a witness has finished direct examination

Curtesy right – The common law right of a widower to the lands owned by his deceased wife

Damages – Money awarded by a court to someone who has been injured by another person, designed to compensate the injured party for the injury and, in some cases, to punish the wrongdoer

De novo – The appeal from a court that is not a court of record, resulting in the re-trying of a case

Deceit – See "fraud," below

Deed of trust – Written record evidencing a form of co-ownership created through a mortgage relationship

Deed – Written record of the transfer of land from one party to another

Defamation – Tort interfering with the personal rights of another in which one person defames the good name and reputation of a second person

Defective product – One that does not meet the reasonable expectations of the ordinary consumer as to its safety

Defendant – In a criminal proceeding, the person accused of a crime; in a civil proceeding, the person or entity who is sued and called upon to satisfy the person who complains of some wrong committed by the defendant

Demonstrative legacy – Gift under a will of a specific sum to be taken from a particular source

Denial – A defense claiming that the plaintiff's claim is untrue

Deposition – Oral examination, recorded by a court reporter, by any party of any person whom the party believes has relevant information to a matter under litigation

Deterrence – Objective of a sentence in a criminal matter: stopping a convicted defendant from committing crime in future

Detrimental reliance – Modern name for "promissory estoppel," below

Devisee – One who is designated in a will to receive real property

Digest – Legal research volume in which information is grouped by topic

Direct examination – Initial questioning of a witness by the prosecutor or plaintiff

Directed verdict – Motion by a defendant under Rule 50(a) that the plaintiff has not proven the essential elements of plaintiff's claim and, therefore, the defendant is entitled to judgment. Made after plaintiff has rested its case but before defendant presents defendant's case

Disciplinary Rule – Rule promulgated by a bar association that must be followed by all members

Discovery – Process of gathering information about a matter prior to trial

Diversity of citizenship actions – Cases involving a dispute between citizens of different states, or between a state government and a citizen of another state, or between an American citizen and a foreign government, or a citizen of a foreign country

Diversity jurisdiction – Case involving disputes between parties who are citizens of different states

Docket – Central record system of motions and other matters ready to be heard and cases ready to be tried and the scheduled dates

Doctrine of judicial self-restraint – Doctrine under which federal courts use certain criteria to designate cases for which they refuse to accept jurisdiction

Doctrine of transferred intent – Theory under which the intent to harm a person is transferred from the intended victim to a second person who is actually harmed

Double jeopardy – Doctrine under which an individual may not be tried more than once for the same allegation

Dower right – The common law right of a widow to the lands owned by her deceased husband

Duress – Severe pressure to force a person to enter into a contract, such as a physical threat or an economic threat

Easement appurtenant – Implied easement that entitles a party to travel over the land of another party to reach the property conveyed to the first party by the second party

Easement – Interest in land, less than an estate, which gives one party the right to make some specified use of the land of another party

Ejectment – Statutory right of a landlord to regain premises and force a tenant to vacate with a minimum of delay

Eminent domain – The power to take private property for public use

En banc – Latin term meaning that all the judges on a court hear a case

Equitable conversion – Doctrine under which a contract for the sale of property creates not only a legal contractual obligation for the seller to deliver a deed, which in turn delivers the legal title to the property, but also an equitable title to the property that arises on behalf of the buyer as soon as the contract is signed

Equitable ownership – Status, in addition to legal ownership, created by the doctrine of equitable conversion and or by a trust

Equity – Principle of justice that enables a worthy plaintiff to present his or her case in court and receive damages when neither the common law nor statutory law provides a remedy.

Escheat – Originally, returning of property to the lord of a manor if the deceased person had no heirs; now, returning of property to the state if no heirs can be found

Estate *pur autre vie* – Estate in land granted to an individual with reference to the lifespan of a second individual

Estate in land – Category of various ownership interests

Estate tax – Federal tax imposed on all property remaining in an estate after debts have been paid, together with other property such as certain trust funds and property held in joint tenancy with right of survivorship, less a deduction allowed for property transferred to the decedent's spouse or to charity

Ethical Consideration – An aspirational ethical rule promulgated by a bar association, such as the American Bar Association or a state bar

Evidence – Documentary or oral statements and material objects that are admissible in court

Exclusionary rule – Rule that evidence obtained in violation of standards set out in the Fourth Amendment must be excluded from court

Exclusive jurisdiction – Specific claims that only certain courts have authority to hear

Executive branch – Branch of the American government containing, on the federal level, the President and the President's appointees in executive departments and, on the state level, the governor and the governor's appointees in executive departments

Executor – Individual named to manage a testator's estate

Exemplary damages – Compensation to the victim of a tort in a sum designed to punish the tortfeasor and to make an example of the tortfeasor so as to warn others from committing such tort

Exhibit – Document or other physical object presented in evidence at a trial

Expectation theory – Concept in contract law that damages should place the injured party in the position he or she would have occupied if the contract had been fully performed

Express contract – Contract in which parties have expressly agreed, orally or in writing, that each is to be bound to do certain things

Express warranty – Representation of fact, promises and descriptions made by a seller under the Uniform Commercial Code

Extrinsic fraud – Fraud wherein the party is aware of the bargain he or she is making but has been induced to make the agreement by a deliberately false representation

False imprisonment – Intentional tort; restraining a person within a bounded area against that person's will

Federal question jurisdiction – Jurisdiction of the federal government over certain questions, such as disputes arising under the United States Constitution or treaties made by the United States; as opposed to state jurisdiction

Federal Rules of Evidence – Rules following by a federal court to determine whether or not evidence is admissible

Federal Rules of Civil Procedure – Rules promulgated by the federal courts to be followed in civil law disputes

Federal Rules of Criminal Procedure – Rules promulgated by the federal courts to be followed in criminal law disputes

Federal District Court – The initial, trial court level of the federal court system

Fee simple – The most common estate in land, representing complete ownership of the land

Fee simple absolute – Fee simple estate with maximum possible ownership rights subject to no conditions whatsoever

Fee simple determinable – Fee simple estate that will expire upon the happening of a specified event

Fee simple subject to a condition subsequent – Fee simple estate subject to certain conditions

Fee tail – Estate in land under which land is granted to a male individual and passed to his lineal descendants until such time, if any, as the line of descendants ran out; common in England

Felony – Major crime for which a severe penalty, such as a substantial fine, imprisonment, or capital punishment, may be assessed

Final decision – Ends the litigation on the merits and leaves nothing for the court to do but to execute judgment

Fine – Sentence under which a convicted defendant must pay monetary damages to the government

Forbearance – The act of refraining from doing something one is entitled to do

Forced heirship statute – Common law doctrine under which a surviving spouse may elect to take the share, if any, given him or her by the will of the deceased spouse and a share specified in the statute of the state

Forcible entry – Prohibited entry by a landlord into a tenant's premises; see "ejectment"

Forcible entry and detainer – Permits the landlord to regain the premises and force the tenant to vacate with a minimum of delay and legal red tape

Foreclosure – Seizure and sale of land by a mortgagor to satisfy the debt owed by the mortgagee

Form book – Book with sample formats of legal documents that may be copied and adapted

Fraud – Knowingly false representation made to a person upon which that person reasonably relies to his or her detriment in deciding to enter a transaction into which he or she would not otherwise have entered

Fraud in the factum – See "intrinsic fraud," below

Fraud in the inducement – See "extrinsic fraud," above

Freehold estate – Category including the fee simple estate, the fee tail estate, and the life estate

General legacy – Gift under a will from the estate in general, as opposed to some specific fund or source

General verdict – Under Federal Rule 49, a statement by the jury as to the side for which it finds, plaintiff or defendant. Contrast with "special verdict," below

General warranty deed – Deed including a promise that the grantor holds good title to the property being conveyed

Grand jury – Official body of citizens brought together to decide whether an accused person should be officially charged

Grand jury indictment – Charge made by an official body of citizens brought together to decide whether a person accused of a crime should be officially charged

Grantee – One who receives an estate in land entitling that recipient to possession and use of the land

Grantor – One who gives an estate in land, conveying title to a recipient

Headnotes – Paragraphs written by editors summarizing important legal points contained in a decision

Heir – Closest surviving descendant

Holographic will – Will entirely in the handwriting of the testator and duly signed by the testator

Hung jury – Jury that is deadlocked and cannot agree on a verdict

Impeachment – Removal from office of an official, such as a judge, for serious misconduct, such as conviction for a crime

Implied in fact – Contract inferred from conduct

Implied in law – Contract when the law imposes requirements on the parties

Implied warranty of fitness for a particular purpose – Warranty under the Uniform Commercial Code that the goods being sold are fit for the particular purpose for which the buyer is acquiring the goods and of which the seller is aware

Implied warranty of merchantability – Warranty under the Uniform Commercial Code that the goods being sold are of average quality, are fit for ordinary purposes, and are adequately contained, packaged and labeled

Implied warranty of title – Warranty under the Uniform Commercial Code that the goods being sold belong to the seller

Imprisonment – Sentence for a convicted defendant sending that defendant to prison for a set length of time

Independent administrator – Executor (see above) who takes charge of a testator's estate without court supervision

Indictment – Decision by a grand jury that a person must be brought to trial

Individual calendar system – System of assigning new court cases under which one judge receives the random assignment of a case and handles that case until the dispute is resolved

Indorsement – Signature of a holder

Injunctions – A prohibitive writ forbidding a party to do some act

Injunctive – An order prohibiting a certain act

Intentional infliction of emotional distress – Intentional tort; conduct so extreme, outrageous, and transcending all bounds of common decency, so as to affect severely another person

Inter vivos **trust** – When property passes by conveyance

Interference with business relations – Business tort under which a tortfeasor attempts to interfere with the conduct of another's business affairs

Interlocutory judgment – Judgment that is not final

Interrogatory – Series of written questions that one party in a lawsuit submits to another party, which questions must be answered in writing and under oath

Intestate succession – Distribution of the property of a person who dies without a will

Intrinsic fraud – Fraud wherein the party is not aware of the nature of the agreement into which he or she is entering

Invasion of privacy – Tort interfering with personal rights in which the right of quiet enjoyment is denied a person

Investigation – Initial step in the criminal justice process, generated by observation of a crime, report of a criminal, or belief that a crime is about to occur

Invitee – One who is on land as a member of the public or to further the business interests of the person owning the land

Irrevocable trust – Trust that may not be revoked by its maker

Joint tenancy with right of survivorship – Form of tenancy in common (see below) that provides for automatic passage of the interest of a deceased joint tenant to a surviving joint tenant

Judgment – Written document containing the decision of a judge. May also mean the amount of damages assessed against a party, as in "obtaining a judgment"

Judgment lien – Security interest against property of one who loses in a lawsuit held by the one who has prevailed in the suit

Judgment notwithstanding the verdict – Request to a judge to set aside a jury verdict and enter judgment in favor of the moving party

Judicial branch – Branch of American government containing the courts

Jurisdiction – Power or authority of a court to hear and decide a particular kind of case; also refers to a geographic territory within which a court's authority is exercised *e.g.*, Iowa; Des Moines County

Jury charge – Written instructions for the jury, offered by each of the prosecution and the defense

Jury panel – Group of citizens from whom a jury is selected

Justice Department – Section of the federal executive branch headed by the Attorney General and responsible for law enforcement

Justiciable controversy – An actual controversy between parties involving their legal relationship that is appropriate for a court of law to determine the outcome. The parties must have adverse interests involving something of value such as money, property, or rights

Law clerk – As used in this book, a fully-qualified attorney who works for a judge doing research and administrative functions. Also, a student in a law school who works in a law firm during summer months or part-time during the school year

Law journal – Legal periodical published by a law school

Law review – Another term for "law journal," above

Leasehold estate – Estate in land giving one party the use of property but not the title thereto, as opposed to a freehold estate; term of years, periodic tenancy, and tenancy at will

Legal research – The process of acquiring information on a legal topic

Legatee – One who is designated in a will to receive personal property

Legislative branch – Branch of American government containing the elected representatives of the people. On the federal level: Congress. On the state level: the elected legislature

Legislative history – Record of the passage of a bill through a legislature, beginning with the initial draft

Libel – Tort of written defamation

License – In real property law, a limited right to use land for a specific purpose; not an estate interest

Licensee – With respect to torts, a visitor on land for a legitimate purpose and with permission of the landowner, but not as an ordinary member of the public or for a business purpose of the landowner

Lien – Security interest

Life estate – Estate in land granted to an individual for the duration of that individual's lifetime

Litigants – Parties who either institute or defend a lawsuit; generally used in reference to civil suits rather than criminal

Litigation – Contest carried on in court in which the legal rights of the parties are determined; often used to mean all the steps taken in a civil case up to and including settlement of a case before a trial becomes necessary

Livery of seisin – Medieval term denoting transferring land by the parties going to the land and the grantor's giving the grantee a clod of earth or twig to symbolize transfer of the land

Malicious prosecution – Tort interfering with personal rights under which one person seeks to bring another, innocent person to trial

Maritime jurisdiction – See admiralty jurisdiction, above

Master – In agency theory, one who authorizes another to act in his or her place

Master calendar system – See "central calendar system," above

Materialmen's lien – Lien (see above) in favor of suppliers of construction materials

Mechanic's lien – Lien (see above) in favor of contractors or workmen

Memorandum opinion – Detailed ruling by a judge containing not only a decision but also specifics of the law on which the judge relied for his or her decision. Initially prepared for the judge by a law clerk

Miranda warning – Oral admonition advising a person under arrest of the rights he or she has under the United States Constitution, such as the right against self-incrimination and the right to have an attorney present

Misdemeanor – Minor crime, varying from a traffic violation to theft of a small amount of money

Mistrial – Declaration by a judge that the trial may not go forward, possibly because of a hung jury, and that the defendant must be tried again

Mortgage – Deed of trust; a lien on or interest in land arising from the consent of the owner

Mortgagee – Owner of the interest in land

Mortgagor – Holder of the property who pays the mortgagee to reside on the land in which the mortgagee has an interest

Motion – Request submitted to the court for a ruling on a particular issue or issues; request that a court act in a certain manner

Motion for change of venue – Request to have the trial held in another geographical site, invoked when the defense counsel alleges that the defendant cannot receive a fair trial at the original venue due to pretrial publicity or some other cause

Motion for judgment on the pleadings – Motion under Rule 12(c), not appropriate until all pleadings in a matter have been filed with the court. Filed by plaintiff claiming that defendant's answers are not sufficient to relieve defendant of liability. Rarely used

Motion for summary judgment – Motion under Rule 56 asking the court to look to evidence beyond the pleadings filed and determine whether there is any genuine issue of material fact. If none is found, the court may decide the issues of law and rule in favor of one party or another without the matter going to trial. Appropriate when both plaintiff and defendant agree on issues of material fact

Motion to compel – Motion under Rule 37 under which one party asks the court to order the other party to respond to the discovery requests filed by the first party

Motion to dismiss – Request that the charge against a defendant be dismissed

Motion to sever – When two or more defendants are accused of the same crime, motion to try each defendant separately

Motion to suppress evidence or to dismiss the indictment – Defense motion claiming that the grounds of the charge are not sufficiently specific or that the evidence against the defendant is inadmissible because it is irrelevant, unduly prejudicial, or was obtained illegally. Motion to suppress is also called a motion in *limine*

Negligence – Tort consisting of four basic elements: a duty to conform to a certain standard established by law, a failure to meet such standard, a cause-and-effect relationship between that failure and the resulting injury, and damages resulting from the injury

Negligence per se – Violation of a statute prohibiting certain conduct, which statute was enacted to benefit a class of persons

Negligent misrepresentation – Business tort under which one person misleads another to induce the second person to enter into a business transaction

Negotiable – Transferable by endorsement or delivery so as to pass to holder the right to sue in one's own name

Negotiable instrument – Note or draft that may be negotiated from one owner to another by endorsement

Nolo contendere – "I will not contest it," an alternate plea to "guilty" or "not guilty"

Nominal damages – Damages awarded the tort victim when such victim has suffered no loss; damages in a very small sum, such as $1.00

Non-exclusive jurisdiction – Jurisdiction by either a federal or a state court, not reserved exclusively to the federal court

Nonconforming use – Use of land that is inconsistent with the land's zoning classification, permitted to remain on the land because the use was in existence at the time such zoning classification was enacted, with the proviso that such use may not be changed or expanded

Novation – Agreement between parties to a contract that a third party will assume some or all of the contractual obligations of one of the original parties

Nuisance – Label given to a variety of torts that are deemed either private or public nuisances

Nuisance per se – Nuisance under all circumstances

Nuncupative will – Will made by speaking

Offer – Communication by one party to another party that reasonably leads the receiving party to believe that the offering party is willing to enter into a contract

Official reporter – Reporter published by a government agency

"One-bite" rule – Assumption that the owner of a cat or dog is not liable for the first time a pet bites a person

Opening statement – Brief statement of a party's position and what the party intends to prove at trial

Original jurisdiction – Jurisdiction under which a matter is first tried

Parol evidence rule – Rule under which statements (either oral or written, but usually oral) outside a written contract may not be used to contradict the terms of the contract

Parole – A conditional release of a convicted criminal from prison followed by the opportunity to serve the remainder of prison term in the community

Partition – Division of land demanded by a tenant in common so that such tenant in common will receive exclusive title of a portion of the land, such portion representing the tenant in common's fair share

Pendent jurisdiction – Right of a federal district court to make decisions on matters that would otherwise be exclusively heard by the state court

Per capita – System of distribution of property in an estate whereby each person entitled to a share of the estate takes an equal share

Per stirpes – System of distribution of property in an estate whereby each descendant of the testator takes a share representing a proportionate distribution of the property at each succeeding generation

Peremptory challenge – Removing a potential juror without any stated reason

Periodic tenancy – Leasehold estate existing for a given period of time and automatically renewing itself unless one party notifies the other party that renewal is not desired

Permissive counterclaim – Defendant's counterclaim arising out of an incident other than the one that is the subject matter of the plaintiff's action

Personal jurisdiction – The power of a court over the people involved in a criminal or civil lawsuit based upon where they reside or can be found, where the alleged illegal acts occurred, or where any property involved in a lawsuit is located. Also called "*in personam* jurisdiction"

Personal recognizance – Promise of defendant to appear at trial, without a sum of money to guarantee such appearance. See "bail bond," above

Plaintiff – The party in a civil proceeding who sues another party, called the defendant, and seeks satisfaction for a wrong the complaining party believes that the defendant has committed

Plea bargaining – Negotiation between the prosecutor and defense counsel to have the defendant enter a guilty plea in exchange for some benefit to the defendant, such as a reduction of charges against the defendant

Pocket part – Annual supplement fitted into the back of a volume containing statutes, keeping the volume current as statutes are amended

Precedent – Principle that when a court has decided a case based upon a set of facts, that decision provides guidance for other courts faced with similar sets of facts

Presentence report – Report compiled by a federal probation officer, summarizing an investigation of the background of a defendant who has been found guilty and recommending a sentence

Pretermitted child statute – Statute that revokes a will if the testator had no living children at the time of making of the will but later had a child who survived the testator by at least one year

Pretrial release program – Program under which a defendant is allowed release until trial in return for paying a small premium on a bail bond called a pretrial release bond. See "bail bond"

Prima facie **case** – The essential elements of a party's claim

Primary source – Information from a direct source of law, such as a court opinion

Private nuisance – Interference with a landowner's right to possession and enjoyment of the landowner's land

Privilege against self-incrimination – Privilege, provided by a clause in the Fifth Amendment of the Bill of Rights, that one shall not be compelled to be a witness against oneself

Probable cause – Evidence that leads a reasonable person to believe that guilt is more than a possibility

Pro bono publico – "For the good of the public"; professional service rendered by legal professionals at no charge or reduced charge

Probate – Presentation of a will to the probate court for public filing

Probation – Sentence under which a convicted person is not imprisoned but must report to a probation officer

Probation revocation hearing – Hearing at which the convicted defendant on probation is called before the court to determine if such probation should be revoked

Procedural due process – Rights and privileges available under the Bill of Rights to the defendant in a criminal matter, such as notice that he or she is accused of a crime, and a fair hearing

Procedure – Step-by-step rules that people bringing or defending a lawsuit or criminal prosecution must follow

Production of documents – Discovery request pursuant to Federal Rule 34, by which a party to a lawsuit may be requested to produce, and to permit the other party to inspect and copy, any designated documents

Products liability – Strict liability tort involving products that are defective and unreasonably dangerous

Profits or *profits a prendre* – Right to sever minerals or crops from land; not an estate interest

Promissory estoppel – Doctrine under which a promise by a promising party should reasonably expect to cause, and that indeed does cause, definite and substantial reliance by the other party and, therefore, requires no consideration

Promissory note – Type of commercial paper evidencing a maker's promise to pay to the order of a lender principal and interest at a future date

Prosecutor – The person who represents the government in a criminal proceeding and who prepares and conducts the case against the accused. At the municipal and state level the person is usually called the district attorney; at the federal level the person is called a U.S. attorney

Protection of the public – Objective of a sentence in a criminal matter: shielding the public from actions of a convicted defendant

Protective order – Under Rule 26(c), order by the court to shield a party from annoyance, embarrassment, oppression, or undue burden or expense

Proximate causation – Concept in tort liability under which injuries result, although not directly, from an action or failure to act

Public defender – Office of attorneys who defend accused persons who cannot afford representation

Public nuisance – Interference with the rights of the public generally

Punitive damages – See "exemplary damages," above

Quasi-contract liability – Liability resulting from a contract implied in law

Quiet enjoyment – Possession of real property without interference

Quitclaim deed – Deed containing no warranties, giving the grantee whatever interest in the property, if any, that his or her grantor had at the time of the deed

Rebuttal evidence – Opposing evidence or arguments

Receiver – Neutral party appointed by the court to preserve property during the course of litigation

Recross examination – Questions of a witness by counsel for the "other side" for a second time

Regional reporter – Reporter dealing with published judicial opinions in a stated geographic area

Rehabilitation – Objective of a sentence in a criminal matter: changing the life style of a convicted defendant so that defendant may return to society

Rejoinder – Rebuttal evidence by a defendant

Remainder – Portion of an interest in property held not by the grantor or grantee but by a third party

Remedy – The means employed to redress an injury

Removal – Transferring a case from the court where a plaintiff filed it originally to another based on a question of jurisdiction

Reporter – Volume of published judicial opinions

Request for admissions – Request from a party to a lawsuit that opposing party admit or deny the truth of matters within the scope of discovery that relate to statements, opinions of fact, or the application of law to fact

Request to produce – Request by a party in a lawsuit to inspect and copy any designated documents

Res ipsa loquitur – Latin term for "The thing speaks for itself"

Rescission – Discharge of a contract ordered by a court under which the contract is declared void and each party returns to the other party or parties any benefits received under the contract

Residuary legacy – Gift under a will of the balance of the testator's estate after all debts and other legacies have been paid

Restitution – In criminal law, part of a sentence that requires the defendant to pay damages to the victim in order to (partially) restore the victim to his or her condition before the crime was committed

Restrictive covenant – Restriction in a deed limiting the use to which land may be put or the individuals to whom the land may be conveyed; not an estate interest

Retribution – Objective of a sentence in a criminal matter; punishing a convicted defendant

Reversion – Portion of an interest in property still held by the grantor

Revocable trust – Trust that may be revoked by its maker

Right of eminent domain – Right to unfettered use and possession of land

Right of survivorship – Upon the death of one joint tenant, that tenant's interest automatically passes to the other joint tenant(s)

Right of way easement – Specified use of land for passing over another's land to reach his or her own property

Ripeness doctrine – Doctrine in constitutional law whereby a federal court will not decide a case before the necessity to decide it

Rule against perpetuities – Common law rule under which an instrument, such as a trust, establishes a time limit beyond which no interest may vest under the instrument

Rules of procedure – Step-by-step rules to be followed when bringing a matter before a court

Rulings – Court decisions on what evidence should be allowed and what law applies

Secondary source – Source of legal research not stemming from government, such as a legal treatise or a law review (see above)

Secrets – Information that the client has requested to be kept secret because it could be embarrassing or detrimental to the client

Secured transaction – Sale of goods covered by Article 9 of the Uniform Commercial Code under which one party obtains a security interest in goods or other personal property owned by another party

Security interest – Same as lien or mortgage

Self-proving affidavit – Affidavit attached to a will executed by the testator and two witnesses before a notary, which by its very existence attests to the proper execution of the will

Sentence – Punishment set by a judge for a convicted defendant

Sentencing guideline – Part of the Federal Criminal Code setting the minimum and maximum sentences that may be assessed for conviction in a federal court

Session law – The text of a statute and amendments thereto, written precisely as they were enacted at a given session of the legislature that passed the law

Settlement – Resolution of dispute without trial

Settlor – One who makes a trust. See "trustor," below

Shepardizing – Using *Shepard's Citations* to establish if a reported case has been followed by a lower court as precedent or overturned by a higher court; determining if a ruling is still "good law"

Slander – Tort of verbal defamation

Slip law – Recently enacted statute printed individually in booklet form

Slip opinion – Recently issued opinion printed in booklet form

Special verdict – Under Federal Rule 49, a verdict in which the jury responds in writing to specific written questions on factual issues. Contrast with "general verdict," above

Special warranty deed – Deed promising only that the grantor is giving the grantee as good a title as the grantor originally received from his or her grantor, further promising that the grantor has done nothing to impair the title to the property during the grantor's ownership of it

Specialized reporter – Volume of court decisions on a particular area of the law, such as securities or bankruptcy

Specific devise – Testamentary gift of a specific tract of land

Specific legacy – Testamentary gift of a specific object

Specific performance – Performance ordered by the court of a party found liable for breach of a contract

Split sentence – Combination of imprisonment followed by probation

Standing – Personal stake in litigation of a sufficient nature to justify bringing suit, as a person must show "standing" in a federal court

Stare decisis – Latin term for principle of law announced by previous courts that judges are hesitant to overturn even though the facts of a current case may warrant a contrary decision

Statute – Prohibition, command, or declaration enacted by a legislative body

Statute of Frauds – 1677 English statute that has been adopted through the United States requiring certain types of contracts to be in writing to be enforcable

Statute of limitations – Period of time during which plaintiff may sue, generally measured from the date the wrongful act the plaintiff complains of first occurred, or was first discovered by the plaintiff

Stipulate – To agree

Strict-liability tort – Civil wrong for which a person may be held liable despite having acted with the utmost care

Subject matter jurisdiction – The authority of a court to hear and decide cases based on the subject matter of the violations or claims involved, and/or the amount of monetary damages requested by the complaining party

Sublease – Transfer by a lessee of fewer than all rights under a lease, making a tenant a "junior landlord" to whom the sublessee owes obligations as a tenant

Substantive Law – Legislative enactments or decisions handed down by judges

Surety bond – Bail bond by which guarantee is made by a second person's promise to pay if the defendant fails to appear for trial

Suspended sentence – Sentence under which a convicted defendant may stay in society under probation and under which, should the defendant violate terms of the suspended sentence, the defendant goes immediately to prison for duration of the sentence

Tax Division – Division of the Justice Department responsible for litigation arising under the Internal Revenue Code, either civil or criminal

Tax lien – Security interest held by the government in property arising from unpaid taxes

Tenancy at will – Leasehold estate terminable without advance notice by either party

Tenancy by the entireties – Specialized form of joint tenancy between husband and wife

Tenancy in common – Means by which two or more persons may concurrently own a single piece of land under which each has an undivided interest in the land

Term of years – Leasehold estate giving a grantee the right to possession and use of real property for a specified period of time; a fixed-term lease

Testamentary trust – Trust created within a will

Testator – One who makes a will

Title insurance – Policy under which an insurance company will make good losses to buyer of real property if, at a later date, it is discovered that a defect exists in title to such real property

Title opinion – Opinion of an title company stating that, based on its research, the seller holds good title to property

Title search – Tracing a chain of grantors and grantees of a property

Tort – Act, or omission to act, that causes legal harm to another, committed under circumstances where the law imposes a duty to refrain from causing such harm; a civil wrong, as opposed to a criminal offense

Tortfeasor – One who commits a tort

Transferred intent – Doctrine in tort law wherein the intent to harm one person is transferred to the person who was actually harmed

Treatise – Legal reference book written by a law professor or other legal scholar ·

Trespass – Intentional tort; interference with a person's right to exclusive and complete possession of land or tangible goods

Trespasser – One who is on land without express or implied permission of the landowner

Trust – Transaction developed by the courts of equity whereby a trustor conveys title to a trustee for the benefit of a beneficiary

Trustee – One to whom the legal title to real or personal property is conveyed in a trust transaction so that trustee may hold such title for the benefit of a third party

Trustor – Maker of a trust, also called the settlor; the one who conveys legal title to the trustee in a trust transaction

Undue influence – Severe pressure of a moral nature that forces a person to enter into a contract he or she would otherwise have avoided

Unfair competition – Business tort under which one person used unlawful means to compete with another in a business setting

Uniform Commercial Code – Model law setting up uniform rules for commerce such as the sale of goods, secured interests, and negotiable instruments that, when adopted by the various states, mitigates the problem of inconsistent state laws that hamper commerce

Uniform Simultaneous Death Act – When testator and beneficiary die almost simultaneously, half the property passes as though testator had died first, and half as though the beneficiary had died first

Unilateral contract – Contract that contemplates actual performance as the form of acceptance

United States Attorney – Attorney appointed by the President with the advice and consent of the Senate for a term of four years, reporting to the Attorney General

United States Court of Appeals – Federal court of higher jurisdiction to which cases from a federal district court may be appealed

United States District Clerk – Supervisor of the record-keeping and service functions of a federal district court

United States Magistrate – Attorney appointed to assist a federal judge with administrative and judicial functions

United States Marshal – Law enforcement officer in the executive branch of federal government, reporting to the Attorney General

United States Probation Office – Section of the federal court system responsible for supervising persons or probation and parole

United States Supreme Court – Highest court of the United States; representative of the third branch of the division of powers between judicial, executive and legislative branches

Unjust enrichment – Doctrine under which one party unfairly receives a benefit not intended

Unofficial reporter – Volumes of reported cases published by a private legal publishing company; in general use because the unofficial reporters appear much sooner than the official reporters published by the government

Utility easement – Specified use of land for utilities

Vendor's lien – Lien in favor of the seller of property to insure that the seller receives the full purchase price

Venue – Geographical location(s) where a court can exercise its jurisdiction; site where a case is being tried

Verdict – Decision of the triers of fact; the jury

***Voir dire* (French term) examination** – Examination of potential jurors

Widow's election will – Will giving the surviving spouse of a testator the option to take what the will gives the spouse or, alternatively, to take his or her own half share of the community property, irrespective of the provisions of the will

Writ of *assumpsit* – Doctrine from which contract law descended, stating that virtually no contract liability can be created except by agreement

Writ of *certiorari* – Petition of a party that a ruling made in the court of appeals be heard again and reviewed by the Supreme Court

Writ of trespass – In medieval times, a quasi-criminal remedy for redress of a direct and usually intentional injury

Zoning ordinance – Local law by which a city regulates the use to which land may be put and structures that may be erected upon the land

CONSTITUTION OF THE UNITED STATES

Preamble

We the People of the United States, in order to form a more perfect union, establish justice, insure domestic tranquility, provide for the common defence, promote the general welfare, and secure the blessings of liberty to ourselves and our posterity, do ordain and establish this Constitution for the United States of America.

Article I

Section 1. All legislative powers herein granted shall be vested in a Congress of the United States, which shall consist of a Senate and House of Representatives.

Section 2. The House of Representatives shall be composed of members chosen every second year by the people of the several states, and the electors in each state shall have the qualifications requisite for electors of the most numerous branch of the state legislature.

No person shall be a representative who shall not have attained to the age of twenty five years, and been seven years a citizen of the United States, and who shall not, when elected, be an inhabitant of that state in which he shall be chosen.

Representatives and direct taxes shall be apportioned among the several states which may be included within this Union, according to their respective numbers, which shall be determined by adding to the whole number of free persons, including those bound to service for a term of years, and excluding Indians not taxed, three fifths of all other persons. The actual enumeration shall be made within three years after the first meeting of the Congress of the United States, and within every subsequent term of ten years, in such manner as they shall by law direct. The number of representatives shall not exceed one for every thirty thousand, but each state shall have at least one representative; and until such enumeration shall be made, the state of New Hampshire shall be entitled to choose three, Massachusetts eight, Rhode-Island and Providence Plantations one, Connecticut five, New York six, New Jersey four, Pennsylvania eight, Delaware one, Maryland six, Virginia ten, North Carolina five, South Carolina five, and Georgia three.

When vacancies happen in the Representation from any state, the executive authority thereof shall issue writs of election to fill such vacancies.

The House of Representatives shall choose their Speaker and other officers; and shall have the sole power of impeachment.

Section 3. The Senate of the United States shall be composed of two senators from each state, chosen by the Legislature thereof, for six years; and each senator shall have one vote.

Immediately after they shall be assembled in consequence of the first election, they shall be divided as equally as may be into three classes. The seats of the senators of the first class shall be vacated at the expiration of the second year, of the second class at the expiration of the fourth year, and of the third class at the expiration of the sixth year, so that one third may be chosen every second year; and if vacancies happen by resignation, or otherwise, during the recess of the Legislature of any state, the Executive thereof may make temporary appointments until the next meeting of the Legislature, which shall then fill such vacancies.

No person shall be a senator who shall not have attained to the age of thirty years, and been nine years a citizen of the United States, and who shall not, when elected, be an inhabitant of that state for which he shall be chosen.

The Vice President of the United States shall be President of the senate, but shall have no vote, unless they be equally divided.

The Senate shall choose their other officers, and also a President pro tempore, in the absence of the Vice President, or when he shall exercise the office of President of the United States.

The Senate shall have the sole power to try all impeachments. When sitting for that purpose, they shall be on oath or affirmation. When the President of the United States is tried, the Chief Justice shall preside: And no person shall be convicted without the concurrence of two thirds of the members present.

Judgment in cases of impeachment shall not extend further than to removal from office, and disqualification to hold and enjoy any office of honor, trust or profit under the United States: but the party convicted shall nevertheless be liable and subject to indictment, trial, judgment and punishment, according to law.

Section 4. The times, places, and manner of holding elections for senators and representatives, shall be prescribed in each state by the legislature thereof; but the Congress may at any time by law make or alter such regulations, except as to the places of choosing Senators.

The Congress shall assemble at least once in every year, and such meeting shall be on the first Monday in December, unless they shall by law appoint a different day.

Section 5. Each house shall be the judge of the elections, returns, and qualifications of its own members, and a majority of each shall constitute a quorum to do business; but a smaller number may adjourn from day to day, and may be authorized to compel the attendance of absent members, in such manner, and under such penalties as each house may provide.

Each house may determine the rules of its proceedings, punish its members for disorderly behaviour, and, with the concurrence of two thirds, expel a member.

Each house shall keep a journal of its proceedings, and from time to time publish the same, excepting such parts as may in their judgment require secrecy; and the yeas and nays of the members of either house on any question shall, at the desire of one fifth of those present, be entered on the journal.

Neither house, during the session of Congress, shall, without the consent of the other, adjourn for more than three days, nor to any other place than that in which the two houses shall be sitting.

Section 6. The senators and representatives shall receive a compensation for their services, to be ascertained by law, and paid out of the treasury of the United States. They shall in all cases, except treason, felony and breach of the peace, be privileged from arrest during their attendance at the session of their respective houses, and in going to and returning from the same; and for any speech or debate in either house, they shall not be questioned in any other place.

No senator or representative shall, during the time for which he was elected, be appointed to any civil office under the authority of the United States, which shall have been created, or the emoluments whereof shall have been increased during such time; and no person holding any office under the United States, shall be a member of either house during his continuance in office.

Section 7. All Bills for raising revenue shall originate in the house of representatives; but the senate may propose or concur with amendments as on other bills.

Every bill which shall have passed the house of representatives and the senate, shall, before it become a law, be presented to the president of the United States; If he approve he shall sign it, but if not he shall return it, with his objections to that house in which it shall have originated, who shall enter the objections at large on their journal, and proceed to reconsider it. If after such reconsideration two thirds of that house shall agree to pass the bill, it shall be sent, together with the objections, to the other house, by which it shall likewise be reconsidered, and if approved by two thirds of that house, it shall become a law. But in all such cases the votes of both houses shall be determined by yeas and nays, and the names of the persons voting for and against the bill shall be entered on the journal of each house respectively. If any bill shall not be returned by the President within ten days (Sundays excepted) after it shall have been presented to him, the same shall be a law, in like manner as if he had signed it, unless the Congress by their adjournment prevent its return, in which case it shall not be a law.

Every order, resolution, or vote to which the concurrence of the Senate and House of Representatives may be necessary (except on a question of adjournment) shall be presented to the President of the United States; and before the same shall take effect, shall be approved by him, or being disapproved by him, shall be repassed by two thirds of the Senate and House of Representatives, according to the rules and limitations prescribed in the case of a bill.

Section 8. The Congress shall have power

> To lay and collect taxes, duties, imposts and excises, to pay the debts and provide for the common defence and general welfare of the United States; but all duties, imposts and excises shall be uniform throughout the United States;

> To borrow money on the credit of the United States;

> To regulate commerce with foreign nations, and among the several states, and with the Indian tribes;

> To establish an uniform rule of naturalization, and uniform laws on the subject of bankruptcies throughout the United States;

> To coin money, regulate the value thereof, and of foreign coin, and fix the standard of weights and measures;

To provide for the punishment of counterfeiting the securities and current coin of the United States;

To establish post offices and post roads;

To promote the progress of science and useful arts, by securing for limited times to authors and inventors the exclusive right to their respective writings and discoveries;

To constitute tribunals inferior to the supreme court;

To define and punish piracies and felonies committed on the high seas, and offences against the law of nations;

To declare war, grant letters of marque and reprisal, and make rules concerning captures on land and water;

To raise and support armies, but no appropriation of money to that use shall be for a longer term than two years;

To provide and maintain a navy;

To make rules for the government and regulation of the land and naval forces;

To provide for calling forth the militia to execute the laws of the union, suppress insurrections and repel invasions;

To provide for organizing, arming, and disciplining, the militia, and for governing such part of them as may be employed in the service of the United States, reserving to the States respectively, the appointment of the officers, and the authority of training the militia according to the discipline prescribed by Congress;

To exercise exclusive legislation in all cases whatsoever, over such district (not exceeding ten miles square) as may, by cession of particular States, and the acceptance of Congress, become the seat of the government of the United States, and to exercise like authority over all places purchased by the consent of the legislature of the state in which the same shall be for the erection of forts, magazines, arsenals, dock-yards, and other needful buildings;—And

To make all laws which shall be necessary and proper for carrying into execution the foregoing powers, and all other powers vested by this constitution in the government of the United States, or in any department or officer thereof.

Section 9. The migration or importation of such persons as any of the states now existing shall think proper to admit, shall not be prohibited by the Congress prior to the year one thousand eight hundred and eight, but a tax or duty may be imposed on such importation, not exceeding ten dollars for each person.

The privilege of the writ of habeas corpus shall not be suspended, unless when in cases of rebellion or invasion the public safety may require it.

No bill of attainder or ex post facto law shall be passed.

No capitation, or other direct, tax shall be laid, unless in proportion to the census or enumeration herein before directed to be taken.

No tax or duty shall be laid on articles exported from any state. No preference shall be given by any regulation of commerce or revenue to the ports of one state over those of another: nor shall vessels bound to, or from, one state, be obliged to enter, clear, or pay duties in another.

No money shall be drawn from the treasury, but in consequence of appropriations made by law; and a regular statement and account of the receipts and expenditures of all public money shall be published from time to time.

No title of nobility shall be granted by the United States – and no person holding any office of profit or trust under them, shall, without the consent of the Congress, accept of any present, emolument, office, or title, of any kind whatever, from any king, prince, or foreign state.

Section 10. No State shall enter into any treaty, alliance, or confederation; grant letters of marque and reprisal; coin money; emits bills of credit; make any thing but gold and silver coin a tender in payment of debts; pass any bill of attainder, ex post facto law, or law impairing the obligation of contracts, or grant any title of nobility.

No state shall, without the consent of the Congress, lay any imposts or duties on imports or exports, except what may be absolutely necessary for executing its inspection laws: and the net produce of all duties and imposts, laid by any state on imports or exports, shall be for the use of the Treasury of the United

States; and all such laws shall be subject to the revision and control of the Congress. No state shall, without the consent of the Congress, lay any duty of tonnage, keep troops, or ships of war in time of peace, enter into any agreement or compact with another state, or with a foreign power, or engage in war, unless actually invaded, or in such imminent danger as will not admit of delay.

Article II

Section 1. The executive power shall be vested in a President of the United States of America. He shall hold his office during the term of four years, and, together with the vice president, chosen for the same term, be elected, as follows:

Each state shall appoint, in such manner as the legislature thereof may direct, a number of electors, equal to the whole number of senators and representatives to which the state may be entitled in the Congress: but no senator or representative, or person holding an office of trust or profit under the United States, shall be appointed an elector.

The electors shall meet in their respective states, and vote by ballot for two persons, of whom one at least shall not be an inhabitant of the same state with themselves. And they shall make a list of all the persons voted for, and of the number of votes for each; which list they shall sign and certify, and transmit sealed to the seat of the government of the United States, directed to the president of the senate. The president of the senate shall, in the presence of the senate and house of representatives, open all the certificates, and the votes shall then be counted. The person having the greatest number of votes shall be the president, if such number be a majority of the whole number of electors appointed; and if there be no more than one who have such majority, and have an equal number of votes, then the house of representatives shall immediately choose by ballot one of them for president; and if no person have a majority, then from the five highest on the list the said house shall in like manner choose the President. But in choosing the President, the votes shall be taken by the states, the representation from each state having one vote; a quorum for this purpose shall consist of a member or members from two thirds of the states, and a majority of all the states shall be necessary to a choice. In every case, after the choice of the President, the person having the greatest number of votes of the electors shall be the Vice President. But if there should remain two or more who have equal votes, the senate shall choose from them by ballot the Vice President.

The Congress may determine the time of choosing the electors, and the day on which they shall give their votes; which day shall be the same throughout the United States.

No person except a natural born citizen, or a citizen of the United States, at the time of the adoption of this constitution, shall be eligible to the office of President; neither shall any person be eligible to that office who shall not have attained to the age of thirty five years, and been fourteen years a resident within the United States.

In case of the removal of the President from office, or of his death, resignation, or inability to discharge the powers and duties of the said office, the same shall devolve on the Vice President, and the Congress may by law provide for the case of removal, death, resignation or inability, both of the President and Vice President, declaring what officer shall then act as President, and such officer shall act accordingly, until the disability be removed, or a President shall be elected.

The President shall, at stated times, receive for his services, a compensation, which shall neither be increased nor diminished during the period for which he shall have been elected, and he shall not receive within that period any other emolument from the United States, or any of them.

Before he enter on the execution of his office, he shall take the following oath or affirmation:

> "I do solemnly swear (or affirm) that I will faithfully execute
> the office of President of the United States, and will to the
> best of my ability, preserve, protect and defend the
> constitution of the United States."

Section 2. The President shall be commander in chief of the army and navy of the United States, and of the militia of the several states, when called into the actual service of the United States; he may require the opinion, in writing, of the principal officer in each of the executive departments, upon any subject relating to the duties of their respective offices, and he shall have power to grant reprieves and pardons for offences against the United States, except in cases of impeachment.

He shall have power, by and with the advice and consent of the senate, to make treaties, provided two thirds of the senators present concur; and he shall nominate, and by and with the advice and consent of the senate, shall appoint ambassadors, other public ministers and consuls, judges of the supreme court, and all other officers of the United States, whose appointments are not herein otherwise provided for, and which shall be established by law. But the Congress may by law vest the appointment of such inferior officers, as they think proper, in the president alone, in the courts of law, or in the heads of departments.

The President shall have power to fill up all vacancies that may happen during the recess of the senate, by granting commissions which shall expire at the end of their next session.

Section 3. He shall from time to time give to the Congress information of the state of the union, and recommend to their consideration such measures as he shall judge necessary and expedient; he may, on extraordinary occasions, convene both houses, or either of them, and in case of disagreement between them, with respect to the time of adjournment, he may adjourn them to such time as he shall think proper; he shall receive ambassadors and other public ministers: he shall take care that the laws be faithfully executed, and shall commission all the officers of the United States.

Section 4. The President, Vice President, and all civil officers of the United States, shall be removed from office on impeachment for, and conviction of, treason, bribery, or other high crimes and misdemeanors.

Article III

Section 1. The judicial power of the United States, shall be vested in one supreme court, and in such inferior courts as the Congress may from time to time ordain and establish. The judges, both of the supreme and inferior courts, shall hold their offices during good behaviour, and shall, at stated times, receive for their services, a compensation, which shall not be diminished during their continuance in office.

Section 2. The judicial power shall extend to all cases, in law and equity, arising under this constitution, the laws of the United States, and treaties made, or which shall be made, under their authority; to all cases affecting ambassadors, other public ministers and consuls; to all cases of admiralty and maritime jurisdiction; to controversies to which the United States shall be a party; to controversies between two or more States; between a state and citizens of another state; between citizens of different States; between citizens of the same state claiming lands under grants of different States, and between a state, or the citizens thereof, and foreign States, citizens or subjects.

In all cases affecting ambassadors, other public ministers and consuls, and those in which a state shall be party, the supreme court shall have original jurisdiction. In all the other cases before mentioned, the supreme court shall have appellate jurisdiction, both as to law and fact, with such exceptions, and under such regulations as the Congress shall make.

The trial of all crimes, except in cases of impeachment, shall be by jury; and such trial shall be held in the state where the said crimes shall have been committed; but when not committed within any state, the trial shall be at such place or places as the Congress may by law have directed.

Section 3. Treason against the United States, shall consist only in levying war against them, or in adhering to their enemies, giving them aid and comfort. No person shall be convicted of treason unless on the testimony of two witnesses to the same overt act, or on confession in open court.

The Congress shall have power to declare the punishment of treason, but no attainder of treason shall work corruption of blood, or forfeiture except during the life of the person attainted.

Article IV

Section 1. Full faith and credit shall be given in each state to the public acts, records, and judicial proceedings of every other state. And the Congress may by general laws prescribe the manner in which such acts, records and proceedings shall be proved, and the effect thereof.

Section 2. The citizens of each state shall be entitled to all privileges and immunities of citizens in the several states.

A person charged in any state with treason, felony, or other crime, who shall flee from justice, and be found in another state, shall on demand of the executive authority of the state from which he fled, be delivered up, to be removed to the state having jurisdiction of the crime.

No person held to service or labour in one state, under the laws thereof, escaping into another, shall, in consequence of any law or regulation therein, be discharged from such service or labour, but shall be delivered up on claim of the party to whom such service or labour may be due.

Section 3. New states may be admitted by the Congress into this union; but no new state shall be formed or erected within the jurisdiction of any other state; nor any state be formed by the junction of two or more states, or parts of states, without the consent of the legislatures of the states concerned as well as of the Congress.

The Congress shall have power to dispose of and make all needful rules and regulations respecting the territory or other property belonging to the United States; and nothing in this Constitution shall be so construed as to prejudice any claims of the United States, or of any particular state.

Section 4. The United States shall guarantee to every state in this union a Republican form of government, and shall protect each of them against invasion; and on application of the legislature, or of the executive (when the legislature cannot be convened) against domestic violence.

Article V

The Congress, whenever two thirds of both houses shall deem it necessary, shall propose amendments to this constitution, or, on the application of the legislatures of two thirds of the several states, shall call a convention for proposing amendments, which, in either case, shall be valid to all intents and purposes, as part of this constitution, when ratified by the legislatures of three fourths of the several states, or by conventions in three fourths thereof, as the one or the other mode of ratification may be proposed by the Congress; Provided that no amendment which may be made prior to the year one thousand eight hundred and eight shall in any manner affect the first and fourth clauses in the ninth section of the first article; and that no state, without its consent, shall be deprived of its equal suffrage in the senate.

Article VI

All debts contracted and engagements entered into, before the adoption of this Constitution, shall be as valid against the United States under this Constitution, as under the confederation.

This Constitution, and the laws of the United States which shall be made in pursuance thereof; and all treaties made, or which shall be made, under the authority of the United States, shall be the supreme law of the land; and the judges in every state shall be bound thereby, any thing in the constitution or laws of any state to the contrary notwithstanding.

The senators and representatives before mentioned, and the members of the several state legislatures, and all executive and judicial officers, both of the United States and of the several states, shall be bound by oath or affirmation, to support this constitution; but no religious test shall ever be required as a qualification to any office or public trust under the United States.

Article VII

The ratification of the conventions of nine States, shall be sufficient for the establishment of this constitution between the States so ratifying the same.

Amendments to the Constitution

(The first ten Amendments were ratified Dec. 15, 1791, and form what is known as the Bill of Rights.)

Amendment 1

Congress shall make no law respecting an establishment of religion, or prohibiting the free exercise thereof; or abridging the freedom of speech, or of the press, or the right of the people peaceably to assemble, and to petition the Government for a redress of grievances.

Amendment 2

A well regulated Militia, being necessary to the security of a free State, the right of the people to keep and bear Arms, shall not be infringed.

Amendment 3

No Soldier shall, in time of peace be quartered in any house, without the consent of the Owner, nor in time of war, but in a manner to be prescribed by law.

Amendment 4

The right of the people to be secure in their persons, houses, papers, and effects, against unreasonable searches and seizures, shall not be violated, and no Warrants shall issue, but upon probable cause, supported by Oath or affirmation, and particularly describing the place to be searched, and the persons or things to be seized.

Amendment 5

No person shall be held to answer for a capital, or otherwise infamous crime, unless on a presentment or indictment of a Grand Jury, except in cases arising in the land or naval forces, or in the Militia, when in actual service in time of War or public danger; nor shall any person be subject for the same offence to be twice put in jeopardy of life or limb; nor shall be compelled in any criminal case to be a witness against himself, nor be deprived of life, liberty, or property, without due process of law; nor shall private property be taken for public use, without just compensation.

Amendment 6

In all criminal prosecutions, the accused shall enjoy the right to a speedy and public trial, by an impartial jury of the State and district wherein the crime shall have been committed, which district shall have been previously ascertained by law, and to be informed of the nature and cause of the accusation; to be confronted with the witnesses against him; to have compulsory process for obtaining witnesses in his favor, and to have the Assistance of Counsel for his defence.

Amendment 7

In Suits at common law, where the value in controversy shall exceed twenty dollars, the right of trial by jury shall be preserved, and no fact tried by a jury shall be otherwise re-examined in any Court of the United States, than according to the rules of the common law.

Amendment 8

Excessive bail shall not be required, nor excessive fines imposed, nor cruel and unusual punishments inflicted.

Amendment 9

The enumeration in the Constitution, of certain rights, shall not be construed to deny or disparage others retained by the people.

Amendment 10

The powers not delegated to the United States by the Constitution, nor prohibited by it to the States, are reserved to the States respectively, or to the people.

Amendment 11

(Ratified Feb. 7, 1795)

The Judicial power of the United States shall not be construed to extend to any suit in law or equity, commenced or prosecuted against one of the United States by Citizens of another State, or by Citizens or Subjects of any Foreign State.

Amendment 12

(Ratified July 27, 1804)

The Electors shall meet in their respective states and vote by ballot for President and Vice President, one of whom, at least, shall not be an inhabitant of the same State with themselves; they shall name in their ballots the person voted for as President, and in distinct ballots the person voted for as Vice President, and they shall make distinct lists of all persons voted for as President, and of all persons voted for as Vice President, and of the number of votes for each, which lists they shall sign and certify, and transmit sealed to the seat of the government of the United States, directed to the President of the Senate;—The President of the Senate shall, in the presence of the Senate and House of Representatives, open all the certificates and the votes shall then be counted;—The person having the greatest number of votes for President, shall be the President, if such number be a majority of the whole number of Electors appointed; and if no person have such majority, then from the persons having the highest numbers not exceeding three on the list of those voted for as President, the House of Representatives shall choose immediately, by ballot, the President. But in choosing the President, the votes shall be taken by states, the representation from each state having one vote; a quorum for this purpose shall consist of a member or members from two-thirds of the states, and a majority of all the states shall be necessary to a choice. And if the House of Representatives shall not choose a President whenever the right of choice shall devolve upon them, before the fourth day of March next following, then the Vice President shall act as President, as in the case of the death or other constitutional disability of the President.—The person having the greatest number of votes as Vice President, shall be the Vice President, if such number be a majority of the whole number of Electors appointed, and if no person have a majority, then from the two highest numbers on the list, the Senate shall choose the Vice President; a quorum for the purpose shall consist of two-thirds of the whole number of Senators, and a majority of the whole number shall be necessary to a choice. But no person constitutionally ineligible to the office of President shall be eligible to that of Vice President of the United States.

Amendment 13

(Ratified Dec. 6, 1865)

Section 1. Neither slavery, nor involuntary servitude, except as a punishment for crime whereof the party shall have been duly convicted, shall exist within the United States, or any place subject to their jurisdiction.

Section 2. Congress shall have power to enforce this article by appropriate legislation.

Amendment 14

(Ratified July 9, 1868)

Section 1. All persons born or naturalized in the United States, and subject to the jurisdiction thereof, are citizens of the United States and of the State wherein they reside. No State shall make or enforce any law which shall abridge the privileges or immunities of citizens of the United States; nor shall any State deprive any person of life, liberty, or property, without due process of law; nor deny to any person within its jurisdiction the equal protection of the laws.

Section 2. Representatives shall be apportioned among the several States according to their respective numbers, counting the whole number of persons in each State, excluding Indians not taxed. But when the right to vote at any election for the choice of electors for President and Vice President of the United States, Representatives in Congress, the Executive and Judicial officers of a State, or the members of the Legislature thereof, is denied to any of the male inhabitants of such State, being twenty-one years of age, and citizens of the United States, or in any way abridged, except for participation in rebellion, or other crime, the basis of representation therein shall be reduced in the proportion which the number of such male citizens shall bear to the whole number of male citizens twenty-one years of age in such State.

Section 3. No person shall be a Senator or Representative in Congress, or elector of President and Vice President, or hold any office, civil or military, under the United States, or under any State, who, having previously taken an oath, as a member of Congress, or as an officer of the United States, or as a member of any State legislature, or as an executive or judicial officer of any State, to support the Constitution of the United States, shall have engaged in insurrection or rebellion against the same, or given aid or comfort to the enemies thereof. But Congress may by a vote of two-thirds of each House, remove such disability.

Section 4. The validity of the public debt of the United States, authorized by law, including debts incurred for payment of pensions and bounties for services in suppressing insurrection or rebellion, shall not be questioned. But neither the United States nor any State shall assume or pay any debt or obligation incurred in aid of insurrection or rebellion against the United States, or any claim for the loss or emancipation of any slave; but all such debts, obligations and claims shall be held illegal and void.

Section 5. The Congress shall have power to enforce, by appropriate legislation, the provision of this article.

Amendment 15

(Ratified Feb. 3, 1870)

Section 1. The right of citizens of the United States to vote shall not be denied or abridged by the United States or by any State on account of race, color or previous condition of servitude.

Section 2. The Congress shall have power to enforce this article by appropriate legislation.

Amendment 16

(Ratified Feb. 3, 1913)

The Congress shall have power to lay and collect taxes on incomes, from whatever source derived, without apportionment among the several States, and without regard to any census or enumeration.

Amendment 17

(Ratified April 8, 1913)

The Senate of the United States shall be composed of two Senators from each State, elected by the people thereof for six years; and each Senator shall have one vote. The electors in each State shall have the qualifications requisite for electors of the most numerous branch of the State legislatures.

When vacancies happen in the representation of any State in the Senate, the executive authority of such State shall issue writs of election to fill such vacancies: *Provided*, That the legislature of any State may empower the executive thereof to make temporary appointments until the people fill the vacancies by election as the legislature may direct.

This amendment shall not be so construed as to affect the election or term of any Senator chosen before it becomes valid as part of the Constitution.

Amendment 18

(Ratified Jan. 16, 1919)

Section 1. After one year from the ratification of this article the manufacture, sale, or transportation of intoxicating liquors within. the importation thereof into, or the exportation thereof from the United States and all territory subject to the jurisdiction thereof for beverage purposes is hereby prohibited.

Section 2. The Congress and the several States shall have concurrent power to enforce this article by appropriate legislation.

Section 3. This article shall be inoperative unless it shall have been ratified as an amendment to the Constitution by the legislatures of the several States, as provided in the Constitution, within seven years from the date of the submission hereof to the States by the Congress.

Amendment 19

(Ratified Aug. 18, 1920)

The right of citizens of the United States to vote shall not be denied or abridged by the United States or by any State on account of sex.

Congress shall have power to enforce this article by appropriate legislation.

Amendment 20

(Ratified Jan. 23, 1933)

Section 1. The terms of the President and Vice President shall end at noon on the 20th day of January, and the terms of Senators and Representatives at noon on the third day of January, of the years in which such terms would have ended if this article had not been ratified; and the terms of their successors shall then begin.

Section 2. The Congress shall assemble at least once in every year, and such meeting shall begin at noon on the third day of January, unless they shall by law appoint a different day.

Section 3. If, at the time fixed for the beginning of the term of the President, the President elect shall have died, the Vice President elect shall become President. If a President shall not have been chosen before the time fixed for the beginning of his term, or if the President elect shall have failed to qualify, then the Vice President elect shall act as President until a President shall have qualified; and the Congress may by law provide for the case wherein neither a President elect nor a Vice President elect shall have qualified, declaring who shall then act as President, or the manner in which one who is to act shall be selected, and such person shall act accordingly until a President or Vice President shall have qualified.

Section 4. The Congress may by law provide for the case of the death of any of the persons from whom the House of Representatives may choose a President whenever the right of choice shall have devolved upon them, and for the case of the death of any of the persons from whom the Senate may choose a Vice President whenever the right of choice shall have devolved upon them.

Section 5. Sections 1 and 2 shall take effect on the 15th day of October following the ratification of this article.

Section 6. This article shall be inoperative unless it shall have been ratified as an amendment to the Constitution by the legislatures of three-fourths of the several States within seven years from the date of its submission.

Amendment 21

(Ratified Dec. 5, 1933)

Section 1. The eighteenth article of amendment to the Constitution of the United States is hereby repealed.

Section 2. The transportation or importation into any State, Territory, or possession of the United States for delivery or use therein of intoxicating liquors, in violation of the laws thereof, is hereby prohibited.

Section 3. This article shall be inoperative unless it shall have been ratified as an amendment to the Constitution by conventions in the several States, as provided in the Constitution, within seven years from the date of the submission hereof to the States by the Congress.

Amendment 22

(Ratified Feb. 27, 1951)

Section 1. No person shall be elected to the office of the President more than twice, and no person who has held the office of President, or acted as President, for more than two years of a term to which some other person was elected President shall be elected to the office of the President more than once. But this Article shall not apply to any person holding the office of President when this Article was proposed by the Congress, and shall not prevent any person who may be holding the office of President, or acting as President, during the term within which this Article becomes operative from holding the office of President or acting as President during the remainder of such term.

Section 2. This article shall be inoperative unless it shall have been ratified as an amendment to the Constitution by the legislatures of three-fourths of the several States within seven years from the date of its submission to the States by the Congress.

Amendment 23

(Ratified March 29, 1961)

Section 1. The District constituting the seat of Government of the United States shall appoint in such manner as the Congress may direct:

A number of electors of President and Vice President equal to the whole number of Senators and Representatives in Congress to which the District would be entitled if it were a State, but in no event more than the least populous State; they shall be in addition to those appointed by the States, but they shall be considered, for the purposes of the election of President and Vice President, to be electors appointed by a State; and they shall meet in the District and perform such duties as provided by the twelfth article of amendment.

Section 2. The Congress shall have power to enforce this article by appropriate legislation.

Amendment 24

(Ratified Jan. 23, 1964)

Section 1. The right of citizens of the United States to vote in any primary or other election for President or Vice President. for electors for President or Vice President, or for Senator or Representative in Congress, shall not be denied or abridged by the United States or any State by reason of failure to pay any poll tax or other tax.

Section 2. The Congress shall have power to enforce this article by appropriate legislation.

Amendment 25

(Ratified Feb. 10, 1967)

Section 1. In case of the removal of the President from office or of his death or resignation, the Vice President shall become President.

Section 2. Whenever there is a vacancy in the office of the Vice President, the President shall nominate a Vice President who shall take office upon confirmation by a majority vote of both Houses of Congress.

Section 3. Whenever the President transmits to the President pro tempore of the Senate and the Speaker of the House of Representatives his written declaration that he is unable to discharge the powers and duties of his office, and until he transmits to them a written declaration to the contrary, such powers and duties shall be discharged by the Vice President as Acting President.

Section 4. Whenever the Vice President and a majority of either the principal officers of the executive departments or of such other body as Congress may by law provide, transmit to the President pro tempore of the Senate and the Speaker of the House of Representatives their written declaration that the President is unable to discharge the powers and duties of his office, the Vice President shall immediately assume the powers and duties of the office as Acting President.

Thereafter, when the President transmits to the President pro tempore of the Senate and the Speaker of the House of Representatives his written declaration that no inability exists, he shall resume the powers and duties of his office unless the Vice President and a majority of either the principal officers of the executive department or of such other body as Congress may by law provide, transmit within four days to the President pro tempore of the Senate and the Speaker of the House of Representatives their written declaration that the President is unable to discharge the powers and duties of his office. Thereupon Congress shall decide the issue, assembling within forty-eight hours for that purpose if not in session. If the Congress, within twenty-one days after receipt of the latter written declaration, or, if Congress is not in session, within twenty-one days after Congress is required to assemble, determines by two-thirds vote of both Houses that the President is unable to discharge the powers and duties of his office, the Vice President shall continue to discharge the same as Acting President; otherwise, the President shall resume the powers and duties of his office.

Amendment 26

(Ratified July 1, 1971)

Section 1. The right of citizens of the United States, who are 18 years of age or older, to vote shall not be denied or abridged by the United States or by any state on account of age.

Section 2. The Congress shall have power to enforce this article by appropriate legislation.

Amendment 27

(Ratified May 7, 1992)

No law, varying the compensation for the services of the Senators and Representatives, shall take effect until an election of Representatives shall have intervened.